How to Do Business with the Japanese

A Complete Guide to Japanese Customs and Business Practices

Boye De Mente

NTC Business Books

a division of *NTC Publishing Group* • Lincolnwood, Illinois USA

1989 Printing

Published by Passport Books,
a division of NTC Publishing Group.
4255 West Touhy Avenue,
Lincolnwood (Chicago), Illinois 60646-1975.
© 1987 by Boye De Mente. All rights reserved.
No part of this book may be reproduced, stored in a
retrieval system, or transmitted in any form, or by
any means, electronic, mechanical, photocopying or
otherwise, without the prior written permission
of NTC Publishing Group.
Manufactured in the United States of America.
Library of Congress Catalog Card Number: 86-62724.

9 0 VP 9 8 7 6 5 4

Contents

System — Those Famous Expense Accounts — Compensation
for Salesmen — The Cash-Wage Syndrome — The Growing
Mobility of Labor — Quitting Isn't Easy — Executive Recruiting
Agencies — Who Wants to Work for a Foreign Company? —
Getting a Nose Job First — Alternatives for Foreign Firms —
Renting Your Japan Staff

Chapter 10
Peculiarities of Japanese Unions 151
The Enterprise Union System — Mutuality of Interests and
Ongoing Negotiations — The National Union Federations —
Foreign Firms and Japanese Unions

Chapter 11
The Makeup of Japan's Consumer Market 157
Shopping in the *Shotengai* — Central Shopping Districts and
Specialty Shops — Department Stores — Supermarkets and
Chain Stores — "Reading" the Japanese Market — The
Importance of "Detailers" — Discovering the Female Market
— Market Is Still "Japanese" — A Case in Point — Enduring
Traditions — Discount Selling — Credit Sales in Japan —
Packaging of Traditional Products — Packaging of Western
Products — Product Displays

Chapter 12
Japan's Distribution Labyrinth 175
Ties That Bind — The Emotional Factor — Direct Sales
Outlets — Exclusive Franchise Shops — Directly Owned Sales
Shops — Primary Wholesalers — Secondary Wholesalers —
Tertiary Wholesalers — "Market Shock" and American
Companies in Japan — Complexity in the Food Business —
The Apparel Industry

Chapter 13
How the Japanese Sell 187
The Japanese Philosophy of Selling — Selling in Department
Stores — Selling in Specialty Shops — Door-to-Door and
Direct-Mail Selling — Changing the Salesman's Image —
Going in Headfirst — Rebates and "Service" — Learning a
Lesson — It Can Be Done!

Chapter 1

Japan Today

Cultures in Collision

Japanese and Western businessmen annually do billions of dollars worth of import-export business with each other. There are several thousand joint Japanese-foreign firms operating at a profit in Japan—and the number is increasing at a rate of four or five a month. Yet, one of the worst mistakes foreign businessmen can make about Japan is to assume that the Japanese are as "Western" as their industry, that business in Japan is conducted more or less as it is in the United States or Europe, or that doing business in Japan is easy.

There have been, in fact, more failures than successes among foreign companies that have set up operations in Japan since 1952. What is even more significant is the number of proposed ventures that didn't get off the ground because of insufficient preparation, misunderstandings, and mistakes made by both sides.

For several years during the 1950s many Westerners and Japanese took it for granted that Japan's "traditional" business system was outmoded and would soon be replaced by the "more modern and efficient" American system. During these years, some small and medium-size firms, a few of which were to achieve extraordinary growth and fame in less than a decade, did adopt to varying degrees a number of the more conspicuous facets of American management. But without fanfare, the bigger and older Japanese companies continued to conduct their business in the Japanese way, serene in the belief that they already had the best system in the world—at least as far as Japan was concerned.

In the early 1960s, Japanese business in general further repudiated American-style management by going back into their history for concepts to buttress the foundations of their own unique system, as well as to pick up practical advice on how to deal with growing competition at home and abroad. Much of this effort involved the avid study of three books: an 18-volume biography of

1

Ieyasu Tokugawa, founder of Japan's last great military dynasty; *Sun Tzu*, the Chinese classic on military strategy; and a new edition of the *Operations Manual of the Imperial Japanese Army*. In brief, the messages the businessmen-readers got from these books were to equate business management with the strategy and tactics of war and to labor unstintingly for the prosperity and glory of their company and their country.

By the mid-1960s, all of the companies, including joint Japanese-American firms, that had adopted (or started out with) a number of American management practices, found that they had to drop them altogether and go back to The Japanese Way or modify them drastically to fit the Japanese scene. Today, despite the many surface changes that have occurred in Japan, the Western and Japanese business systems still differ radically—in ways that provide the foreign businessman in Japan with an endless source of frustration, anxiety, and wonder.

You can perhaps begin to appreciate some of the differences between the Japanese and Western ways of doing business when you consider that generally in the West the conduct of business creates tension in an atmosphere of personal competition, while the main theme of the Japanese way is to eliminate or reduce tension and individual responsibility, promote group spirit, and maintain harmony. The Japanese traditional business system, based on superior-inferior personal relations, seniority, and a strong authoritarian-paternalistic approach, contradicts many of the attitudes and practices American and European businessmen hold dear. The resulting conflicts are often traumatic to Japanese, as well as to foreign, managers.

The Japanese Abroad

Foreign businessmen who find themselves suffering from culture shock in their efforts to do business in Japan may take some solace in the fact that Japanese businessmen operating abroad are even more susceptible to this very human malady.

There are now some 10,000 Japanese enterprises operating overseas and close to half a million Japanese businessmen and family members living abroad. The combined effect this traumatic experience is having on the traditionally insular-minded, xenophobic Japanese is turning out to be a plus for foreign businesses because it is forcing the Japanese to become more open-minded and more international in their attitudes and policies. As more and more of these expatriate Japanese businessmen are rotated back to their home offices, the easier it will be for foreign businessmen to deal with Japan.

Japan's Second Opening

The liberalization and deregulation measures implemented by Japan in the mid-1980s have gone a long way toward internationalizing the Japanese market. The door is not yet wide open, but there is no denying that there has been a fundamental shift in both private and public policies to give foreign companies broader access to the Japanese marketplace. For the foreign enterprise willing to learn how to operate in the Japanese environment and to make the necessary investment in time, energy, and money, Japan can be a new frontier.

The genuine internationalization of Japan is proceeding at a snail's pace, however, despite appearances to the contrary. The number of Japanese businessmen who can speak English is rising at a significant rate, but it is still insignificant in the overall picture. The number of younger Japanese executives who have been educated abroad and/or spent years abroad on foreign assignments is also growing rapidly, but they are limited in what they can do outside the Japanese system. Some Japanese companies, including the great trading combines like Mitsubishi and Mitsui, began as early as the 1960s to virtually "collect" Japanese who had earned MBA degrees from Harvard and Stanford, despite the fact that they had no way of using them in their seniority-oriented management system.

Most of these companies still have not changed enough to take advantage of their MBAs. One newly hired MBA was sent out to a factory and ordered to "scrub off" what he had learned at the Brookings Institute in Washington, D.C. Unable to go back to the Japanese way of doing things, half or more of all the Japanese who have earned MBAs in the United States have ended up joining foreign firms or joint ventures on the foreign side.

Problems in TQC Land

The Japanese concept of Total Quality Control (TQC), now spreading around the world, had its roots in the quality control system introduced into Japan shortly after the end of World War II by Professor W. E. Deming of the U.S. But it was the Japanese Union of Scientists and Engineers (JUSE) in the early 1980s that created and launched the philosophy and system that is credited by many with the continuing success of Japan's economy. The primary goal of JUSE was to help Japan cope with the two oil crises that occurred in the 1970s.

The quality-control program launched by the JUSE bears little resemblance to the quality control system espoused by Dr. Deming. In their usual fashion, the Japanese took the root idea and developed it into a full-blown management philosophy that helped Japanese factories become the most efficient in the world. In fact, TQC, the current phase of the Japanese obsession with quality control, is regarded by many as the root cause of the trade imbalance between Japan and the U.S.

TQC as practiced by many Japanese companies has been likened to a religious cult in which adherents work with a fervor and commitment that is unmatched anywhere else. While the system has streamlined Japanese companies and virtually eliminated waste, some critics add that it has turned Japanese workers into robots and that a growing number of them end up burned out.

These same critics say that many Japanese companies have become so entranced by TQC that they have lost sight of market movements and have become totally dependent on TQC experts. The critics also contend that the warm, humanistic management for which these companies were famous has given way to a preoccupation with cold, impersonal data and that work has become monotonous and job satisfaction has diminished.

There is considerable and growing evidence that these critics are right. But like religious zealots, a significant proportion of Japanese managers remain hooked on TQC despite what appear to be strongly detrimental effects on overall management, either because managers cannot see what is happening or because they are so caught up in the quality craze they are unable to resist its pervasive influence.

4

Foreign Successes in Japan

It often seems that companies that take the plunge into Japan either succeed admirably or fail miserably. A recent summary of the companies that have been conspicuously successful in Japan showed that foreign firms have 92 percent of the market for dry soup mixes; 80 percent for instant coffee, safety razors, and paper cartons; and over 50 percent of the market for a number of other items ranging from golf balls to types of computers.

As these statistics indicate, some of the most conspicuous American marketing successes in Japan have been in the food and beverage areas—and most of these involve companies that have gone into joint ventures with Japanese firms, licensed Japanese companies to make their products in Japan, or established wholly owned subsidiaries in Japan. These companies include Nabisco, General Foods, Del Monte, Heinz, Campbell, and Coca-Cola.

As usual, there is a common pattern to the success stories of these companies. They made a long-term commitment to the Japanese market. They were well financed. Their food or drink formulas were redesigned to suit Japanese tastes. Their packaging was redone to appeal to the Japanese and to meet various other market demands. They went into relationships with well-known, successful Japanese manufacturers and/or wholesalers. They went out of their way to hire highly experienced Japanese managers with good personal connections in the trade, and they had the advantage of employing exceptionally capable American managers to head up their Japan operations. In addition, their products were new to Japan, had ego appeal, or were qualitatively or technically superior.

It sounds simple enough, but it wasn't and it isn't. Each of these companies—and the others that have succeeded in getting a share of the Japanese market—had to struggle for several years and perform a multitude of tasks correctly. A very significant factor in all of these success stories was the role that key Japanese managers played in helping bring them about. Without these very special people, the companies probably would not have succeeded.

The existence of some 400,000 wholesalers in the food distribution system, for example, was one of the many factors that had to be dealt with. One of the reasons for so many wholesalers is that there are some 700,000 retailers in the food trade—and a majority of them expect deliveries in lots as small as six units of something or other. Futhermore, most food outlets in Japan pay in cash, which has to be collected in person within a 60-day period after delivery. Finally, the primary allegiance of the wholesalers is to the retailers, not to the manufacturers.

The message that comes through from the experiences of each of these companies is that the key to success in Japan is recognizing the cultural components of the Japanese marketplace and then, with the help of very competent Japanese participation, devising strategies to deal with them.

Regardless of how many of the above factors apply, the foreign businessman in Japan must recognize and accept the fact that the Japanese are the most demanding consumers in the world. They demand unfailing quality not only in the products they buy, but in the packaging as well.

There is, in fact, no secret to achieving success in the Japanese market. It is a matter of having a product or service that the Japanese will accept and then working very hard and very carefully to win their acceptance. Notes Larry Blagg, president of Ore-Ida Japan Inc.: "You have to be almost perfect in terms of your packaging and your product and freshness and a lot of things that the Japanese people take for granted here every day."

A Serious Mistake

Many American companies that entered Japan in the immediate postwar decades made a serious mistake by taking the easy way out and going through Japanese trading companies and distributors. As a result, they learned little or nothing about the market. Many American companies trying to enter Japan today are attempting to repeat the same mistake, ignoring the fact that there is now very little incentive for Japanese trading firms and importers to aggressively market American-made products in Japan.

By almost totally ignoring the cultural component of selling in the Japanese market, American business as a whole is about 20 years behind the times when it comes to dealing with the Japanese and getting a share of the Japanese market. Fortunately, this time lag can be overcome fairly quickly if the American company is willing to make the necessary changes in its attitude and approach to the Japanese market.

There are three basic principles to business success in Japan. You must have a product or service that the Japanese want to buy; you must have an extensive network of contacts in Japan that you can orchestrate to achieve your goals; and you must have sufficient cross-cultural communication skills to gain the confidence and goodwill of the Japanese and make them comfortable in dealing with you.

It helps tremendously if you are starting out with a product that has been successful in the American market. Often, the first criterion the Japanese apply to any foreign-made product is how successful it has been in its own home market.

In Japan, even more so than in the United States, every product has a distinctive identity, image, acceptable role, and what Japan marketing specialist Earle Okumura calls its "contact infrastructure." To successfully market a product in Japan, one must be aware of all of these factors and use them correctly. One of the major differences between the Japanese market and the American market is that the contact infrastructure in Japan tends to be far more deeply entrenched and far more influential in the marketing of any product. It is therefore often necessary to do more marketing research in Japan and to spend more time at developing personal relationships with these contact points. Once you have established your network, it is also necessary to spend more time nurturing it to keep it working smoothly.

The best product, the best research, and the best network in the world may all go for naught in the Japanese market if you are not really good at communicating with your Japanese contacts in the appropriate cultural context. And this is the area in which most Western businessmen, particularly Americans, are the most likely to fall down.

We tend to believe that a good product will sell itself in any market, which is almost always not the case in Japan, and to ignore or downplay the importance of the cultural factor. In Japan, ignorance of the cultural aspect of business is the most fatal of all handicaps.

While the strategy and tactics that a foreign company should use in any attempt to enter the Japanese market are obvious, it is astounding how many foreign companies fail to recognize or do the obvious.

The first characteristic of business in Japan is its personal nature. The second characteristic, in virtually every category, is its competitiveness—fierce competitiveness that drives the engine of the economy domestically, as well as internationally. There is competition for land, for capital, for workers, for raw materials, and for the attention and the money of consumers. The obsession for exquisite design, high quality, an almost unlimited amount of aftermarket service, and a steady stream of new products makes the Japanese marketplace the most competitive in the world.

Foreign companies doing business in Japan face the same kind and degree of competition. But marketing conditions in Japan are becoming more receptive to the American approach to merchandising. The market is changing from the commodity approach, in which products are simply placed on shelves, to one in which "product pull" is the key to success. This gives foreign companies, which have been honing their consumer-pull marketing skills for over 100 years, a distinct advantage in Japan if they can get beyond the cultural barriers.

Cultural insensitivity and casual-to-arrogant attitudes remain the greatest handicaps afflicting many foreign businessmen interested in the Japanese market, Americans in particular. Americans generally rank at or near the bottom in sensitivity to other cultures. We continue to downplay or ignore the importance of speaking the language of the people we want to do business with. We do not give sufficient value to the life-styles, habits, likes, and dislikes of Japanese consumers.

It goes without saying (to use a favorite Japanese expression) that virtually all the successful American businesses in Japan understood and worked *with* the cultural forces instead of against them. This is such a simple concept that it appears moronic to harp on the subject continuously, but the reality is that a significant percentage of American businessmen appear congenitally incapable of stepping outside of their cultural skin when dealing with the Japanese.

Becoming culturally sensitive *and* knowing enough about another culture to operate in it—or with it—efficiently is not easy. For most of us, it does not come with a few days or weeks of exposure. It is something that usually requires years of study and practice. In Japan, it is a very fine art that the Japanese themselves are acutely attuned to, are very conscious of, and take pride in mastering and practicing with all the finesse of a master violinist.

The typical American businessman who goes to Japan is not only handicapped by little or no appreciation or training in cross-cultural skills, he is also immediately subjected to cultural differences that are absolute and thereafter influence every nuance of his thought and behavior. He is severely limited in what he can say and do, to the extent that much of his education and professional training become virtually useless.

His first impressions on arriving in Tokyo are usually misleading. The city is mostly Western in appearance. His hotel is often well above international standards in architecture, decor, and services. He has no serious problem communicating as long as he limits himself to addressing only lobby hotel staff or restaurant and shop personnel within the hotel. So far, the fact that he is in a new and very different world has made little impact.

But problems begin the moment he tries to deal with anyone else or steps outside the hotel. He finds that he cannot read signs, talk to people, locate addresses, go anywhere, or do anything except stroll around (near the hotel) without getting help from someone who speaks English. Not being able to come and go without help or to make his own appointments or to track down business leads puts the businessman in the hands of whoever he gets to help him.

If he has Japanese contacts, he generally depends on them for virtually everything he does while he is in Japan, except perhaps for some shopping. The Japanese are very polite and amazingly generous with their time and money in hosting foreign visitors. The foreign businessman is shuttled to a series of meetings, luncheons, dinners, and visits to cabarets and massage baths that begin early and often continue until midnight or after.

All this time, the typical foreign businessman tends to feel he is functioning well, and the idea of culture shock seldom if ever enters his mind. In the meantime, he has usually been behaving in a manner that is totally out of character. Unless he has something valuable the Japanese really want, he is at a serious disadvantage in negotiating any kind of relationship. Even the advantage of having something the Japanese want generally lasts only until an agreement is made and a contract signed.

It is virtually axiomatic that problems between Japanese and foreign companies begin immediately after the celebration following the signing of a contract. These problems are often already present in seed form because the two parties were unaware that they did not fully understand each other prior to the signing, or they were conscious of their misunderstanding but signed anyway, expecting to work the problems out between them afterward.

How to Do Business with the Japanese

Even if both sides fully understood each other, problems begin immediately anyway because they will invariably interpret the aims of the relationship differently. If they do not anticipate this possibility and fail to nurture the relationship carefully and on a regular face-to-face basis, the arrangement gradually breaks down or becomes more and more Japanese—for better or worse.

The good news is that there is a growing awareness among Japanese on all levels, but particularly in the highest government and business echelons, that Japan must become more aggressive in effectively integrating its economy with that of the world—or they will suffer the ultimate alienation and isolation, and loss of life as they know it today.

This, plus the fact that social changes in Japan have reached a high frenzy, and are changing both attitudes and lifestyles so rapidly that Japanese businessmen in general cannot keep up with them.

Japanese consumers are in a constant state of metamorphosis—a process that is being influenced and aided by the hundreds of foreign companies in Japan, by the fact that several million Japanese travel abroad each year (during which time they shed a little more of their Japanese skin), and by an ongoing dialogue and debate within the heart of the nation about the need to understand, be understood, and very quickly come to terms with the great forces they themselves unleashed.

The problem is not that of Japan alone. American businessmen and American consumers, and their counterparts around the world, have been willing and eager accomplices in the emergence of Japan as a super economic power that threatens to take over more of the world economic pie than is fair.

It is past time for both foreign consumers and businessmen to understand the role they played in Japan's rise to superpower status, and jump on the bandwagon they first pulled and are now running to catch up with.

The question of whether or not it is worth the effort for American and other foreign businessmen to try to do business with Japan—or do it better if they are already doing it—is no longer the issue. If they want to continue doing business in their *own* country—as well as elsewhere in the world—they have no choice . . . and that includes their own neighborhood markets.

The Japanese are on a global roll, and the only way foreign companies around the world can stay in the game is to learn how to play the same game. Otherwise, the Japanese will win by default.

This new imperative is a challenge of major importance, but it should not be viewed as malicious or threatening. Rather, it should be seen for what it actually is—an opportunity to advance the economic, social, and cultural level of the world at a vastly accelerated pace, and an opportunity to bring unprecedented benefits to mankind in one generation.

The future that the Japanese envision for themselves—in fact, the future they are planning and working toward—is very exciting. Just a glimmer of how the Japanese see their future, how they would like for it to be, should be enough to inspire the competitive and cooperative spirit of business and government leaders everywhere.

Chapter 2

Problems Facing Westerners Doing Business in Japan

"The more I visit Japan, the less I understand about what is going on!"
—A veteran American importer

The Obstacles

The obstacles facing Westerners doing business in Japan are many, and several are unique. They begin with the language barrier; proceed to basic differences in philosophy, values, motivation, living style, etiquette, and social sanctions; and then go on to geographical, historical, economic, and political factors.

The personal reaction of foreign businessmen when they encounter these obstacles varies with circumstances. The short-term visitor who comes here as a guest, on a "firemen's" tour, or on a "fact-finding" mission, is generally impressed with what he sees and with some of the apparent advantages enjoyed by Japan's business leaders, without having more than a vague idea of what lies behind those advantages.

The foreigner who travels to Japan with a number of business goals to accomplish in a limited period of time will most likely get an entirely different impression. He is apt to find himself in the strange position of being both frustrated and fascinated—literally unable to believe things could possibly be as they seem.

For example, Japanese companies often decide on the dividend they are going to pay stockholders long before they know whether it is earned. Some base their dividends on what others in the industry are paying. You can imagine the consternation that is caused when the Japanese partner in a joint venture announces at the beginning of a term its intention of paying such-and-such a dividend at the end of the year!

How to Do Business with the Japanese

One Tokyo-based American sales executive offered another example: "If we present a promotion idea to our Japanese staff and they like it immediately, it frightens us. This is a pretty fair sign it isn't any good. It has been our experience that good ideas can generally be expected to result initially in a negative reaction. To get around this, we allow the negativism to run its course and then lead them back to the same proposition by another route."

Of course, the American businessman in this example is presuming that his ideas really are "good" and that the Japanese are wrong in rejecting them.

In negotiating with Japanese businessmen, most Americans try to get them to take immediate or quick action. Since this is not the Japanese way of doing business, they are forced into a corner where they have no chance but to say no—usually by employing delaying tactics that often lead the frustrated foreign businessman to throw his hands up in angry defeat. Describing a typical business experience in Japan, the sales manager of a large American manufacturing firm said: "Last year I worked for six months setting up a deal for a Canadian company. Then the top technical executive came over to sign the contract. He expected to have it wrapped up in two days. I estimated seven. It took 15. Shortly after he returned to the home office he informed me that he had negotiated and signed exactly the same kind of contract with an American firm in two working days."

In a lengthy comment, the Japanese manager of an American buying office observed: "We deal with around 100 suppliers. Out of this number, only a few will let us know in advance if they cannot deliver on the date specified. With these few suppliers our relationship has become more than just business. It is a highly personal affair. Most sundry suppliers here will say anything to stall you off after a delivery date comes due. We know this, but we always feel there is a chance they will come through the next time. But time and again they put us off on a day-to-day basis until it is too late to cancel the order and attempt to place it elsewhere.

"Another of the most frustrating policies of Japanese trading firms—the large ones, as well as the small ones—is their system of assigning only one man to each business account. If your man is out—and he is about 30 percent of the time—nothing can be accomplished until he returns. Worst of all, however, is the planned disappearance of this man when anything goes wrong—the very time you need him most. This game of hide-and-seek often goes on for days. We contact the company time after time, and nothing happens. Everybody in the man's company, including his superiors, are 'sympathetic' but say they are powerless to help you.

"In most cases, this is nothing more than a stall, and the whole company participates in the conspiracy. It sometimes happens that the man has been handling your account outside the firm, either as a private individual or with another supplier from whom he receives a commission. When I first arrived in Japan I took all this very seriously and was sick for two years. Now I live by the 'duck's back' philosophy—and just let everything slide off."

While I do not believe this man's experience is typical today, it nevertheless points up areas of potential trouble for the foreign businessman in Japan.

The Personal Approach

It is important that businessmen wanting to enter the Japanese market take into consideration the religious aspects of Japanese culture and business. The larger and more successful the firm, the more likely the company's practices will be based on essentially religious precepts and, in fact, include a number of annual religious ceremonies.

The huge and multinational Toyota Motor Company has a Shinto shrine in its headquarters compound in Toyota, Aichi Prefecture. On January 5 each year, all of the company employees, from the president and other ranking executives on down, line up and pray for the continued growth and success of the company.

Japanese sociologists often comment on the religious ardor with which the Japanese engage in business and compare the attitude and activities of Japanese company employees abroad with that of missionaries—almost blindly dedicated to their cause and sacrificial to the point of martyrdom in their efforts to succeed.

The point is not that the Japanese are strict Buddhists or Shintoists per se, but that they approach work and business success with the dedication and persistence that is more typical of a burning religious commitment. Like a religion, the affairs and interests of the company pervade every aspect of the employees' lives.

As a result of the personal nature of the Japanese business system, the daily activities of business naturally hinge around interpersonal considerations rather than the cold, rational logic favored by Westerners. This difference may sound insignificant, but its overall implications are of great importance to the foreign businessman working in Japan.

It means, first of all, that not being Japanese, the foreigner is not subject to the web of personal obligations that provide the foundation of Japan's business ethics. Because of his non-Japanese identity, plus the long list of pervading cultural barriers that are for the most part insurmountable, the foreign businessman cannot fully assume these personal obligations even if he wants to. He is in the widest sense culturally barred from fully meeting the Japanese on their own home ground—or on *any* common ground, for that matter, since the average Japanese finds it just as difficult to step out of his unique business world as the foreigner does to step into it.

In practical terms, this means that the foreign businessman cannot approach a Japanese company as he would a Western company with any chance of getting similar results in a like period of time. From the first moment of contact, the Japanese businessman is more concerned with how you got his name, whether you have an introduction, and, if you do, whom it came from, than with the purpose of your visit. If you do not have an introduction, you are off on the wrong foot and may make no progress at all. If you have one, but it is from someone with whom the Japanese businessman or his company has no important relationship, it may do you very little good.

As a rule, Japanese businessmen do not feel safe until they know who you are, and they are not likely to make any commitment or respond in any positive way until you have identified yourself and provided them with sufficient guarantees that you are a respectable, responsible person who is not likely to cheat or deceive them. There is really nothing irrational about this attitude, even from the Western viewpoint. Businessmen everywhere treat people differently when they come to them recommended by friends or important contacts.

But in Japan, this difference is far more extreme than it is elsewhere. Conditioned to respond positively only to people in his own group or with whom he has an established relationship, the Japanese businessman is seriously limited in his reaction to people he doesn't know or has no reason to trust.

If you do have a strong introduction, the Japanese businessman is then interested in the size of your firm, your title, your age, and even your university. Last on the list, as far as he is concerned, is what you want to see him about.

The initial contact you make in a Japanese company is of prime importance. You should show the same interest in him that he shows in you—his age, how long he has been with the company, whether he has had a promotion recently or is on the verge of getting one; all these are vital factors. If he has just had a promotion or expects to get one within a matter of weeks or months, he will be even more reluctant to get personally involved in something new. In any case, it is almost always more effective if your introduction is to someone on or above the *bucho* (department head) level. After you get acquainted is the time to ask him which *bucho* or *kacho* (section head) is in charge of your product or area of interest.

Personal relations are generally more important than price in Japan's business system. Maintaining harmonious relationships that involve mutual trust, mutual help, and guarantees of reciprocity take precedence over profit. An important example of the personal approach to business in Japan is gift giving. Most companies keep careful records of clients and customers and twice each year send them gifts.

Another example is the extensive entertainment of clients and customers by Japan businessmen in cabarets and restaurants. An American director of a joint venture company who has made a detailed study of this aspect of doing business in Japan said: "The average foreign business resident in Japan really knows very little about the Japanese business world, which recognizes little difference between night and day and emphasizes regular late-night entertainment."

The customary way to initiate close personal relationships with Japanese businessmen is to meet and entertain them on their own stamping grounds. To do this, it helps considerably if the foreign representative has "face" at appropriate cabarets, bars, and restaurants. That is, he has to be known by key hostesses and managers of several places and be welcomed there. He has to be accepted to the extent that he can charge bills.

Said the above-mentioned joint venture representative: "When I first came to Japan, I used to take my Japanese associates and clients to nightclubs that catered to foreigners. It didn't take long to see that nobody enjoyed these outings, including myself. So I suggested that we go to a typical Japanese cabaret: small, intimate, and well-stocked with hostesses who hadn't been de-Japanized by exposure to foreigners. The transformation was startling. In their

17

own element, my Japanese companions really let their hair down. All formalities and pretensions disappeared. I made note of this and immediately began a systematic campaign to develop the necessary "face" at selected places. Now, when I take Japanese guests to these places, I'm treated like a nabob. I have "face," which often means more to a Japanese than business acumen. Now, these people go out of their way to help me do my job in Japan."

Higher-level Japanese business executives, however, seldom, if ever, go to cabarets or public bars. They patronize only very exclusive restaurants—which are either private or in hotels—or so-called *geisha* houses, which are exclusive restaurants/inns that call in *geisha* when requested by known patrons. It is not recommended that the foreign businessman invite these executives to any other kind of place.

While the amount and intensity of business entertainment has declined significantly since the heydays of the 1960s and 1970s, it is still one of the major industries in the country, involving hundreds of millions of dollars a year.

The role that entertainment plays in business in Japan is a traditional one sanctified by more than a thousand years of custom. Few agreements are made without it. One of the best-known examples of sealing bargains and contracts with entertainment concerns two of Japan's military heroes. During the revolutionary turmoil surrounding the Meiji Restoration (1868), Takamori Saigo, of the famous Satsuma clan, met Shinshu Takasugi, of Choshu. To emphasize the respect with which he regarded Saigo and the closeness of the relationship he desired with him, Takasugi immediately suggested they go to a whorehouse together. After the two men participated in the excursion, they became blood brothers from the Japanese point of view.

"This doesn't mean that the foreign executive in Japan has to become a regular customer at houses of ill-fame," a Japanese businessman added, "but it is good sense for him to take his top Japanese associates out to a restaurant or cabaret on fairly regular occasions." Foreign businessmen should keep in mind that among high-ranking Japanese businessmen, as well as many in middle-management, the golf course is now more popular than the *geisha* house.

The foreign businessman should also remember that gift giving and entertaining will have a negative effect if they are done without good reason. When there is no obvious excuse for either activity, the Japanese are inclined to become suspicious and wary. The time to entertain is at the beginning of a project when you are going to ask your staff or suppliers to make an extraordinary effort to do something particularly hard or important. Entertaining is also appropriate when something has been done well, and a celebration is called for. On both of these occasions, the monolingual foreign businessman is often well served by having a Japanese spokesman who can speak for him and say the right things.

Some Japanese companies have done away with gift-giving custom altogether, and the trend is for others to follow suit. Commenting on this subject, Earle Okumura, a veteran consultant on doing business in Japan, with extensive hands-on experience, said: "Foreigners should not try to follow the gift-giving custom because it is too subtle and really not necessary where they are concerned. Getting involved simply isn't productive, and there is no reason for the foreign businessman to try to compete with the Japanese in this area. This is something the Japanese fully understand and appreciate. On the other hand, a card at Christmas is neither complicated nor costly and is appreciated."

Maintaining Correct Relations

It is not easy for a foreign businessman to achieve and maintain good relations with his Japanese staff and counterparts in other companies. But trying to meet them on their home ground is important. It requires a thorough knowledge and at least a partial acceptance of the interpersonal relationships that control not only individuals, but whole companies, as well as a considerable skill in manipulating the various elements. The primary requirements, according to Japanese psychologists, are three: (1) getting into the family circle, (2) establishing a strict hierarchy, and (3) maintaining surface harmony with business associates.

The first requirement—becoming one of the family or group—is most important because the Japanese idea of group/family incorporates an exclusivity to the point of hostility to nonmembers. As a result, the only way anyone, foreign or not, can become close to a Japanese is to become symbolically a member of his group. In business, this is accomplished in two ways: by granting special favors to one's Japanese subordinates and by eating and drinking with them. Of the latter, drinking is the most important because it

19

allows one to throw off all inhibitions and to display emotion. Complete drunkenness is required for the two parties to reach full communion. If for some reason a person can't or doesn't get completely drunk, he should simulate drunkenness.*

Having been out on the town a number of times with your Japanese business associate, you may want to invite both him and his wife to your home for dinner. This is not as natural as it sounds. It is not customary for Japanese businessmen to socialize in this way with their co-workers or counterparts in other firms. They will usually do so with foreign businessmen, however, when the opportunity arises. In many cases, the wife of the Japanese businessman may never have been in a Western home, may speak little, if any, English, and is likely to be afraid (particularly if she is past middle age) of embarrassing everyone.

Just the smallest amount of proficiency in the Japanese language by yourself and your wife will help put the Japanese wife at ease. Once this is accomplished, you have established a relationship with your Japanese associate in what are to him the three most important areas of his life: (1) the official company-to-company relationship, (2) the man-to-man contact during pleasure time, and (3) the family relationship. When you have accomplished this, you have demonstrated, in the only way acceptable, your interest in and appreciation for Japan and the Japanese.

Establishing a hierarchical system means requiring subordinates to contribute to a superior's prestige and status by the use of "respect" language, by making periodic visits to his desk, and by giving him seasonal gifts—although gift giving to superiors is also being discouraged by a number of companies. A subordinate must cooperate with a superior in all things and not attempt to repay any favors he receives—because this would be a sign that he considers himself the superior's equal.

The hierarchical system in Japan is illustrated whenever two Japanese meet for the first time. They are always very careful of what they say and how they act until they find out their respective hierarchical positions. If they happen to be members of the same company, and there is no discernible age difference, they are both uneasy until they know when each entered the company, how far

*Recent strict enforcement of drunken-driving regulations has taken some of the fun out of getting tipsy. If you are the guest, however, the Japanese host usually provides a car and driver to take you home.

they went in school, which schools they attended, and what "group" they belong to in the company. Once these facts are established, the two men immediately either assume senior-junior roles or act toward each other as equal.

This sharp superior-inferior difference between all Japanese is defined by the three words *sempai* (senior), *kohai* (junior), and *doryo* (equal rank). The first two words are heard often—the latter not so frequently because even among people of equal rank one will usually be superior to the other in some way. Japanese etiquette requires that all *kohai* attach the honorific "san" to the name of any *sempai* they address. When speaking to a junior, a senior often uses the last name and "kun" instead of "san." Equals use "san" when addressing each other in formal and public situations. If they are very close personal friends from school days, they will often refer to each other by their last names when they are on outings and when they are drinking together.

The last of the three major requirements for maintaining "correct" relationships in any Japanese group or company dictates that subordinates must never show up superiors in any way. If a project succeeds, the superior must appear to have played the leading role. If a project fails, the superior must appear to be blameless. This protects the stability of the hierarchy. As a result of this system, it often appears that many young employees in Japanese firms do very little because they are afraid they might upset the hierarchical balance. Years ago, there was a saying to this effect that was popular among employees who aspired to be executives—*yasumazu* (never take a holiday); *okurezu* (never be late for work); and *hatarakazu* (never do any work). If the junior executive could abide by these rules, it was implied that he would have the reputation of being a steady, dependable fellow and that he would automatically rise in the managerial hierarchy, eventually taking his place at or near the top. Young would-be executives must still be extremely cautious about upsetting hierarchical harmony, but today they are expected to work diligently at whatever task they are assigned.

The Very Important Aisatsu

The *aisatsu* (aye-sot-sue) is another Japanese institution that foreign businessmen must know and use in order to function effectively in Japan. By itself, the word means "greeting," but over the centuries it has come to mean much more. The first meeting between high executives of two companies just beginning a relationship is known as an *aisatsu*. In this instance, the purpose of the meeting is to establish an official, recognized relationship between the two companies, give the principals a chance to size each other up, and set the stage for follow-up meetings between lower-ranking personnel.

There is almost never any detailed discussion of business at this meeting. Often, the Japanese executive will not know anything about the matter at hand and will not be directly involved in either the following negotiations or any subsequent business relationship. Any attempt by the foreign side to begin serious discussions at an *aisatsu* would be a mistake.

Once a relationship is established with a Japanese company and business is underway, there are frequent occasions during the year when it is customary to pay *aisatsu* (courtesy) calls on your counterpart and key contacts in the Japanese company. These calls may be made when business is going especially well or especially badly, when someone is promoted or dies, or when there is some other special event—just before the end of the year, for example, and immediately after offices open following New Year's.

Being in the Right Place

One of the things the foreign businessman in Japan has to get used to is being told where to sit. Where one sits in Japan is a matter of rank and hospitality, and it is a deeply ingrained custom that plays an important role in all meetings and gatherings, including such mundane ones as riding on a train or in a car.

The ranking member or guest is invariably directed to the "seat of honor" (*kami za*) in any Japanese situation. In a room, office, or restaurant, the seat farthest from the door is the seat of honor. In a train, it is the window seat facing the front of the train, and in an automobile it is the seat behind the driver. There is even a "place of honor" on elevators—the left rear corner.

Your awareness of this custom—and your using it when you are hosting Japanese—will go a long way toward demonstrating your understanding of Japanese culture and your sensitivity to the feelings of your Japanese colleagues or guests.

It is also a demonstration of friendship and goodwill to accompany your Japanese guest to the door or the elevator when he or she leaves your office. The final gesture is to push the button that brings the elevator to the required floor and then to make your farewell comments after your visitor is on the elevator and has turned to face the door.

Another barrier to Western businessmen operating in Japan on an equal footing with the Japanese is that most of the various associations and power groups are closed to foreign membership. As the Japanese would say, the idea of letting foreign firms join all of these groups is "unthinkable—like clasping the enemy to your bosom." In the associations that foreign firms are allowed to join, they are treated as outsiders and generally have little or no influence.

Asked for the best advice he could give to foreign businessmen dealing with Japanese, a top Japanese executive said: "First of all, the foreign businessman should not behave as if Japanese companies were identical or even similar to Western companies. In the United States, in particular, companies are made up of individual people with distinct personalities. Japanese companies consist of a hierarchy with semitotalitarian management. They have to be treated like small feudal states. The larger the firm, the more likely its top executives are to consider themselves modern day feudal lords with all the traditional responsibilities and prerogatives implied in the title."

These few comments are enough to indicate that the Western businessman visiting or working in Japan cannot automatically take for granted many of the business practices he is accustomed to in his country. To the Western or European mind, for example, the idea of studying military strategy and tactics as a means of enhancing the chances for business success is incongruous, to say the least. To the Japanese, it is a natural inclination and is reflected daily in their use of military terms—infiltration, invasion, landing—to describe foreign capital coming into Japan.

For the foreign businessman to succeed in business in Japan, it is essential that he know a great deal about how Japanese businessmen (and government bureaucrats) think and what they regard as normal behavior. This understanding requires an extensive knowledge of the environment of Japan and specifically how it has shaped the character, personality, and attitudes of the Japanese businessman.

Chapter 3

The Japanese Businessman

"We Japanese have policies but no principles."

—Dr. Kazutaka Watanabe
Liberal arts authority, author, lecturer

Doing Business Upside Down

Cultural circumstances have made the Japanese unique in a number of ways and have resulted in a business system that, from the Western viewpoint, often appears upside down. From earliest times, the lives of the Japanese have been guided by vertically structured personal relations within the family, with their neighbors, with their clan, with other clans, and finally with the overall ruling power. Individualism, personal ambition, and other characteristics that we look upon as being among the birthrights of man were subordinated to the interests of these carefully defined groups.

As the centuries passed, the necessity for the Japanese to faithfully discharge their personal obligations to those above and below them became formalized into meticulously detailed ceremonies. Finally, these obligations became sanctified as the fundamental "principles" of life. Good and bad were not abstract theories derived from some metaphysical heaven or hell. Actions and thoughts that did not disrupt personal relations were good—or possibly neutral—while anything that threatened disruption was bad.

At no time did this obligation-based society function perfectly. It was constantly being subverted to some degree by the universal human inclination toward selfishness—the desire for wealth and power. But on the whole, no system has ever been applied as successfully anywhere over such a long period of time.

With the deterioration of the country's rice economy in the eighteenth and nineteenth centuries, the framework of the system suffered grievously. The introduction of Western socioeconomic ideas and industrial technology, following the downfall of the feudal dictatorship in 1868, further weakened the remaining framework and undermined to a significant degree the philosophical foundations of the superior-inferior system. But a system that differs in no great degree from a religion cannot be destroyed or even partially eclipsed in one or two lifetimes. Furthermore, when industrialization began, it was natural for the Japanese to establish companies based on the hierarchical arrangement and obligation system that was the root of their society.

During the American period in Japan in the late 1940s and early 1950s, this system came under extraordinary pressure to change. For the most part, these changes were limited to the family system, not the company system. By the late 1950s, Japanese business leaders who had been flirting with the American way of doing business had found it wanting. And, in concert with many intellectuals, they began to draw once again on traditional Japanese concepts and customs as the foundation for their business system.

As the crumbling of the hierarchical structure of the family continued to weaken the web of obligations binding the members to one another, the company gradually replaced the family as the basic unit in Japanese life. The degree to which traditional concepts are being applied today differs with each firm. The larger and older the company, the stronger the system tends to be. It is easily discernible, however, in every company in Japan.

The Family System in Business

The typical ranking Japanese businessman tends to believe with religious zeal that a company should be run as a huge family, with the president as both mother and father of the employees. Workers should be bound to the firm by a filial type of love, respect, and loyalty that transcend all desire for material gain. Everyone is expected to be perfectly selfless and labor in happy unison for the mutual benefit of them-

26

selves, the company, and Japan. Thus, the important Japanese businessman sees himself as a benevolent dictator whose guiding principle is respect and love for humanity. The products of this philosophy—the control over behavior and the deeply personal way in which Japanese firms are operated—are the factors that directly and decisively affect the foreign businessman in Japan.

The fact that the leader of a Japanese company is regarded as a surrogate parent is advantageous to both the leader and the company. After he retires from the company, he does not give up his authority as parent he continues to exercise a certain amount of influence and authority until he dies. In the case of such founder-leaders as Konosuke Matsushita, he, like many emperors and *shoguns* in Japan's past, remained just as powerful in retirement as they were when they were running their organizations on a day-to-day basis. In fact, many such men retire early to free themselves from daily affairs in order to spend their time thinking and working out long-range plans for their companies.

To the short-term visitor, the family system of Japanese companies may appear to function smoothly. But in many cases, beneath the surface of enforced conformity, discontent and ferment occasionally erupt. The problems of the individual in this system are popular themes in sociological studies, and the system no longer escapes unscathed. But it prevails.

How Managers Are Developed

The Japanese way of training future managers to fit into and perpetuate the family system in business is interesting. Responsibility for this important function is usually left to middle-aged managers who, though well respected, have not been and will not be chosen to become company directors by the age of 45 or so and who, when they reach 55, are likely to be promoted to the top management of subsidiary or affiliated companies. These "trainers" are never the direct superiors of the young managerial trainees and may have no authority over them.

Trainees are "assigned" to a particular manager on the basis of school ties and a "general understanding" that is not clearly defined. Peter Drucker once referred to these manager-train-ers as "godfathers," and I can't think of a better term. The relationship lasts for about ten years, usually ending when the godfather retires or is transferred. During the intervening years, he is expected to act as an adviser to the young men "attached" to him (in a large company, there may be several dozen), to help them with personal problems within or outside the company, and to introduce them to the art of en-tertaining business associates or clients in cabarets and *geisha* houses.

In the course of this relationship, the godfather is expected to become sufficiently acquainted with each young man un-der his care so that when the time comes he can give top man-agement an accurate appraisal of his ability, character, and potential. When the personnel department begins looking for a man for a new assignment, it is the godfathers who are consulted.

The Toyota System

Toyota is an outstanding example of the Japanese companies that use the godfather system of training managers. At Toyota, it is called the Advisory System. Managerial candi-dates coming into the company are assigned to group leaders who are two job-ranks above them and who are responsible for the training of the fledgling managers during the rest of their careers. Training revolves around actual work situations and problems on the job. Each year, some 500 Toyota em-ployees are officially appointed advisers.

In addition, Toyota also conducts ongoing seminars for its managers, utilizing both in-house executives as trainers and bringing in well-known managers and specialists from the outside. The president and chairman of the board of Toyota regularly participate in these training sessions as speakers.

Toyota teaches its managers foreign languages and tries to give them an international perspective. Foreign employees are similarly trained. They learn Toyota's management style, especially how to transfer their technological know-how and managerial skills to their subordinates—something that Ameri-can and European managers often do not do.

At Toyota, administrative, as well as technical, personnel are rotated to other jobs every three to five years. This means that their on-the-job training continues throughout their working careers. On the shop level, employees are rotated within their work group, which is called *han* (hahn), the old word for provincial clans in feudal Japan. This constant rotation of office and plant personnel is aimed at enhancing the individual development of employees and continuously reenergizing the workplace.

One of the primary aims of Toyota's collective educational programs is to make sure that employees are familiar with company policies and understand the performance expectations and responsibilities required at the different levels of management. Another important aim is to help them develop special skills and grasp new technologies. Toyota differs from most other Japanese companies in that people originally recruited as factory workers can be promoted to white-collar management positions.

Changes Coming

Management and news media in Japan are filled with warnings that Japan must adapt its traditional management system to meet today's challenges, not only internationally but domestically. The marketplace is changing so rapidly that the older, larger, and more bureaucratic companies are losing touch on an accelerating scale, despite efforts to constantly update the training of their employees.

In a throwback to the 1950s, many of the training programs inaugurated in the early and mid-1980s, especially management schools that are private enterprises, were patterned after those used for decades by Harvard and other American business schools. In a growing number of corporations, something very close to MBA-type training is *in*. These various programs are all designed, in one way or another, to foster the development of *jinzai*, or "men of talent"—meaning people who can think and act independently.

This trend will surely continue, and some time in the next two or three decades, Japanese and Western-style management should meet somewhere in the middle.

The Importance of Company Spirit

The foreign businessman dealing with a larger Japanese company must recognize the importance of the company spirit with which the employees are imbued. It is a product of Japanese culture in general and of the training each employee undergoes after joining the company.

The training centers of many Japanese companies are operated very much like military camps for such elite groups as the American Marines or the Green Berets. The rules are strict, and the training is both physically and mentally demanding. The new "recruits" are literally brainwashed in the spirit of the company.

At the Matsushita training center, for example, all trainees are assembled each morning in a military-type formation after an exercise session. Then the director of the center, standing before the group on a platform, unfolds a scroll on which are written the precepts of the company. He leads the trainees in a loud and rousing reading of the Matsushita credo, which includes the line: "We shall perform our duty as employees, make efforts to improve social life, and contribute to the development of world culture!"

The extraordinary conformity that has been the hallmark of traditional company training programs in Japan is now under attack, however, and there are some who are saying that such conformity has created a vacuum; that in order to compete domestically and internationally in the future, Japanese managers will not only have to maintain their individual spirit and initiative, they will have to learn how to be independent-minded and individually decisive instead of the reverse. These critics of the traditional system say that virtually every characteristic that used to be considered taboo in a good employee is now not only desirable, but vital to the survival of individual companies and Japan.

In the early 1980s, major companies began recruiting more widely from universities than they did in the past. They also began hiring more people who had been educated abroad or worked in other companies for several years—both previously out of the question for the typical large firm.

Not surprisingly, many Japanese companies are looking at the training programs and hiring procedures of more successful American and European firms as models. Still, these changes are slow in coming. It will take decades before the overall way of doing business is significantly changed—but change is inevitable.

Japanese Logic

One of the fundamental problems that often upsets the foreign businessman is the difference between Japanese and Western logic. Japanese logic is not inflexible and unchanging. It is like a wrapping cloth that can assume any shape and can be made large or small. It is based on circumstances rather than principles. Like a chameleon, the Japanese businessman automatically attempts to take on the protective coloring of his surroundings. An example of the adaptability of the Japanese was especially well illustrated in a comment by a well-known Japanese writer-lecturer who said of himself: "I am a Christian in faith, Buddhist in philosophy, and Shintoist in my views on society."

This same attitude makes it possible for the Japanese businessman to maintain, without apparent conflict, views regarding values, contracts, commitments, time, and other relationships that the Westerner tends to feel are both contradictory and irrational.

Values of Japanese Businessmen

The guiding principle of most Western businessmen is that profit must be made. This standard pervades virtually all our endeavors and actions. We give only secondary consideration to the needs of our employees, if we consider them at all. We tend to look upon society at large and our government as separate entities and we often think of government as an adversary.

Leading Japanese businessmen, on the other hand, automatically identify themselves as Japanese first and entrepreneurs second. Their guiding principles are: (1) their overall responsibility to Japan; (2) their responsibilities to their employees; and (3) the need to be successful in business in order to fulfill the first two obligations.

It should be noted that the pure profit motive does not appear in the "guiding principles" of leading Japanese businessmen. This is not to suggest, of course, that Japanese businessmen do not try to make a profit. But time and again, in situations in which the Western businessman's behavior is determined entirely by profit, the Japanese businessman's behavior is determined largely by other considerations. He will strive to maintain harmony in the company, in the market, or in the country; avoid laying off employees; or enhance his reputation—in a manner that often distresses foreign businessmen who are dealing with him.

Most Japanese businessmen identify very closely with their government. They consider their interests and those of the government to be essentially the same, and they expect the government to exercise significant control over their industry. Where the government has not taken a direct hand in the conduct of business, the businessmen have formed associations and cartels with others in the same industry and then sought government approval and guidance. Behind the scenes, it is often impossible to see any difference between the policies and actions of the leading industrial firms and the policies and actions of the government. The two are often so closely related financially that, for all practical purposes, there is no difference.

Finding Where the Buck Stops

Another characteristic of Japanese companies and individual Japanese businessmen is that no single person is "in charge" in the Western sense, regardless of the title he may have. With very rare exceptions, individuals cannot make decisions binding their sections, departments, or companies. They must gain the consensus of the entire group.

It is therefore difficult, if not impossible, to find one person who is expected to take full responsibility for anything, except serious accidents or failures! Because it is impractical to hold large groups of people collectively responsible for important mistakes or misfortunes, the Japanese developed the system of allowing one man—usually the leader—to assume full responsibility for the setback and to make atonement by resigning his position. Examples of this occur frequently in both business and politics in Japan. A typical case is when a company is threatened by bankruptcy or suffers an accident that results in the loss of many lives.

When a president or department director or section head takes personal responsibility in such cases, however, it is only a formality. He is not particularly dishonored and customarily collects his retirement allowance. Not too long afterward, he usually returns to business or politics in some other capacity.

The Group Way of Doing Business

As stated earlier, the foreign businessman in Japan must understand that business with larger companies is done on a group, rather than individual, basis. You cannot single out a particular individual and deal with him or her. You must learn how to deal with several interrelated groups at the same time. This puts a serious strain on the person who is unaccustomed to investing the time and energy required to maintain good communications and rapport with so many people.

The general structure of Japanese companies is a series of relatively equal clusters rather than a hierarchical chain (as might be expected) that is typical in Western companies. The various departments in a Japanese company have been likened to villages that are connected by a number of informal networks. The networks are usually headed by section chiefs (*kacho*), who meet regularly with other *kacho* and *bucho* (department heads) to coordinate and synchronize their activities.

It is therefore vital that the foreign businessman establish a good working relationship with the *kacho* in whatever company he is involved with because nothing happens without their understanding and effort. It is most essential to get the cooperation of the *kacho* himself, but it is also important to make sure that none of the members of the *ka* lose face or are slighted in any way, because every member of the group will take it personally.

The cultural component in every relationship with a Japanese businessman should be studied and considered. This begins with the initial contact (an introduction) and goes on from there to encompass the proper use of the name card, the getting-acquainted process, maintaining close personal contact, and following protocol on all other occasions.

It often seems that the less businesslike you are (in the American sense), the better are your chances of success in Japan. One friend recounts how he desperately wanted the backing of a bank in a building project. He finally got in to see the chairman of the board of the bank and spent some 45 minutes with him, but the banker never once gave him an opportunity to discuss the purpose of his visit. A few days later he was informed by the local branch manager that his application had been approved. "I'm still not sure what happened," he says.

Another peculiarity of the Japanese way of doing things—and the barriers that foreign business often face—was revealed in the experience of an American veterinarian who opened an office in a Tokyo suburb. There were immediate complaints from Japanese veterinarians. He was then subjected to a series of warnings that his license would be revoked and his visa withdrawn. After prolonged negotiations, it was agreed that he could stay in Japan and practice "if he treated only foreign dogs."

How Decisions Are Made

In a vertically structured, group-oriented business system that is operated under a pattern of inferior-superior relations with no individual responsibility, it is obvious that individual members within the system cannot make decisions on their own, except in matters of no consequence. There are exceptions, particularly in so-called one-man companies and in quite small firms. But, in general, decision making in Japan is a communal affair requiring unanimous approval by management.

Most Japanese companies of any size use some form of a system of decision making known as *ringi-seido* (document system). Somewhere in the lower ranks of management, usually at the *ka* (section) level, a manager drafts a proposal—after achieving consensus within his own group—for a project he wants to initiate or has been asked to initiate. The document stating the proposal and its rationale is circulated to the heads of other sections and departments. These heads study the proposal. If they approve, they stamp their name seals on it. If they disapprove, they either refuse to stamp it or put their seals on it upside down. In either event, the document is then passed up through the different levels of management until it reaches the president, who may or may not take it up with the board of directors.

If everyone stamps the *ringi-sho*, it becomes company policy. If all do not stamp it, it is usually sent back to its originator with the suggestion that the proposal would benefit from more staff work. Thus, middle managers in companies using the *ringi* system perform almost all the planning functions for the company, deciding what will be done, when, and how. The president and directors in many such companies have other duties or are little more than figureheads.

The larger the company or organization, the more complicated decision making will be because it involves dozens of people whose primary concern is their own personal interest and the interest of their department or division. These division and department chiefs, following normal Japanese behavior, tend to consider other executives in the company as direct competitors and are prone to be uncooperative and sometimes downright hostile toward them. In addition to making decisions difficult, this factor also hinders to a considerable degree the efficiency and potential of a company in other ways.

Even at board-room level, all decisions are unanimous in principle. To prevent this tradition of unanimity from being completely stultifying, however, many Japanese organizations have a man in a position somewhat like that of elder statesman, whose services are used in times of crisis. When it becomes obvious that unanimous agreement on a particular subject cannot be reached, this man—who may be a retired president or director or a member of the family owning a majority of the company's stock—is called in. After listening for as long as it takes to hear all sides, he presents as his own view what has emerged as the majority opinion. The minority is permitted to agree that he must be right, so the tradition of unanimity is maintained.

Whenever a foreign businessman approaches a Japanese company with a proposition, the same decision-making process applies. Even if the outside businessman happens to represent a company with which the Japanese want to do business and makes them an offer that they are willing to accept, an affirmative decision still requires much more time than would be the case in the United States or Europe.

If, on the other hand, the company is not interested in the foreign businessman's proposition—and it may not arrive at this position for some time—it generally will not reject the offer immediately. It will show enough polite interest to make a naive businessman think that a deal is forthcoming. On occasion, a department or division chief will go even further (because he doesn't want to turn the offer down on his own authority) and allow the foreign businessman to assume that everything is settled. The outsider may thus spend weeks of time—and large amounts of effort and money—under this impression, only to be told at the final stage that no deal exists.

The best way to avoid this situation is for the foreign businessman to have the company concerned sounded out by a Japanese, who may be an employee of the foreigner or someone who has connections with the Japanese firm. Either way, the Japanese company will usually tell him — directly or indirectly — whether it is interested in the foreign company's proposition. If its reaction is sufficiently positive, the foreigner can be fairly certain that he is not being given the runaround.

The major points of agreement between a foreign company and a Japanese company—as between high-ranking diplomats from two countries—should in most cases be settled by lower-level go-betweens before the top foreign representative puts in his first appearance. This goes against the grain of most American businessmen, but they should adjust to it if they want to succeed. (See Some Suggestions on Negotiating in Chapter 7).

"The dynamic, fireball type of executive who comes to Japan expecting to change the system is reduced to running around in circles before he has been here three months. He either acclimatizes, has a nervous breakdown, or else gets out," said an ex-fireball.

Unless the foreign businessman uses the go-between system, he can never be sure whether and to what extent the Japanese company with which he would like to do business is interested. Even with a go-between there are usually areas of confusion and uncertainty.

In conferences, the Japanese use a method of reaching agreement (which does not allow anyone to stand on principle) called *matomari*, or adjustment. At a meeting, each participant, usually beginning with the senior member, makes an opening statement that may hint at his preference but does not commit him to a specific idea or course of action. As the talk continues, the members feel each other out and gradually adjust their own views so that a consensus emerges. If one does not emerge, the leader usually suggests that they take more time to study the subject, and they schedule another meeting at a later date.

Americans can make instant decisions, but the decisions often take six months or more to implement and seldom come out as intended. The Japanese often take three to six months to make sure that everyone is in full agreement before they make a decision; then they implement it immediately.

On a day-to-day operational basis, the most effective way for the foreign businessman to get his thinking into the general consensus within a Japanese company, so that it becomes a part of the overall decision-making process on all levels of the company, is to regularly hold casual, informal chats with key personnel. These conversations can occur at lunch or at other informal get-togethers. The key people are the *kacho* (section chiefs) of all the sections that are concerned with—or are going to be concerned with—the project. The American businessman should present his ideas reticently and indirectly—a form of communication that epitomizes the Japanese way.

Another key point for the aggressive businessman to keep in mind is that the Japanese do not react positively to the preaching or pep-talk approach.

In recent years, the Japanese government itself has gone to great lengths to explain how corporate decisions are made in most larger Japanese companies. The explanations begin with the premise that there are a number of conditioning factors that may make the process different from what it is in other countries:

(1) Although the structure of Japanese companies appears to be the same as or similar to that of Western companies, important differences exist in the formal and informal lines of communication between and through lower, middle, and upper management.

(2) Japanese employees tend to be very much alike in their educational background, attitudes, and aspirations, and—despite the vertical structure of both management and society—all tend to be and expect to be treated alike within their age and educational categories. Rank is primarily based on age and seniority rather than ability, and rewards are psychological rather than financial or political. It therefore becomes essential that decisions be made by groups after careful discussion.

(3) Japanese managers are trained to be generalists rather than specialists and are regularly rotated to different departments and jobs. Authority for decision making is diffused among all the various sections and departments that might be affected by a project under consideration. Thus, all managers have participated in decision making in various departments.

(4) An employee's ability to develop and maintain close relations with people in his own section, as well as in other sections, and his ability to obtain input from the other people in the company and

transmit it to upper management weighs heavily in personnel evaluations and promotion to upper-level management in a Japanese company.

(5) The overall approach to management in a Japanese company, which involves everyone in the decision-making process, requires outsiders to deal with the company as a group, not with individual managers.

These basic factors cause decision making in Japan to be a very cumbersome and time-consuming process, but, once again, when a decision is finally made, it can be implemented quickly and easily because everybody involved is familiar with the project and knows what has to be done.

One of the peculiar features of decision making in Japan is the importance of the role of middle management—not only in making decisions, but in coordinating them after they are made. This means that the foreign businessman who wants to succeed with a Japanese company must work closely with middle management at all stages of the project. He must make sure that they know everything they need to know in order to do their own job, which includes convincing upper management that the project is worthwhile, and keep them informed as the relationship develops.

The Japanese emphasize that not all decisions are made or proposals originated at the lower or middle management level in Japanese companies. Those involving major investments and financing are made by top management.

Decision making is summed up in this way: While authority to oversee operations as a whole is vested in the top managers of Japanese firms, the power to make or break decisions is diffused throughout upper and middle management to a far greater degree than it is in Western firms. The Japanese company, with its winding channels of information, its shifting policy coalitions, its teams of relatively powerless but extremely active and influential middle managers, and its complex web of familylike social ties bears a resemblance to a political organization rather than an army.

While the Japanese system of decision making *is* complex and time-consuming, it helps companies avoid mistakes and makes close teamwork mandatory. And while the system is often frustrating to the outsider, it can also pay off in the long run because he must get acquainted with a fairly large number of people in the company, learn a great deal about how the company works, and keep close liaison with the company thereafter.

Foreign businessmen who want to do business in Japan should keep the following points in mind:

(1) Very careful attention must be given to meeting and getting acquainted with middle managers and then providing them with the information they need to make your case to upper management. It is a serious mistake to try to go over the heads of middle managers. They will resent it strongly and will not be fully cooperative afterwards, no matter what happens. At the same time, there are occasions when it is important—and acceptable—for you to meet top executives, because they will be the ones to make the final decisions.

(2) Upper level managers do not make fast, on-the-spot decisions. You must take this into consideration when you are planning to make a presentation to a Japanese company.

(3) Foreign businessmen negotiating with a Japanese company should avoid showing any kind of favoritism toward one individual or depending on a single individual, especially someone who happens to speak English. This will alienate the other managers. And your perception of which of your Japanese contacts is the most capable or the most influential will often be wrong.

(4) Foreign businessmen should spend a substantial amount of time planning and preparing for a meeting with a Japanese company, keeping the decision-making process in mind, and anticipating the reaction and the needs of the Japanese managers.

(5) The only way to perfect your negotiating skills with the Japanese is through actual experience, and it usually requires a period of years. If you have not had this experience, and the project is a major one, you are strongly advised to engage the help of a bilingual, bicultural adviser who can participate in the meetings with you. The person who is both inexperienced in negotiating with the Japanese and unfamiliar with the subtle, often nonverbal, cultural cues is at a serious disadvantage.

The Japanese way of decision making, especially the tendency for all power to be concentrated in management at corporate headquarters, is often as much of a problem to the Japanese as it is to foreign companies wanting to do business with them. This particularly applies to Japanese branches and subsidiaries overseas, where even the smallest matter is often referred to headquarters rather than being decided on the spot.

Foreign businessmen negotiating with Japanese branches abroad continue to find themselves frustrated by delays caused by this corporate system. The system prevails primarily because the Japanese managers dispatched abroad have had no experience whatsoever in making decisions on their own or assuming personal responsibility for their actions. Once abroad in very unfamiliar territory, their fear of failure is magnified and, becoming even more cautious than they ordinarily are, they prefer to let headquarters make the decisions.

This attitude must change if Japan is to maintain its competitive position in the world economy, but it is not going to change drastically any time soon.

Tyranny of the Majority

The Japanese do not believe in the principle of majority rule in business or politics, pointing out—and rightly so—that it is unfair for the opinions and preferences of a majority (which may be only 51 percent) to absolutely bind a minority. The Japanese way is to work out a compromise that takes into consideration the desires and feelings of both the majority and minority.

The Japanese are especially incensed when any majority tries to impose its will on a minority by the crude process of a vote, as in a board meeting or "democratic" election. They are also angered when any majority or a powerful individual figure behaves in an arrogant or aggressive ("high posture") manner. Because all opinions in any given situation have to be taken into consideration, arriving at conclusions and decisions in Japan is a time-consuming process.

The Business Go-Between

In Japan, it is not proper etiquette to make a direct "cold" call on a businessman or government official whom you do not know. The custom is to arrange for a mutual friend or connection (like a bank or some other company) to call first and introduce you—to give assurance that you are a reliable person, to "guarantee" you.

Many Japanese firms have traditionally employed well-known political figures, retired government officials, and sometimes ex-royalty as "go-betweens"—called *komon* or *sodan-yaku* (consultant) in Japanese—in order to make use of their connections in arranging appointments with businessmen and officials they want to meet. This is an accepted technique that more Western businessmen in Japan, especially those involved in joint ventures, could use to considerable advantage. A reputable *komon* with prestige can often accomplish the impossible in getting proposals and papers processed through company or government red tape.

The Shokai-jo

Less effective than the *komon's* personal contact, the *shokai-jo*, or introduction, is much used in Japan. A friend or connection provides you with a written introduction to a person he knows and whom you want to meet. After he writes something like "Please do what you can for the bearer" on his name card, you take it to the person for whom it is intended. A *shokai-jo* may also be in the form of a letter sent directly to the third party or delivered by you. Verbal introductions are used, but they are less acceptable and less impressive than written ones.

Introductions work best if they are from a high-level executive in a bank or company with which the firm you are interested in has close relations, from one of the professors of the person you want to meet, or from a close family friend.

The Japanese View of Contracts

Just as they do not like to set precedents or make unalterable commitments, Japanese businessmen do not like to sign detailed, restrictive contracts. To them, no agreement is final for the simple reason that circumstances change, and they want to be able to change with them. They prefer a loose arrangement based on sincerity and goodwill—one that will allow them leeway to change the character of the relationship as the situation demands. The binding power of this type of contract is determined by the amount of "mutual understanding," goodwill, and sincerity demonstrated by both sides—characteristics that the Japanese regard as fundamental to business relationships.

The flexibility provided by this type of contractual arrangement gives the Japanese a tremendous advantage over those who are bound by tightly limiting contracts. If they do sign an American contract with lots of fine print, they will usually abide by the terms until conditions change; then they renegotiate.

The Japanese do not use lawyers in their negotiations and seldom consult them in the case of disputes (there are only some 15,000 attorneys in the country, as opposed to nearly 700,000 in the U.S.). Disliking the legalistic approach to contracts or business, they have taken a very strong position against foreign legal firms operating in Japan.

In 1955, Japan effectively barred foreign lawyers from practicing in the country, a policy that has continued to the present time with only slight changes. With but few exceptions, the foreign attorneys in Japan have been relegated to the status of "trainees" who draft documents and handle legal English, but are officially prohibited from giving legal advice. When foreign problems arise, Japanese attorneys and their foreign "trainees" regularly consult with overseas law offices via telex and facsimile.

The few foreign attorneys now able to practice in Japan established their offices there before the 1955 law went into effect.

The legal profession in Japan is tightly controlled by the Ministry of Justice (which keeps the number of law graduates to approximately 500 a year) and the Japanese Federation of Bar Associations (JFBA). In 1976, the Ministry gave its approval for foreign attorneys to open offices in Japan if they passed the equivalent of the bar examination, which is so difficult that only *two percent* of the Japanese law school graduates are able to pass it on an annual basis. No foreign attorney has ever passed the test.

But there has been increasing pressure from many sources, both foreign and Japanese, to liberalize the legal marketplace, as well as the product market, because so much of Japan's business is now international, and virtually every foreign relationship requires some kind of contract in English.

The position of the JFBA is that cultural differences make it inappropriate for foreign attorneys to have unrestricted access to Japan and that if foreign law firms could establish offices in Japan they would soon dominate the tiny Japanese legal profession. The issue remains unresolved, and it is heating up as both the need for and the opportunities for foreign-trained lawyers increase in Japan—a situation that is leading more and more Japanese to attend law schools in the U.S., where they are welcomed as students, as well as practicing attorneys, after they finish their education and take the bar exams.

The Importance of Human Rights

Foreign employers in Japan are often accused of treading on the "human rights" of their employees. On most occasions, the employers have done nothing more serious than insisting that employees get to work on time or installing time clocks without getting the "approval" of the workers. The complaints may also be the result of asking personnel to do something they consider to be outside their area of responsibility. Whatever the source of the complaints, they point up one of the most interesting facets of doing business in Japan—the importance of human rights.

Before 1945, the common people of Japan had certain specific rights that were theoretically guaranteed by their superiors in their personal hierarchy; by their superiors' superiors; and, finally, somewhere in the hazy heights, by the Emperor himself. These rights really didn't go very far and were frequently ignored by official, as well as private, authorities.

When democracy was "introduced" into Japan by the United States military forces following the Pacific war, the average Japanese took it to mean that his personal rights, which for the most part had always been denied him, were now guaranteed by Japan's new constitution. To some Japanese, however, democracy means that they are entitled to think and act without regard for others. Democracy, translated as human rights, therefore, became a justification for the young to be both socially and morally irresponsible. Some students misbehave in school and frequently attack their teachers, who cannot punish them because that would be a violation of the student's human rights. The known thug on the street can't be searched without his permission. The businessman who asks a girl who is not a tea-server to serve tea to visitors is leaving himself open to a charge of violating her human rights.

Exactly what does the adult Japanese today consider to be his human rights? First, he must not be embarrassed in any way. Second, he should not be asked to do any work outside of his duties, as he sees them. Third, he should not be criticized for expressing individualism. And fourth, he should not be forced to do anything against his wishes—unless it serves the interests of the group. The foreign businessman should be aware of these important factors in his relations with his Japanese employees.

The Role of Humility in Japan

As a control device to help weld together their vertically graded social fabric, the Japanese developed the concept of humility to an extraordinary degree. The language, as well as the traditional manners, of the Japanese are a direct reflection of this factor. But more than just language and outward behavior of the Japanese were affected by millenniums of such conditioning. Humility became a way of life for all except the privileged elite, and even they were not excused from at least acting the part.

Humility is still of vital importance in Japan today in every area of life. In fact, humility is an important facet of Japanese ethics. Just as Westerners consider ethics important and yet are often not ethical in thought or action, the Japanese are not always humble. But such lapses are not so easy for foreigners to discern since the face the Japanese show to the public comes masked in manners that may hide any number of contrary realities.

When a man or woman is in a very high position in business, politics, entertainment, or any other profession in Japan, he or she is expected—forced is more accurate—to maintain a "low posture toward the public." That is, he must present himself as the humblest of creatures, deprecate his achievements, and cater to the masses, especially to the press, as if he were undeserving of any praise and obsequiously grateful for any scrap of recognition that comes his way. The Japanese cannot stand anyone outside their own immediate hierarchy who acts conceited or superior in any way, and they tend to be hostile and critical toward such people to a degree that foreigners consider grossly excessive.

Westerners in Japan are in an extremely awkward position because large areas of our normal behavior appear to the Japanese to represent the worst kind of arrogance. I have often had Japanese remark to me that while they "appreciated" the good intentions of many foreign businessmen who approached them, it was "very hard to put up with their superior attitude." As a result, many Japanese are much relieved when, for any reason, these people take their business elsewhere.

There are two techniques the Japanese use to overcome the problems inherent in their humility-oriented system. The first is the practice of throwing themselves on the kindness or mercy of a superior (or whoever they want to get something from). This entails a big show of humility toward and complete dependence on the other party. As used by the Japanese, this procedure often entails an almost complete negation of the self, and the displays of wet-eyed emotion involved can be quite repelling to foreigners.

There is the strong implication, of course, that once you have put yourself in a position of receiving a favor from someone (including businessmen and government officials, whose duty it is to serve you), you are obligated to him and must somehow repay him. This payment may take the form of a rebate, a gift, entertainment, or some other favor. In numerous cases, the bribe is given first, and then the favor is asked for.

The expression of humility, especially the way it is practiced in Japan, may be so repugnant to Westerners that they may be unable to adopt the technique. Its importance, however, should not be underestimated. If the foreigner wants to use it, he might think of it in terms of modesty.

The second technique is more familiar to foreigners but is not thoroughly understood or appreciated. This is the practice of apologizing. Over the centuries, life in Japan was so hedged in by limitations and laws, both expressed and implied, that the Japanese could hardly breathe without breaking some code or custom. In order not to have to inflict punishment on so many people so often—because it would have been impractical and because the Japanese are generally a humane people—it became customary to accept apologies instead of calling for the enforcement of legal or social sanctions.

Finally, the practice developed to the point where fairly serious transgressions were excused if the culprit confessed his guilt and apologized humbly. Examples of this can be seen daily in Japan. A bank clerk embezzles millions of yen, goes to Atami Hot Springs with a girl friend, and proceeds to live it up for several days. Then he has a change of heart and gives himself up. Or a relative influences him to come back, or he is captured quickly by the police. If he has a story of hardship and mental anguish to tell and will throw himself on the mercy of the court and apologize to everyone concerned, he can often get off with a suspended sentence. Japan's modern-day Columbus, Kenichi Horie, who left Japan without going through immigration and crossed the Pacific in a small boat, was arrested on his return to Japan but was eventually freed because "he showed humility and apologized to all the authorities concerned."

The foreigner in Japan (or China or Korea) who runs afoul of the law and is found guilty, unfailingly gets off easier if he confesses and humbly apologizes.

In business in Japan, the use of the apology technique is a highly developed, integral part of the day-to-day routine. It comes into play when there is a dissatisfied client or when there is any kind of friction between one firm and another or between a firm and some government office. These occasions arise with such monotonous regularity that many Japanese companies employ someone just to write *shimatsu-sho,* or official apology letters. Other firms employ lawyers for this purpose. As can be imagined, there are surely few, if any, original excuses left to explain away a company's mistakes or delays or failures; so it is customary that only the cleverest men are assigned *shimatsu-sho* writing duties. They are prized in accordance with their ability to come up with new twists for old themes.

Western businessmen working in Japan or dealing with Japan should keep this custom in mind. I do not suggest that it be used in the sometimes unethical and almost always misleading way it is used in Japan. But there is an advantage in knowing about it and times when it may be used legitimately—such as when you are at fault, and you need the help of the Japanese side to get out of a tight bind.

The Japanese View and Use of Time

Some Western businessmen see the Japanese concept of time as one of the biggest problems confronting the foreign firm. Said one businessman: "Their time values are a great deal more lax than ours, and if you press them into agreeing to schedules that are not realistic from their viewpoint it is 'your fault' when they don't follow through. When you ask a Japanese businessman when something is going to be finished or when some action is going to be initiated, he will generally say 'as soon as possible.' This is a sign that you shouldn't press him for an exact date, time, or sales forecast, because he doesn't know. On the occasions when I've tried the hardest to get someone to commit himself and then stick to it, I've gotten the worst results."

For Western businessmen who have had no direct experience in Asia—or in several European and Latin American countries where the situation is similar—this time problem comes as an unpleasant shock. Even after a certain amount of exposure to cultures with different time values, many Americans in particular find themselves unable to accept the Japanese view of time and fight it with a determination that sometimes borders on the maniacal. They are unable to see any reason why the Japanese businessman cannot change this part of his nature by a simple act of will.

While we have been conditioned to live by the minute—and sometimes by the second—the Japanese have traditionally connected the passage of time with moods, events, and seasons, which are unpredictable to some degree. It often appears that the Japanese businessman is completely oblivious to the passage of time. Unless he has been strongly influenced otherwise, his view of time covers only his own personal situation, not that of any outsider or any commitment to an outsider, because he knows that whatever project he is involved with will move forward only when the group is ready to move.

The only practical solution to this problem is threefold: (1) to comprehend how the particular company functions; (2) to pinpoint the key individuals in the company (and they may not be titled executives or even managers); and (3) to do your best to help them achieve what you want.

To succeed at this kind of "interference" in the internal affairs of a Japanese organization, you must be both subtle and clever. You must keep in mind that no individual in the company can be expected to take any risk for you because it would put him at odds with his fellow workers and probably ruin his entire career.

The technique is to find or make an excuse to talk to the key men, get your points across indirectly, or explain that your own job is on the line. Since communication between sections and departments in Japanese companies is typically slow—and sometimes nonexistent—you must also find ways to act as a "bridge" between them. This is an extremely difficult role to play, requiring that you maintain a "low posture" and keep your dealings personal.

Aesthetics in Business

Japan is the only country that has ever tried, over a period of many centuries, to raise aestheticism to the level of a religion and to promote its tenets and practices among the entire population. The wellsprings of this tremendous, sustained effort probably lie in the extraordinary appreciation for natural beauty that developed very early in Japanese culture. This love of beauty was followed by the learning of Chinese ideograms—with which the Japanese began to transcribe their language some time around the fourth century A.D. More than just a system of writing, the ideograms are an exercise in aesthetics, and in earlier times people who attained unusual skill in the drawing of the symbols were praised as master calligraphers. The greatest won immortal fame.

Mastering the difficult ideograms still takes up the first several school years of every Japanese student. As a result, the roughest laborer is a skilled artist.

But even before the introduction of the ideograms into Japan, the Japanese had developed from their nature worship a number of practices that were aesthetic in both form and substance. These consisted of the studied appreciation of beauty in natural phenomena, either through poetry, painting, or contemplation. By the Middle Ages, many of these practices had become "nationalized," and there was virtually no one in Japan who did not participate in some type of aesthetic exercise several times a year. To hundreds of thousands of people, particularly the large class of nobility, as well as the *samurai* warriors, exercises in aesthetics were one of their most important daily activities.

In Japan today, this tradition of aestheticism as an essential part of daily life remains very strong. It is no longer as obvious in practice, but its influence on the character and philosophy of the Japanese is unmistakable. It colors every thought they have and every action they take. In their private lives, it gives them an advantage that should make them the envy of the rest of the world. In their modern business relations with foreign companies, however, it is a mixed blessing.

The inbred aesthetic nature of the Japanese first of all contributes to their being emotional and very sensitive. It also contributes to their looking at everything from a personal viewpoint, even when their purpose would be better served by a cool, objective attitude. One of the most conspicuous areas of business that is adversely influenced by the aestheticism is the English-language advertising they prepare. They regularly divide and separate words and sentences for the sake of aesthetic balance, without regard for what happens to the readability or meaning of the message. Further, the message itself is very often obscured in a moody word or phrase picked for its sentiment rather than its sense. The result is that many of their ads are understandable only after a recombining effort that would do credit to both a cryptographer and a clairvoyant.

Although the aesthetic character of the Japanese may thus handicap them in certain areas of business, it is also a source of tremendous creativity, which is equally apparent in Japanese-language ads, product designing, packaging, displays, promotional aids, and so on. The aesthetic bent of the Japanese is also another homogenizing factor in their culture, as well as an important source of spiritual contentment and national identity.

Businessmen as Philosophers

The most influential philosophers in Japan are businessmen. In fact, all Japanese executives tend to be businessmen-philosophers, and their thinking is deeply imprinted on the character and conduct of their companies. In most cases, their thinking is very much alike, but there are two extremes—one beautifully exemplified by the late Sazo Idemitsu, outspoken founder of the Idemitsu Oil Company, and Konosuke Matsushita, founder of the fabulously successful Matsushita Electric Company (National-Panasonic) empire. Idemitsu exemplified the group that believes in the family concept, with a mixture of authoritarianism and humanism as its motivating force. Matsushita represented the group that believes the primary motivating factors should be experience, inspiration, and instinct—all charged with an abundance of that almost mystical quality called *yamato-damashii,* usually translated as "Japanese spirit."

Matsushita is especially known for his use of meditation as a means of developing his intuitive powers, which he credits with helping him develop his unique management practices.[*] Some of the ideas that are instilled in Matsushita employees include: How you do your job is an indication of your loyalty to your country; a business should always be operated for the public welfare and not for private profit; always think of your customers and express gratitude to them for their patronage; good management benefits society, poor management hurts it. Matsushita's business phi-

[*]For a detailed study of these practices, see Rowland Gould's *The Matsushita Phenomena,* published by Kodansha International Ltd.

losophy has been described as sounding like a question-and-answer session with a Zen master.

While deeply involved with metaphysics, Japanese businessmen do not base their philosophy on logic, but on a variety of human and spiritual factors. This pluralistic way of looking at things allows them to accept differences and conflict without suffering any damage to their psyche and without changing their beliefs. Their philosophy thus gives them a decided advantage over Westerners.

Humanism and Idemitsu's Pax Nipponica

While the Japanese businessman prefers to call his distinctive business philosophy "humanism," it is generally referred to by Westerners as paternalism. All of Japan's top companies are outstanding examples of paternalistic enterprises, but the underlying philosophy is more than just paternalism, as this word is understood and used in the West. A number of detailed studies of Japan's business philosophy have been made in recent years by both Japanese and American observers, but no one has explained the subject and its underlying principles more thoroughly than Sazo Idemitsu, founder and long-time president of Idemitsu Oil Company.

On the occasion of the launching of a new oil tanker for his company in 1962, the then 77-year-old businessman released a statement for publication that without doubt is one of the most remarkable expressions of moral and economic philosophy ever made. He said in part:

"Upon completion of my fourth round-the-world trip in 1961, I came to the conclusion that the world was in a state of anxiety from political and economic confusion. What we should do henceforth is to shift from materialism to humanism to transcend money, organization, and other things. There can be no distinction between capitalism or communism or between individualism and totalitarianism. I feel that the Japanese people are capable of bringing this message to the world."

Idemitsu went on to say that the majority-rule principle (of democracy) is undemocratic and disregards humanity; and that individualism, civil liberty, democracy, and freedom are meaningful only if they are based on selflessness—which he saw as the key to world peace and human happiness.

"I believe," he added, "that it is the duty of the Japanese people to lead mankind to this road of humanity and peace, since we have been taught the significance of selflessness and pursued it for over 2,000 years."

Idemitsu denounced capitalism and communism in favor of his own brand of authoritarian-paternalistic humanism and blamed not only union problems in other companies, but the problems of the world in general on "emotional self-centeredness which does not go beyond the framework of materialism." Explaining how his system had produced "respectable and dependable people" from the day he founded the company in Moji just after the turn of the century, Idemitsu said:

"At first, mothers came to my company with their sons fresh from primary school. At their request for me to take care of their children, I made up my mind to bring them up in place of their mothers. Since then I have translated into action maternal love on every occasion and in every appropriate form to my employees. This is what is now called paternalism. The employees that I raised are never dismissed. We are one big family and have no need for such things as time sheets, time clocks, and labor unions. When my employees or their children get married I give them housing and family allowances. I profess myself to be their mother and take a maternal attitude toward their joys and sorrows. In short, affection and loving-kindness produce respectable people. My company has many employees who carry on my maternal love, guaranteeing the perpetuation of my ideas."

Idemitsu concluded: "Now I come to the essential point of the mission of the Japanese people as peacemakers in this confused world. As a result of 50 years' experience, we at Idemitsu have learned that society exists for men and is made by them, and for this reason men must be its center. Men must be above money, material, organizations, democracy, capitalism, communism, and law. As a result of our experience, we are in a position to give suggestions to the State and to society. Even 30 years ago, on the twentieth anniversary of our company, I declared that our business had already set an example for Japan and that we should go out into the rest of the world to teach what we had learned. Regrettably, however, Japan lost the war and our plan was frustrated. Yet new humanism has again sprouted in our test tube in these postwar years, and the time is again ripe for us to share our way with the rest of the world."

Not all Japanese businessmen who believe in the family company system have such grandiose views of its manifest destiny in world affairs, but many go further in practical application than Idemitsu's Pax Nipponica. A typical example is the Jeeklite Chemical Mining Company in Osaka. Some of the benefits given by this company are free wedding ceremonies and receptions, free honeymoons, free housing, free baths, and free haircuts. The employees also enjoy the benefits of meals for which they are charged only a nominal sum. All these extras are available not only to the employees but to their families, as well, and they continue to the end of their lives. When an employee dies, the company pays all the funeral expenses.

Says the president of Jeeklite: "Every employee should be considered a member of the family and must be taken care of until he dies." In line with this philosophy, Jeeklite does not require its employees to retire when they reach a particular age. They continue working as long as they feel like it. When an employee decides he is too old to work, he retires but continues to receive his full base salary. The company has several factories and several thousand employees.

The president of Jeeklite sees himself as the head of a giant household, but he does not insist on ramming company benefits down the employees' throats. If an employee wants to have a private wedding, the company pays part or all of the cost. Outsiders sometimes condemn Jeeklite's miniature welfare state as an advanced form of feudalistic paternalism designed to keep the workers in a state of moral bondage to the company. The employees are regularly advised to form a union and "throw off their feudal bonds." But the employees like it and wouldn't think of trying to upset the system.

The famous selfless dedication to group and national goals that has traditionally been characteristic of the Japanese—and is still today promoted in ranking companies—is rapidly becoming a thing of the past, however, according to the Statistical Research Institute (SRI) of the Ministry of Education. The SRI, which conducts an ongoing study of the character of the Japanese, says that individualism and self-interest had become dominant among adults as far back as 1964. A 1968 survey of "public consciousness" by the Office of the Prime Minister substantiated SRI's findings. Less than 20 percent of the people, and these were nearly all above the age of 50, continued to demonstrate the qualities attributed to "true Japanese," according to these findings.

These survey findings should not be taken as an indication that the unique Japanese character and Japanese business system are doomed to an early disappearance. It is now more than two decades later, and there have been changes. But both the traditional Japanese culture and the business system it spawned are far too deeply embedded in the life and thought of the country to fade away so easily. Both will be around for the foreseeable future.

Kenichi Ohmae, internationally educated management strategist, speaker, and best-selling author of numerous books and articles on business strategy and Japanese culture, says that one of the secrets of Japan's phenomenal economic success is that most Japanese businessmen, who have no formal education in business or management, have a tremendous natural insight into the relationship between a company and its products, customers, and competition. He says that the strategy they apply is instinctive and that many Japanese are successful business strategists because of a state of mind—a cultural and intuitional state of mind—that is opposed to the rational, analytical approach that is typical of Western businessmen.

Another characteristic of Japanese businessmen that Ohmae identifies is their tendency to segment their markets and identify key elements that will take them to the top in the shortest possible time. Once they get there, they attempt to consolidate their position by using their profits to broaden their base. In his words, they concentrate their efforts and are consistent; their planning is so meticulous that they deliberately program telephone calls and meetings in the early morning when people are more likely to be positive and decisive.

Ohmae says Japanese managers are generally overtrained and overqualified for the work they are expected to do and are therefore especially efficient in carrying out their assignments. It is generally seven or eight years before the Japanese managerial candidate receives his first promotion. Western employees are likely to be promoted before or shortly after they reach basic competence in any job and therefore remain undertrained and underqualified for whatever position they are in.

Another difference between Japanese and Western managers that Ohmae emphasizes is the tendency for Westerners to be primarily concerned about their specific job, while the Japanese are conditioned to be concerned about the company as a whole. Japanese managers are trained as generalists instead of specialists and are therefore very flexible and able to accept rapid change without getting out of step.

Like good military strategists, the Japanese will not confront a larger, stronger competitor directly. Their primary strategy is to change the field of battle—to go around, under, or over a competitor with a new product or a new approach. By choosing the arena of competition, as well as the rules, they are often able to outflank their competitors.

The Japanese also have a compulsive desire to obtain and use the latest technology because they see it as a means to quickly catch up with and overtake domestic, as well as foreign, competitors.

Chapter 4

Profile of Japan's Business World

"The state no longer exists; only the enterprises remain."

—**Kazayaki Miyasaki**
Asahi Chemical Industries

The David-Goliath Structure

When the Japanese government undertook a crash program to industrialize the country in 1868, all-out effort was made to introduce new manufacturing techniques into Japan and to assist in the establishment of a number of large-scale manufacturing companies. But no corresponding effort was made to modernize the handicraft and cottage-type basic consumer industries that dated back to the first appearance of community living some thousands of years before. These tiny family shop-factories continued to operate as they had in the past. With the introduction of Western consumer products into Japan, however, a new type of cottage industry began to appear, gradually at first and then, as everything foreign became a fad, in a tremendous crescendo.

Except for the frequent use of small gasoline engines and a few other labor-saving devices, these new shop-factories were set up and managed in the traditional feudal pattern. In the early stages, most of what these shops produced was sold locally, but profit-minded Westerners soon realized that here was an exporter's gold mine. Before the turn of the century, chinaware, cheapened lacquerware, bambooware, etc., were already being exported in large volume. By 1930, Japan was a leading exporter of textiles, toys, flatware, and novelties, with some 90 percent of the nation's trade in the hands of a few large (*zaibatsu*) trading firms.

A few hundred of these new consumer goods manufacturers grew into medium-size firms employing from 30 to 300 people. But the overwhelming majority remained on the shop level, with three to nine employees, and worked primarily as subcontractors (*shita-uke*), depending on traditionally powerful wholesalers and the recently developed *zaibatsu* trading companies for financing and all marketing functions. Thus was developed a split-level industrial structure in which some 90 percent of the enterprises in the country had fewer than 20 workers each, employed approximately three-fourths of the industrial labor force, and turned out 60 percent of the nation's production. The remainder was in the hands of the *zaibatsu* combines and a few medium-size independent firms.

Today there are nearly five million enterprises constituting Japan's business world. Over 600,000 of these are in manufacturing, but only about 700 of them account for the majority of the country's production. Seventy-five percent of these manufacturing companies are not incorporated. The 25 percent of the companies that are incorporated employ 65 percent of the work force.

In the manufacturing category, firms with less than five employees account for half of the total, and fewer than 5,000 firms employ more than 300 persons. In the wholesale and retail trades, which have a total of some 2,300,000 establishments, well over 1,800,000 of these have one to four workers; over 300,000 have from five to nine employees, 141,000 have 10 to 29 employees; 20,000 have 30 to 49 employees; 10,000 have 50 to 99 employees, and only 5,000 have over 100 employees.

Of the 700 largest enterprises of all kinds in the country, some 200 are key members of the *zaibatsu* groups (Mitsubishi, Mitsui, Sumitomo, Fuji, Kawasaki, Hitachi, Furukawa, and Nissan). Sixty of these major corporations are owned by individual families, and the remainder are more or less controlled by their industrial group. Several companies that have developed independently of the *zaibatsu* groupings are substantial complexes within themselves. Toshiba Electric Company, for example, has some 70 subsidiary companies, 60 sub-subsidiaries, and 120 sales companies.

The Great Trading Companies

Trusts, combines, and cartels centering around the old trading firms, banks, the petrochemical industries, and the giant electrical manufacturers constitute the primary features of big business in Japan today. Each of the 31 major business categories in the nation's economy is dominated by 2 to 15 or so giant firms, which altogether number approximately 200. The most unusual of these large and important enterprises are the huge trading companies that were unique to Japan until they were copied by Korea in the 1960s and 1970s.

Altogether, there are some 4,000 trading companies in Japan (with over 9,000 branch offices around the world). The ten largest firms account for some 60 percent of the country's imports, 50 percent of the exports, and 20 percent of the wholesale trade. These ten include Mitsubishi Shoji, Mitsui Bussan, Marubeni-Iida, C. Itoh, Nissho-Iwai, Sumitomo Shoji, Toyo Menka, Nichimen, and Kanematsu-Gosho. If we add the next 20 largest trading companies, the total of 29 do over 70 percent of the country's exporting and some 80 percent of the importing.

Each year, for the last several years, the trading companies have increased their share of the nation's trade, despite the fact that the number of manufacturing companies bypassing the trading companies to handle their own foreign trade directly has also increased (there now being approximately 2,500 such companies).

The larger trading companies perform a number of key functions in the nation's overall economy. They import the bulk of the raw materials the country uses and in many cases have joint venture tie-ups with foreign material suppliers. In Japan, they finance numerous manufacturing operations, provide market information for makers, distribute, and act as freight forwarders and as consulting agencies. All of the big trading companies are involved in joint venture operations with foreign companies, and all are in or getting into such areas as education, travel service, recreational centers, resort spas, housing development, cattle ranching, and space exploration.

In many cases, the primary value of the large trading firms is their close connection with the various government offices concerned with trade and their ability to get paperwork through these bottlenecks. With offices throughout the world, they act as a central supply system, providing raw materials, machinery, and financing to manufacturers, as well as providing a global sales network that no single manufacturer could afford.

Prior to 1945, all the large trading firms except Mitsui and Mitsubishi tended to specialize in certain lines. Now all of them try to handle everything. In prewar days, the trading firms had a very high profit margin and were extremely wealthy. Today their profit margins are relatively low, and they often ally themselves with affiliated banks for financing.*

There are four categories of trading companies in Japan: (1) the giant multilateral firms that handle a wide variety of goods and materials and provide numerous services; (2) the large-scale firms important in a few specialized lines; (3) the so-called window trading companies serving specific manufacturers—like Toshiba Electric's Trading Company and Nissan Motor's Nissan Sales Company; and (4) the wholesale firms specializing in domestic transactions. The first category is made up of the ten leading firms listed earlier, along with a number of former "special traders" (important in a few specialized lines) that more or less succeeded in becoming multilateral in the 1960s. Then there are several smaller firms specializing in textiles (Chori, Itoman, Shinko Sangyo, Ichida, Sankyo Seiko, and Takashima); food (Toshoku, Meiji Shoji, and Nozaki Sangyo); machinery and metals (Osaka Kozai, Toyoda Tsusho, Shinko Shoji, Okura Shoji, Seiko Sangyo, Tokyo Sangyo, Yuasa Kanamano, Kano Tekko, and Kobayashi Sangyo).

Not all the large trading firms have the same system and philosophy, and they present different images to the business world. In the Mitsui group, ties are considerably more relaxed than in the others. The trading side, for example, handles only about one-fifth of the gross sales of Mitsui manufacturing companies. A spokesman says that Mitsui attempts to wield effective control over the group through ability rather than stock holdings.

Mitsubishi Trading, on the other hand, is noted for the amount of control it exercises over the Mitsubishi group. The largest of Japan's enterprise groups, with a nucleus of 26 key "lineal" companies, plus 18 others, the Mitsubishi complex is ruled through a so-called Friday Club made up of the presidents of the 26 leading companies. The club meets on the second Friday of each month, with the presidents of Mitsubishi Bank, Mitsubishi Heavy Industries, and Mitsubishi Trading Company taking turns as chairman. No member of the group is allowed to march out of step with the senior firms.

---

*The most important trading firms and their bank affiliations are Mitsubishi/Mitsubishi Bank; Mitsui/Mitsui Bank and Fuji Bank; Marubeni Corporation/Fuji Bank; C. Itoh/Sumitomo and Daiichi-Kangyo Bank; Kanematsu-Gosho/Bank of Tokyo; Sumitomo/Sumitomo Bank; Nissho-Iwai/Sanwa Bank; Nichimen/Sanwa Bank; Toyo Menka/Tokai Bank.

The Mitsubishi group maintains particularly close relations with the leading political factions, contributing large amounts of money each year to the major parties. The largest donation, however, goes to the Liberal Democratic Party.

In addition to entering such new fields as city housing, ocean development, oil research development, pollution prevention, and space development, Mitsubishi established Japan's first "think tank" (Mitsubishi Research Institute) in 1970. Of the 30 largest firms in Japan, six are Mitsubishi enterprises.

While a few of the larger Japanese firms are unhappy with this control, the majority—and particularly the small and medium-size companies—consider it proper and natural. Most of the larger firms generally find government sanction of monopolies and cartels to their advantage.

Because of their traditional dependence on and cooperation with some type of bureaucratic authority, Japanese businessmen have learned how to live with it. On a higher level, it is often hard to distinguish between businessmen and politicians. Ranking officials in tax offices and various government bureaus are in many cases working for and receiving pay from private interests long before they retire at the early age of 55. After retirement, they officially join the commercial enterprises, while their influence in the organizations they left remains little diminished until their death. Senior officials from the Ministry of Finance and the Ministry of International Trade and Industry (MITI) are particularly sought after by large manufacturing and trading firms. They usually enter such companies at a director or vice-president level.

In addition to being closely connected with the various ministries of the government on a personal and familial basis, as well as employing retired bureaucrats, Japanese businessmen in such industries as oil, transportation, iron and steel, utilities, and trade maintain a regular program of "buying political stock." This means that each year they contribute millions of dollars to the different political factions, with the greatest amount going to the ruling Liberal Democratic Party.

The New Trading Company Image

Japan's huge trading companies, which played such a pivotal role in the country's so-called economic miracle and then lost some of their prominence as more and more Japanese manufacturers began doing their own exporting and importing, have now become entrepreneurs, and they are involved in everything from health clubs to sports centers.

The larger trading companies, with their worldwide network of officers and communications systems, remain one of the keys of Japan's continuing economic success. The communications center of Mitsubishi Shoji, for example, takes up an entire floor in its huge Tokyo headquarters building. In the center are dozens of telex and facsimile machines and computer terminals linking 190 offices in 77 countries. The center processes over 50,000 messages each working day.

Mitsubishi Shoji the largest of the trading companies, now emphasizes technology, financing, and new ventures. One of the primary goals of the company is to build up its in-house staff of young people who understand new technology and to continue developing policies and programs to train older staff members in the use of high-tech. Mitsubishi is giving special emphasis to telecommunications and computer-related businesses. It owns 60 percent of Space Communications Corporation (the remaining 40 percent is owned by Mitsubishi Electric, a sister company).

Power Groups in Japan's Business World

There are five business associations in Japan that represent the major interests of the primary power blocs. These are the Keizai Dantai Rengo Kai (Federation of Economic Organizations), better known as Keidanren; the Keizai Doyukai (the Association of Economic Leaders—also known as the Japan Committee for Economic Development); the Nihon Keieisha Dantai Renmei (Federation of Employers Association), or Nikkeiren, and the Nihon Shoko Kaigisho, or Japan Chamber of Commerce and Industry—often abbreviated as Nissho. The fifth association is an unofficial group known simply as Zaikai (Financial Circles).

The character and roles of the first four of these important bodies are distinguished by what Japanese business commentators refer to as financial or economic "currents." The first current, associated with the Keidanren, is made up of those who dislike government intervention in the free flow of business. This group is also said to resist the tendency for banks to control business in Japan. The second current, represented by the Japan Committee for Economic

Development, emphasizes the need for developing business morality. Nikkeiren, making up the third current, is mostly concerned with management and labor relations. The fourth current (Japan Chamber of Commerce and Industry) is said to advocate government control—or at least government participation—in business, and it is distinguished by its close political affiliations.

The importance of these associations is that they give all the various business groups a formal body headed by a recognized leader to represent their interests to the government . The government, in turn, finds them an ideal means for dovetailing its policies and aims with those of industry.

Keidanren was established in 1945 to help restore economic order to a defeated Japan. Its membership comprises 120 leading industrial organizations and 850 of the largest corporations in the country. It has three key functions: to represent the interests of big business to the government; to exchange views and information with foreign businessmen and governments; and to act as a public relations agency for Japan's business community.

The *Keidanren* has 48 standing committees, each chaired by the chief executive of a leading company, which deal with various issues facing the business community. The activities of the committees are coordinated by a Secretariat, which has 170 members who are recruited from the best universities in the country. The opinions and desires of this elite group carry considerable economic and political clout.

The *Keidanren* also has a political arm called the National Political Association, which collects billions of yen each year, most of which is distributed in the form of donations to the Liberal Democratic Party (LDP).

The *Keizai Doyukai*, or Committee for Economic Development, was formed on April 30, 1946, by a small group of middle managers who dedicated the organization to "building a newborn Japan." It was to be a freethinking give-and-take kind of group that would help democratize Japan's corporate management, with unions helping to run companies. This did not appeal to the business community, and over the years the *Keizai Doyukai* developed into a think-tank kind of organization that addressed medium- and long-range problems having to do with the roles of government and business.

The group has 1,030 individual regular members and a 262-member board of trustees, which meets on the third Friday of each month at Tokyo's Industrial Club Building. It is said, however, that most decisions are made by the chairman and seven vice-chairmen of the board, who meet on the first Friday of each month.

Outside experts are frequently invited to address "study meetings" of the organization, and it has recently become more active in establishing contact with economic organizations abroad. In a major break, the Keizai Doyukai announced on July 18, 1986, that it would accept ten foreign companies as special members.

Not surprisingly, as the founding members of the KD got older, the age of the leadership also went up, and now, like virtually all of the major business organizations in Japan, it is dominated by men in their 60s, 70s, and 80s.

The Japan Federation of Employers Associations, or *Nikkeiren*, was founded on April 12, 1948, during a nationwide labor dispute that was threatening the stability of the government. Labor unions, turned loose by the American Occupation forces, were primarily leftist and quickly became powerful and arrogant. The Nikkeiren was established to represent management in the often violent confrontation with labor.

With the support of the *Nikkeiren*, one strike-bound Japanese company after another won victories in labor disputes, as a result of which the *Nikkeiren* became a powerful voice in Japan's economy. Presently, *Nikkeiren* membership consists of 47 prefectural-level industrial associations and 57 national associations, representing a total of 31,000 corporations in all branches of industry (making up nearly one-third of all workers in Japan).

Nikkeiren is most active during the spring of each year, when the national labor federations mount their annual "spring offensive" as part of their negotiations for new wage contracts. *Nikkeiren* is responsible for the social and corporate education of employees and for making the corporate policies of its members known. The organization founded the Fuji Management Development Center in 1965 to teach enlightened management techniques. Some 20,000 management-level personnel participate in programs at the center each year.

The Japan Chamber of Commerce and Industry (*Nissho*) was originally organized under the aegis of the Tokyo Chamber of Commerce Law, instituted in 1878, and revised as the National Federation of Chambers of Commerce in 1922. The JCCI, incorporated in 1953, has 481 members and represents 1.2 million commercial and industrial companies that have 20 or more employees.

One of the primary reasons for its influenc
economy is that the JCCI has traditionally b
powerful businessman who had direct access t
political and business leaders.

Nissho publishes several English-language guides, jo
directories, including the massive *Standard Trade Index* and an illustrated product catalog, *Japan: New Products & Marketable Commodities.*

The JCCI participates in 14 annual international conferences,
and it is expanding its activities and influence abroad.

In early 1971, the *Mainichi Daily News* carried a series of articles
on the *Zaikai*, which was described as being an unofficial but formally recognized group of Japan's top business leaders, who in effect are the "directors" of Japan, Inc. This was the first time that
most foreign businessmen in Japan had heard the word *Zaikai* used
in this connection.

The word itself has been around at least since the early 1900s—
and as used in conversation it means "business leaders." But it was
not until the *Mainichi* series that the *Zaikai* was linked so promin-
ently with the ruling powers in Japan. According to the *Mainichi*
story, the *Zaikai* is the largest and strongest pressure group in
Japan.

The *Zaikai* is directed by a subgroup of 24 elite members who
make up the *Sanken*, or Industrial Problems Study Council, which
was established in March, 1966. These 24 key *Zaikai* men include
the presidents and board chairmen of 24 of the country's leading
business enterprises.

It is said that the *Zaikai* exercises considerable influence over the
government, not only in deliberative councils (a number of important government councils are headed by *Zaikai* men), but also by
making large financial donations to the ruling party, as well as to
opposition parties. Companies court both the *Zaikai* and politicians because of the importance of maintaining good relations with
both groups. Commenting on this fact, the *Mainichi* reported that
twice a year a "certain construction company" holds a party in Ka-
ruizawa (a mountain resort northwest of Tokyo) for the wives of
top *Zaikai* men and politicians. "Dishes on the tables are filled with
jewels, so that the ladies can take home whatever they like. The
event naturally causes a sensation among the ladies, and this in
turn brings benefits to the company," said the *Mainichi.*

It was the *Mainichi's* contention that the *Zaikai* virtually run *Japan, Inc.* According to the paper's analysis, the *Sanken* was directly responsible for Eisaku Sato's election as prime minister, for the successful Yawata-Fuji Steel merger, and for numerous other important events since its formal inception. If so, the *Sanken* has apparently assumed much of the power and many of the functions of the *Keidanren, Nikkeiren, Keizai Doyukai,* and the JCCI, all of which are headed by *Sanken* members. The *Mainichi* concluded that the 24 *Sanken* members constitute the real government in Japan and that there is no limit to their political or economic power.*

Another of the important government bodies is the Economic Planning Agency, which is attached to the Prime Minister's Office. The EPA accumulates business and economic data, analyzes them, and then makes projections and recommendations. The most powerful of the government agencies, as far as business is concerned, is the Ministry of Finance, because it exercises control over monetary and credit policies through the Bank of Japan. Government influence over business that is applied directly is referred to as Administrative Guidance. Indirect government control through the banking system is called Window Guidance.

To identify properly any Japanese firm, it is necessary to know its relationships with the government and with other firms in the industry—whether it is a subsidiary of a larger firm, a subcontractor attached to a parent firm, "aligned" with any particular group as a result of stock holding, and so on. Affiliated companies are known as *keiretsu kaisha.* Aligned companies are *kankei kaisha.* All related companies have specific status within the group; all know and are very conscious of their rank.

The Ubiquitous Tegata

Japan, Inc. operates primarily on credit. About the only thing that is still occasionally paid in cash is wages, though most major companies are rapidly switching to electronic deposit. Most payments

*In a typical year, the *Zaikai's* executive group (*Sanken*) was made up of the chief officers of the following companies: Tokyo Electric, Nippon Steel, Industrial Bank of Japan, Fuji Bank, Showa Denko, Mitsubishi Heavy Industries, Mitsubishi Bank, Toray Industries, Toyobo, Mitsubishi Shoji, Mitsui & Co., Nissan Motors, Nippon Electric, Nikko Securities, Nippon Rare Metals, Sumitomo Chemical , Nippon Seiko, Hitachi Ltd., Sumitomo Metal Industries, and the president of *Keidanren* and the senior managing director of *Nikkeiren.*

are in form of a *tegata* ("note of hand"), or promissory note, with a due date anywhere from 90 to 180 days. Occasionally, the note is for nine months, in which case it is sometimes referred to as a "pregnant *tegata.*" The fact that domestic business is primarily done on deferred payment has provided one of the compelling incentives Japanese companies have had for exporting, because this is done mostly on confirmed letters of credit that can be discounted for immediate cash.

How Japanese Companies Are Organized

Foreign businessmen who have been perplexed by the corporate structure of the typical large-scale Japanese company and possibly frustrated in their efforts to understand how such an apparently inefficient organization could be effective, as well as dynamic, need not feel lonely. "Japanese businessmen themselves do not have logical explanations of the mystique surrounding the Japanese corporate organization," says Bunichiro Hijikata, professor at Rikkyo University.

The department in the typical Japanese company that most confuses Westerners is the *Somu-Bu*, or General Affairs Department. The *Somu-Bu* does everything that the other departments don't do. It steers visitors to the right department, handles company mail, coordinates interdepartmental relations, maintains the company's official files and stock ledger, and handles public relations.

One of the basic aspects in Japanese company organization can be seen in almost any department. First, the managers seldom, if ever, have private offices. All are located in one or more large rooms, with the desks so arranged that the manager, assistant manager, and section heads are in front of the different sections. The sections are divided by functions, and the desks within the sections are arranged in what Professor Hijikata calls boxes. Each of these boxes constitutes a team headed by a supervisor. Within the boxes, there is very little job demarcation. All members of a section, including the supervisor and section head, usually do the same kind of work. A section usually consists of young men and women fresh out of school, up to the section head who will have from seven to ten years seniority. Those who are experienced tutor the newer employees on an informal basis—teaching them what to do and how to do it. As a person becomes more skilled and effective, more or less by unspoken consent of the team, he is allowed more and more discretion in his contribution to the team's efforts.

In a Japanese company, there is very little distinction between the manager and the managed. Duties, responsibilities, or authority do not change very much, if at all, upon promotion into the lower managerial ranks. The newly promoted manager gets a raise in pay and his status goes up, but he is not set apart from the other employees.The primary discernable difference is that the higher one rises on the rank ladder, the larger his chair becomes and the less work he does. Age is another indication. The older people in an office are almost always senior in rank, as well.

How Does the "Box System" Hold Up?

The various advantages of the box/section system of organization are fairly obvious. Their disadvantages include the fact that they do not usually contribute to the development of specialists; the managers are usually more dependent on the teams than vice versa; and it is difficult to bring anyone new into a box except at the bottom. Another characteristic of this system is that the prestige and power of a manager within his own company is primarily determined by how many sections he has under him and their importance to the company as a whole. Some sections rank high, some low. If a manager is assigned to a box that is ranked lower than what his seniority usually warrants, the message is quite clear.

Professor Hijikata says the corporate structure in Japan is derived from three influences: (1) the traditional conceptual and behavioral patterns of the Japanese; (2) the legalistic thinking and bureaucracy of the German system, which was used as a model for new companies set up in the 1870s; and (3) the adaptation of some American management practices emphasizing a formalistic approach.

The Executive Hierarchy

There are three levels of organization in most Japanese companies. The highest level is the *keiei* (management), which includes the president, vice presidents, and the directors. The second level is the *kanri* (administrative), which takes in the department heads (*bucho*), section chiefs (*kacho*), and assistant section chiefs (*kakaricho*). The third level is the *ippan*, or staff, which includes both the so-called white collar workers (*shoku-in*) and the blue collar workers (*ko-in*). All of these who are permanent employees of the company are also generally known as *sha-in* (company employees). Employees hired on a temporary basis are either *rinjiko* (people employed from the outside when extra help is needed) or *shokutaku* (former permanent employees who are rehired on a temporary basis when they reach the compulsory retirement age of 55 to 58, depending on the company retirement policy).

Both the executives on the administrative level and the general staff—white collar, as well as blue collar—consider themselves salarymen (*sarari-men*), which has a very strong mystique in Japan. As far as educational levels are concerned, most blue collar workers went only as far as grade school. High school graduates are hired for white collar work and usually do not go beyond middle management. College graduates begin as ordinary white collar workers, but they more or less automatically move into upper and top-level management positions.

The *keiei*, or top level of management in a Japanese company, begins with the directors (*torishimariyaku*) and goes upward to the *jomu* (managing directors), *senmu* (senior managing directors), *fukushacho* (vice presidents), *shacho* (president), and finally the *kaicho* (chairman of the board). *Keiei*-level executives in Japan are known generally as *juyaku* (which translates as "director"). Anyone below this level is not considered very important. In joint stock companies, Japan's Commercial Code requires that there be two or three directors who are given power of attorney to represent their companies. Known as representative directors (*daihyo torishimariyaku*), they are appointed by the board from among its members. The Code also requires that each joint stock company have an auditor (*kansa-yaku*), who must be an outsider. In practice, this position usually goes to a retired senior executive of the company. His only duty is to appear at the annual stockholders meeting and announce that he has received the company's financial statement on behalf of the stockholders—for which he usually gets paid a full year's salary.

In most Japanese companies, the position of chairman of the board is little more than retirement-with-pay for an ex-president. The chief executive officer is the president. The president and other senior members of the board usually handpick new directors from among ranking division heads and sometimes from among the presidents of smaller, affiliated companies. It is not common for directors to be brought in from nonrelated companies or the outside in general.

Larger Japanese corporations often have 20 or more directors and senior executives. No doubt because of this, most of these companies have an executive committee (*jomu-kai,* or managing directors' board) made up of the president and a number of key directors who make up what real power there is at the head of a Japanese company.

Top executives of Japanese firms who do not become president and chairman of the board are usually required to retire between the ages of 60 and 65. But the president and chairman can go on for as long as they have the will and the health. The president almost invariably has the right to pick his own successor. This usually is his number-one follower (*kobun*), who has been with him for his entire business career.

What a Japanese Company President Does

Given the nature of Japanese management (the *ringi* system of decision making, which usually originates at the middle-management level, etc.) the duties of a Japanese company president, particularly in larger companies, differ markedly from those of his counterparts in the West. His role is not that of the dynamic innovator, the skilled technician, or the master salesman. He is an expert in human relations who has proven his ability over the years as a group leader. His primary responsibilities are two: to watch over the harmony and spirit in his own company and to make and maintain the necessary personal connections with other companies, associations, government agencies, banks, and important clients.

A Japanese president also gives a great deal of his time and energy to the selection and training of new employees. He is acutely aware that most likely they are going to be with the company for the rest of their lives and that some day one of them will occupy his chair.

Who gets promoted to the *keiei* level in a Japanese company depends to a great extent on school ties, family connections, ability to get along with others and to work within the system, seniority, intelligence, and good health. Not everybody with these qualifications can reach the top because the pyramid narrows, and the directors and president stay on beyond the retirement age for non-*keiei*

level employees. In recent decades, the larger enterprises have grown fast enough that excess executives could be placed in plants or branch offices, sent overseas, or assigned to joint ventures. Others have been encouraged and helped to set up subcontracting operations catering to the parent firm.

Many large Japanese companies have what is known as the *Shacho-Shitsu* or President's Room, which is a group assigned to do staff work on behalf of the president.

The Extraordinary *Sokaiya*

The *sokaiya* are a special breed of minor stockholders, said to be descended from the various gangs of old Japan (and still closely associated with the *yakuza* of modern Japan), who for decades operated one of the world's most unusual extortion rackets. Each year, the *sokaiya* shook down Japan's largest companies for millions of dollars in a way that made them impervious to the law. Their method of operation was very simple. They owned small amounts of stock in each of their victim companies, and they attended all stockholder meetings. As long as the company cooperated and paid off (in some cases, up to a quarter of a million dollars a year), the *sokaiya* made sure the meetings proceeded quickly. Any other stockholder who wanted to comment, ask a question, or voice a complaint was shouted down by the *sokaiya* or was intimidated by threats and rough behavior. For this "service," the *sokaiya* billed the companies for millions of yen.

The annual battle between the *sokaiya* and ranking Japanese firms finally came to a head in 1982, when a new law was passed to control their behavior and make it illegal for them to solicit fees for providing their particular kind of service.

All of the results are not in yet, but smart money is betting that the *sokaiya* will find some way to circumvent the law and go about their business of extorting money from major companies.

In the past, the funds used to pay the *sokaiya* fees were taken from *tsukiai ryo*, or "friendship fees"—the Japanese equivalent of a public relations budget.

The Five-Day Week

The five-day week is an important factor in Japan's business world. But the smaller the company, the less likely it is to have a five-day week. Only about five percent of the companies with 30 to 99 employees work five days a week. This goes up to approximately 15 percent for companies with 100 to 999 employees and then leaps to over 50 percent of the firms with 1,000 or more employees.

Over half of the smaller companies work six days a week, as do a quarter of the medium-size firms. Some four percent of the big companies give their employees only one day off a week. Between these two extremes are companies that give employees anywhere from one to three Saturdays off each month.

Almost 75 percent of the Japanese firms that converted to the five-day week during the 1960s and 1970s claim that their productivity increased as a result of the shorter week. Nearly half of them say that the system has proven beneficial in hiring new employees. The same survey revealed that in 46 percent of the firms, management had taken the initiative in introducing the system, and in 43 percent of the firms it was the employees' idea.

Ranking political leaders both in and out of the government favor the five-day work week. The Socialist Party would like to see a law passed to make the five-day week mandatory. In any event, it seems likely that the system will continue to spread rapidly among large-scale Japanese companies and at least slowly among the smaller enterprises.

Paid Summer Vacations

Most Japanese workers now seem to be more interested in summer vacations and paid holidays than in the five-day week. Summer vacations really began to catch on in Japan in the latter part of the 1960s. Such large firms as Nissan Motors and Hitachi took the lead in closing their factories completely for a week or ten days in late July and early August—the hottest days—and letting all their employees go on paid vacations at the same time.

The Japan Productivity Center and the Japan Federation of Employers' Associations estimate that well over 70 percent of all major enterprises have adopted the summer vacation system. The larger the company, the larger the number of paid holidays employees get. The largest companies give 15 to 19 paid days off each year.

The Expanding Market-Share Syndrome

The Japanese company has an overwhelming need to produce more and to continually expand its share of the market because its labor costs automatically increase each year as a result of the seniority-based wage system, the fact that permanent employees are generally not laid off, and the general inflationary movement. This need for getting and maintaining an increasingly larger share of the market was one of the primary reasons why Japanese companies traditionally preferred to introduce established products into the market rather than invest the time and money necessary to develop new products on their own.

There is now tremendous pressure for Japanese manufacturers, particularly in consumer categories, to come up with new products regularly. They continue to scour the world for product ideas, and more and more companies have their own new product development departments.

Until the 1960s, companies in Japan were usually listed according to their paid-in capital and their share of the market. Now they are more likely to be listed by their market share, possibly followed by their capital.

A Mental Madhouse?

Japan's dreams of achieving greater and greater heights of economic grandeur could be shattered by any of a number of factors— one of which could be the mental collapse of the bulk of the labor force. Years ago, the chief psychiatrist at a Tokyo hospital said that approximately one-third of all Japanese salarymen were in the preliminary stages of neurosis. A recent survey by the Ministry of Labor indicated that emotional and mental disturbances among Japanese workers was reaching epidemic proportions.

Among the workers' complaints shown in the Labor Ministry report: having to work too fast, incapable supervisors, unappreciative management, crowded working and living conditions, traffic and pollution problems, and having to maintain the delicate human relations that are the basis for the Japanese business system.

As early as 1971, Matsushita Electric Industry Company established a Self-Control Room at one of the firm's Osaka factories to help its employees relieve some of their frustrations. At the entrance to the special room are concave and convex mirrors that give the visitor a distorted view of himself as he enters. On the inside is a small gymnasium where the worker can punch bags, pedal bicycles, and take other forms of exercise. The most popular facilities in the gym, however, are two dummies seated on a raised platform, which are there for the workers to beat, slash, and stab to their hearts' content—while "picturing in their minds anyone who is bugging them at the moment." There is a counselor next door in case the worker still feels frustrated after leaving the Self-Control Room.

The Labor Ministry hopes to relieve this very serious problem through special educational programs aimed at instructing business managers in how to treat employees—a sure sign that the old Japanese way of humanistic regard and harmony is weakening.

Chapter 5

Areas of Friction Between Japanese and Western Businessmen

"An ever popular theme in many Western writings about Japan is the so-called 'Mystery of the Orient.' Actually, there is probably no people on the face of the earth as explainable as the Japanese due to their formalized culture and systemized role-playing which influences the deepest and most personal levels of behavior and attitudes. In fact, the Japanese themselves suffer from a malady that might be called the 'Mystery of the West.' They often react to us according to old and well-preserved stereotypes with behavior patterns that are incompatible with their normal conduct. Thus it happens that we are often reacting to abnormal Japanese behavior that is in itself a reaction to us."

—G. H. Lambert
Psychologist/Japanologist

Cultural Differences

The basis for most of the friction that occurs when Westerners engage in business with the Japanese is the failure of both sides, but particularly the foreigners, to recognize and take into consideration the cultural differences. Americans in particular habitually assume that they can deal with the Japanese the same way they deal with their own countrymen. After all, we rationalize, they're just like us, once you get around the language barrier. This, it happens, is not so. The cultural differences that divide Japanese and American businessmen include not only language, but values and beliefs that, more often than not, are directly opposed. Americans doing business in Japan are constantly running into strongly held

73

opinions and attitudes that from our viewpoint have absolutely no logical basis.

When General Douglas MacArthur was Supreme Commander of the Allied Powers occupying Japan, he once remarked that the Japanese were like 12-year-old children. This remark was widely publicized in the Japanese press, but no one disputed it. In the words of a Japanese liberal arts authority, Dr. Kazutaka Watanabe: "It was contemptible to speak of a nation in that manner. But the Japanese took it calmly and philosophically. We knew it was true. Yes. We Japanese have a dual personality. We are like 12-year-olds, and yet at the same time we are 40 years old. These two persons are in our body and have two completely different outlooks on life. Moreover, we are not troubled by this contradiction. As individual people, we are 40 years old. But as members of society we are adolescent children."

Dr. Watanabe continues, "When Americans deal with Japanese, whether as friends or as employers, they are generally unable to determine whether they are dealing with the 40-year-old or the 12-year-old. If the Americans treat the Japanese as children, their adult side will be cynically critical of the Americans. If the Americans treat the Japanese as adults, the child side of the Japanese will be disappointed and critical because the Americans 'don't understand' them."

The reason for this dual personality of the Japanese, according to Dr. Watanabe, can be traced to Buddhism, Confucianism, and feudalism, which teach that the individual should not exist as a private entity but should be submerged within the group. "As a result," Dr. Watanabe says, "we in Japan have discovered neither Man nor Society. We are animal-like individuals who have been baptized in the philosophy of the nonexistence of 'I,' the emptiness of phenomena, and the tragic beauty of nothingness. We are therefore animals, but animals steeped in metaphysics. This is why we have learned teachers who zig-zag in street demonstrations shouting like madmen. They demonstrate as animals, not as thinkers."

In Dr. Watanabe's view, continuous thought in Japan is therefore found only among those people who have somehow managed to become individuals, "overcoming the dark, grey social pressure that seeks to smother their personal selves." As group-oriented people, most Japanese find it difficult or impossible to act as individuals. This explains, he says, why they are so obedient and effective as a mass, but generally so restrained and ineffective as individuals.

There are two distinct categories of Japanese attitudes toward American businessmen. The most important one is that of tremendous respect and admiration, which derives from their overall image of the accomplishments of American businessmen as a group, not of American businessmen as individuals. The other category, which stems from regular direct contact with American businessmen who do not uphold their idealized image, ranges from ordinary respect to contempt. Both Japanese and Americans have been culturally conditioned to have an innate distrust of and dislike for each other, and there is a small percentage on both sides who, while persisting in doing business with each other, magnify these feelings out of proportion. As one Western businessman observed: "The foreigners' distrust of the Japanese is often misplaced. They are frequently accused of being deceitful, but we have found that they are intensely loyal if you play the game fairly with them."

Because of racial homogeneity and centuries of geographical and cultural isolation from the West, the Japanese are "foreign conscious" to a degree that is frequently paranoid. They are acutely conscious of all racial and cultural differences and find it impossible to accept an outsider, particularly a Caucasian, without numerous reservations. No matter how long a foreigner resides in Japan or what his qualifications are in any field, to the Japanese he is still a *gaijin*—an "outside person." Caucasian businessmen who were born and raised in Japan are regarded just like the man who stepped off the plane yesterday. Neither can the Westerner ever feel at home, because he is never accepted. This induces a unique kind of frustration that constantly works on the foreigner who stays in Japan a long time. He never feels permanent or secure. He is never without a gnawing, irritating feeling that he is marking time out of place and that he should go home.

Many older Japanese businessmen in the export field have a very low regard for Jews, despite the fact that very few know a Jew from a Gentile. This has apparently come about because, in addition to adopting to some degree the well-known and often expressed Gentile prejudices, many Japanese exporters have suffered or believe they have suffered from the unscrupulous activities of a small number of Jewish importers operating out of New York. Stories of these incidents have been widely circulated in Japan, and exporters who have any difficulty with any importer are likely to lay the blame on "a Jewish buyer."

Japanese-Americans in Japan

Foreign businessmen in Japan who are of Japanese ancestry—that is, foreign-born descendants of Japanese immigrants, commonly called *nisei* (second-born generation), *sansei* (third-born), etc.—are in a special category. Until the mid-1960s, the Japanese tended to be critical of *nisei* and *sansei*. Caucasian American executives who employed them in their Japan operations were frequently told by Japanese clients that they preferred not to deal with the *nisei* on the staff. Most of these same American businessmen praised their *nisei* staff highly, however, pointing out that they were especially valuable as managers in administrative functions.

The most common way the Japanese expressed their disapproval of *nisei* was to criticize their Japanese language ability, since few of the *nisei* who went to Japan in the years immediately following the Pacific war spoke fluent, modern Japanese.

In practical day-to-day affairs, the treatment that the *nisei* received in Japan depended on their position. If they were in powerful positions, as buyers or persons of authority on the administrative side of business, they were usually treated with the same formal respect given to Caucasian foreigners in the same position. But if they were in a sales or liaison position, they were often not accepted on their own merits.

By the end of the 1960s, Japanese attitudes toward *nisei* and *sansei* had changed significantly. Renewed self-confidence and improvements in their own foreign-language ability made it possible for the Japanese to be more objective in their appraisal of Japanese-Americans. Now, the tendency is for them to expect more of a Japanese-American than of a Caucasian-American businessman and to have little patience with those who do not measure up to their high standards.

On the personal side, Japanese-Americans in Japan continue to have a number of advantages. First, they don't stand out from the crowd unless they draw attention to themselves and therefore are not constantly under a microscope, as Caucasian foreigners are. Second, they are usually able to speak enough of the language to communicate (many, in fact, are now quite fluent) and to avoid many of the problems that plague non-Japanese-speaking foreigners. Third, their wives and children adapt to local conditions and fit into the local scene much more readily. Fourth, most overseas-Japanese have relatives in Japan. They also have a much more compelling desire to be accepted and feel at home—but even they find it difficult, if not impossible, to feel as though they belong.

Getting Along with Your Staff

There is very little social intercourse between most Western businessmen and their Japanese employees or their counterparts in Japanese firms beyond the company party, the reception, and the golf course. The two groups are kept apart, not only by a mutual inability to communicate, but by a different life-style. When they do get together at the above functions, except where the few English-speaking Japanese are concerned, all they can do is shake hands, smile, and offer each other drinks. Actual personal relations are very limited and usually revolve around a few English-speaking Japanese employees of their company who are "used" by the foreign businessmen to help them take care of personal problems.

As a Japanese employee of an American firm said: "One of the most common mistakes made by foreign businessmen in Japan is to ask members of their staff during office hours to help them with their personal affairs, which range from maid problems to pregnant girlfriends. It is all right to ask their help if you explain in private that you have a personal problem on which you would like advice. Ideally, this would not take place in the office at all, but at a casual lunch or perhaps a coffee break. Handled this way, the Japanese feels that the foreigner is expressing confidence in him and as a result will invariably go considerably out of his way to be of assistance. All of this has to be handled very diplomatically; otherwise, the foreigner loses the respect of his Japanese staff."

Since the Japanese are reluctant to show any annoyance at being used for such personal purposes as go-betweens, solicitors, and peacemakers, most foreigners overdo it and some turn valuable employees into serious enemies without being aware of it.

Another human relations problem that many foreigners in Japan are unaware of—or ignore—is the question of what to call their Japanese employees. While it is true that the Japanese customarily call each other by their last names, adding the honorific "san" indiscriminately, it is not always the best idea for foreigners to adopt the same custom—for a reason that will probably surprise many. Westerners, particularly Americans, habitually call each other by their first names. But they have heard that local etiquette requires that all Japanese be addressed by their last names with the "san" attached. Foreigners obviously find this custom very awkward and a considerable strain, especially after they become well-acquainted with the Japanese concerned or when it involves an older executive addressing an office boy. But they usually force themselves to observe proper etiquette.

Some foreigners occasionally break tradition and bestow their own choice of nicknames on Japanese employees. If they discover that a Japanese employee has a foreign nickname, they seize upon it with obvious, if self-conscious, relief. For the most part, however, they observe the "last-name-plus-san" with strict formality.

The surprising part is that the Japanese find this social custom just as awkward as their Western employers do. In fact, it is the source of a considerable amount of frustration. They see and hear the foreigners call each other by their first names in an atmosphere of complete acceptance and informality. It rankles them that they cannot attain the same acceptance and comradeship, and they consider the first-name, last-name problem to be one of the chief obstacles. When the foreign executive calls his American staff and perhaps one or two of the Japanese by their first names, it grates on the rest of the staff's sensibilities.

Years ago, I wrote an article entitled "100 Million Nameless Japanese" for a Japanese magazine, lamenting the almost inhuman barrier formed by the custom of calling people only by their last names and recommending that the custom be dropped. It was not until the Reagan/Nakasone era, however, that the ancient custom began to crack. When President Ronald Reagan and Prime Minister Yasuhiro Nakasone began calling each other Ron and Yasu, it was a signal that personal names were acceptable in Japan. Now, much to my great delight, almost all the younger Japanese I meet immediately call me by my first name.

It should be safe enough now for Westerners to begin using the first names of new Japanese friends, colleagues, or employees soon after meeting them—with the exception of those who are senior in age or in superior positions.

Responsibilities of the Foreign Employer

Most foreign businessmen in Japan take it for granted that their Japanese employees are satisfied as long as they don't complain. But about the only time Japanese employees ever approach their foreign superiors is to hand in their resignation—which generally comes as a complete surprise to their employers. Japanese employees expect their supervisors to take a personal interest in their welfare and keep themselves posted on the workers' personal problems. A Japanese friend explained: "The Japanese are extremely reluctant to take the initiative in bringing their personal affairs to the attention of their superiors. They expect the superiors to demonstrate their interest automatically and to watch over them like a mother. When this interest isn't forthcoming, the Japanese employee feels that he isn't accepted and is being constantly slighted. For example, in a Japanese company, after the wife of an employee has a baby, the employee's immediate superior may quite seriously tell him that he shouldn't have intercourse with his wife until a certain amount of time passes. The husband-employee knows this, of course, but it gives him a feeling of belonging, of being wanted, when his superior demonstrates such a personal interest in his affairs."

One of the most sensitive areas in the relationships between Western employers and their Japanese employees has to do with company parties and drinking in general. The Japanese traditionally have accepted the idea that if you party-it-up with someone you accept him as your equal and commit yourself to the type of obligations that equals have to each other. Because of this, when Japanese supervisors or managers attend a company party or drinking bash, either as host or guest of their employees, they never stay the whole evening. The usual custom is for the boss to slip his juniors a sum of money when he leaves so they can continue the party.

As long as the big boss, whether he is Japanese or foreign, stays on at the party, the employees feel obligated to restrain themselves. They can't relax and really enjoy themselves. Not realizing this, many Western managers stay on until the end, as if it were their duty. It is also common for foreign hosts to indiscriminately invite members of the party out for a second, semiprivate party after the main affair ends. The idea is very democratic, of course, but it is an error in management psychology in Japan. It is customary

79

for a higher executive to invite his immediate subordinates out on such occasions, but not rank-and-file employees. Foreigners who make this error not only alienate their Japanese managers, but also disrupt the chain of command by hobnobbing with the lower staff at the expense of their Japanese supervisors.

Added a Japanese businessman: "We Japanese also do not like the idea of Americans inviting us to the American club or other places that are exclusively for foreigners. To some, of course, it makes no difference. But I'm sure the average Japanese business-man considers such invitations as condescending gestures." A major hotel is always neutral ground.

Another Japanese executive observed: "Most of the British, German, and other European firms that were in Japan before the war have good relations with their Japanese employees. But post-war American firms that have operations in Japan have not been nearly so successful. Probably the most conspicuous example of past years were some of the airlines. The turnover among their Japanese personnel was tremendous. One of them was commonly referred to as a training center for Japanese airline personnel." Ex-plaining why this was so, the executive said: "The American staff assigned here were not trained in personnel management. Few of them bothered to become familiar with Japanese attitudes, work customs, or labor laws. Some didn't even know their own jobs."

He added that this was not a problem unique to American firms. "Japanese companies with offices in the United States have the same problem. It is customary for Japanese firms, particularly trading companies, to send their junior executives abroad for prestige purposes. This custom is known as *haku wo tsukeru*, or coating something in gold foil. These young men stay overseas just long enough to learn how to get from their apartment to the office. American, as well as Japanese, management will have to learn to some extent to respect and conform to the conditions of foreign markets."

Discipline, Sophistication, and Culture

It is necessary to have a different type of relationship with your Japanese staff, observes an experienced American sales executive in Tokyo. "There must be a continuous educational effort on your part to teach them the advantages of individual responsibility. Authority must be exercised with a great deal more studied firmness than is required in the United States. It is necessary to be on the borderline between being firm and being dictatorial, depending on the reception. You cannot be too firm or too soft and compromising. It is a very thin line and takes up a great deal of the mental and physical effort of foreign management in Japan."

"We are still learning," said another executive. "Everything is changing. When we look at it on a day-to-day basis, things sometimes appear to be standing still. But looking back to how business was done here in prewar years, the change has been fantastic. For one thing, the foreign businessman's attitude toward the Japanese has changed. During those years, most foreign businessmen dealing with Japan automatically distrusted their Japanese counterparts. This is no longer true except among a certain type of importer whose operation is essentially larcenous and who attributes to his Japanese suppliers his own character."

Another personal factor that had far-reaching effects on the reputation of United States businessmen who visited Japan in the 1950s and early 1960s was their attempt to be both polite and encouraging. As a rule, both businessmen and visiting economists lavished effusive and often ill-considered praise on certain Japanese products, plants, and management processes. At first, the Japanese eagerly accepted this praise with varying degrees of pride and gratitude. By the mid-1960s, things had changed. The Japanese knew they were good. They knew that in many instances their techniques and products were the best in the world. They were no longer impressed with praise that was often meaningless, and they began to look down on the stream of people who continued to distribute this sort of polite pap year after year.

Rather than having continued to emphasize the development of techniques, many top Japanese executives had long since begun to emphasize the pursuit of culture. Several of the largest firms in the country had established training schools for their high-level executives in which the object was not to study business administration, but to raise the executives' cultural level. Virtually all successful Japanese businessmen have a cultural hobby of some kind. They are inclined to think less of anyone who has no such interest. Thus, ranking American businessmen who want to get on

81

with their Japanese counterparts should not be caught with their cultural pants down.

European business interests tend to be much more sensitive to cross cultural problems than Americans. In 1979, several European chambers of commerce joined together to establish an 18-month Executive Training Program (ETP), in cooperation with *Keidanren* (Japan's leading businessmen's group) and a number of Japanese companies, to provide European managers with specialized training in the Japanese language and in Japanese business methods.

The program is primarily designed for participants from small and medium-size enterprises that make a strong commitment to the Japanese market. During the first year of the program, participants spend six hours a day in the formal study of Japanese, with an additional three hours of home study required. This is followed by six months of on-the-job training in a Japanese company.

Throughout the 18-month course, there are seminars on the general aspects of Japanese society and business, with topics ranging from history to management techniques and from commercial regulations to the role of women in Japanese society. Other seminars cover specific fields of related interest, such as banking and finance, the consumer industry, etc.

The European chambers of commerce involved in the Executive Training Program take a long-range view, to the time when these Japan specialists will be running their companies.

It was not until May 1986 that a group of American congressmen announced they were supporting the establishment of a Japan-U.S. Trade Center in Tokyo to help American firms expand trade with Japan—a move that I and others first began advocating in the early 1960s.

The special problems facing foreign firms wanting to enter Japan also led to the appearance in the early 1980s of a number of Japanese firms especially established to act as go-betweens. These firms include Seibu International Ltd., set up by the Seibu department store group, which is designed specifically to help smaller foreign firms find business partners in Japan and secure outlets in the Japanese market.

Seibu International—along with Intro Japan—a firm set up by Temporary Center, which provides temporary office staff, was the first Japanese company established to cater to small and medium-size foreign firms wanting to do business in Japan. The larger ad agencies and a number of consulting firms, as well as law offices and banks, have been providing a similar service for larger foreign companies since the 1960s.

Seibu International, with offices in Paris and New York, pools proposals from abroad for joint ventures, commodity sales, real estate ventures, and so on. Intro Japan, which has a branch in Los Angeles in partnership with an American consulting company, does market surveys, test sales, and product exhibitions, and aids in setting up, equipping, and staffing offices in Japan.

Chapter 6

Japanese Consumer Attitudes and Foreign Product Image

*"We are very much concerned about the
undesirable national habit of the Japanese to lavish
praise on imported products."*
—Tokyo Chamber of Commerce & Industry

The Sanctity of Japanese Products

Older Japanese are extraordinarily proud of the native products of
Japan. Until the 1960s, the feeling the Japanese had for their traditional implements went further than pride. It bordered on a form of
worship. No observant foreigner in Japan for more than a few days
could fail to encounter this peculiar characteristic. This special
regard the Japanese had for their products came from a combination of several factors: their Shintoistic reverence for beauty as expressed in objects made of natural materials; the tremendous
amount of professional artistry reflected in all their handmade
products; geographical and cultural isolation that prevented most
Japanese from ever seeing a foreign-made or foreign-type product
until well into the nineteenth century; and the discovery upon the
opening of Japan to trade with the West that the only thing about
Japan that Westerners could immediately understand and appreciate were such things as its beautiful lacquerwares, ceramics, and
handmade paper products.

The Japanese wanted very badly to be accepted by Westerners,
and when foreigners accepted the products but not the people who
made them, the Japanese automatically went along with the discrimination. From the beginning of their intercourse with the
West up to recent decades, the Japanese had to be content with

basking in the deluge of praise lavished on their soup bowls, tea pots, scrolls, and other traditional utensils and decorative items. As the years passed, this extraordinary praise for their native products led the Japanese to imbue them with a degree of sanctity that Westerners usually reserve for religious objects. It also led the Japanese to look on the cheapened, Western-type products they made for export with considerable contempt.

This latter attitude began to diminish in the early 1960s and to be replaced by the feeling of superiority previously applied only to traditional products. This trend has continued and eventually may become strong enough to counteract the almost compulsive desire many Japanese still have to buy and use foreign-made products, whether they are superior or not.

In earlier years, the sanctity of traditional utilitarian Japanese products had little bearing on foreign businessmen interested in selling in Japan. However, the attitude is now being transferred to virtually everything made in Japan, and the hypnotic attraction that imported merchandise has had for the Japanese is beginning to wear off with familiarity. If this trend should continue and go too far, it could become a serious problem for foreign manufacturers wanting to sell their products in Japan.

Opposition to Foreign-Made Products

Until the latter part of the 1960s, a significant percentage of the bureaucrats making up the body of Japan's government opposed importation of foreign products on nationalistic, as well as economic, grounds. Commenting on this attitude, one Japanese businessman said: "While Japanese consumers who can afford to are anxious to buy imported merchandise, MITI officials and other government bureaucrats, deep down, are opposed to foreign goods coming into Japan on a strictly nationalistic basis."

A number of years ago, many Japanese manufacturers put themselves in the same boat. Mass campaigns were launched in an effort to destroy the attraction of imported consumer goods and enhance their own merchandise. The central theme of the campaign was emotional and racialistic. Their message: "If you are Oriental, you should use only Oriental products." And they quoted Kipling's well-known saying that "East is East and West is West."

In addition to playing on the racial feelings of the Japanese consumer, both government and business circles conducted all-out, strongly nationalistic "antiforeign goods" campaigns designed to encourage the use of made-in-Japan products. The rush of foreign imports into Japan following partial liberalization several years ago was characterized as a second "Black Ship Invasion," referring to the revolutionary chaos helped along by the arrival in Japan of Commodore Perry in 1853.

The campaigns were not successful. Economic commentator Tatsuo Mitarai summed up the view of most consumers: "It was a sly attempt to stimulate national sentiment and a cunning approach to barring foreign goods altogether. The government should encourage industry to . . . promote the slogan: 'Buy Japanese products if they are good!' Not 'Buy Japanese products because you are Japanese!'"

At this point, the admiration and desire for imported merchandise remains strong. Even when Japanese products are as good or superior to foreign imports, the tradition of snobbery that attaches to such things as Swiss watches, French perfume, Italian accessories, and American golf clubs still prevails in the minds of the majority of Japanese shoppers.

Young Japanese consumers are so status-conscious that they pay double or even triple the home-country price for foreign brand-name items. Heavy advertising has helped condition them to foreign brand names or at least to names in English, even if the products are not made abroad. Whether stemming from a desire for better quality merchandise, curiosity, or racial and cultural frustration—but most probably a combination of all of these—the pent-up demand for foreign goods or at least foreign-style goods is a living thing. There is probably not a household in Japan that does not now make regular use of imported or domestic-made Western products.

Japanese manufacturers learned in the early 1950s that all they had to do to increase their sales by as much as a hundred percent was to print their product labels and trade names in English. This trend has continued and expanded. In many cases, it is difficult to tell where a product is made.

How the Japanese See the United States

Any real understanding of Japanese attitudes toward the United States and toward American business must, of course, take both cultural and historical factors into account. Although the Japanese traditionally felt a greater cultural kinship with the French and Germans than with the Americans (from aesthetic and intellectual viewpoints), they have had much closer relations with the United States since the Restoration period in the late 1860s than with any other country.

Following a traditional pattern first established with Korea and China centuries ago—and despite numerous cultural barriers that did not exist in their Asian contacts—the Japanese were primarily interested in American techniques, which they grafted willy-nilly onto native roots. This situation persisted until the end of the Pacific war in 1945, when those roots were abruptly wrenched from the ground and exposed to the withering winds of social and economic change. As the roots were gradually replanted in a more capitalistic soil, the Japanese businessman began to see that there was more to modern business than just the techniques of production. Since that time, he has been forced to adopt American merchandising methods (but not American reasoning!) at an incredible pace, whether he likes it or not.

The big difference between the wholesale adoption of industrial techniques from 1868 to the early 1900s and the process going on now is that the industrial revolution was imposed and carried out by the government. The present marketing revolution was introduced by businessmen and is progressing at an ever-increasing rate because of its own inherent characteristics. Because this entails inevitable changes in the formal behavior and thinking of the Japanese, however, there is some resistance and a considerable amount of subversion in fitting the changes into Japanese patterns.

The Imperialist Image

The Japanese, including those who admire the system, cannot help but feel that the American way of doing business is imperialistic. This feeling derives from their traditional belief that all relations should be on a personal basis and that these relations should adhere to established patterns of behavior. Already socialistically inclined—because socialism is only a little removed from their own brand of humane feudalism—Japanese students, teachers, politicians, and businessmen who are successful are inclined to consider the impersonal, aggressive commercialism of American businessmen exploitative in nature and dangerous to society.

Much of the criticism by the Japanese concerns what they consider to be "inhuman characteristics" in the American economic system. The central theme of the Japanese system has traditionally been the safety, security, and harmony of the group. In return for this, the Japanese had to give up most of their individuality. But after centuries of living within feudalistic cooperative groups, they came to feel that it was the preferred way. While conditions have changed and are changing still, the overwhelming majority of all Japanese born before 1960 have been conditioned to this type of existence and find it difficult to conceive of any other. Furthermore, most older businessmen in Japan are thoroughly and irrevocably convinced that their paternalistic, hierarchical, feudalistically administered system is both ethically and morally superior to the American system. They believe that any significant inroads made by the American system in Japan would be disastrous.

The American idea of one man or one family pitted against society is still alien to most Japanese. To them the cold, objective approach of the American businessman who hires and fires mechanically and whose primary concern is to make as much profit as possible is not only inhuman but morally sinful.

Demise of the "Winning Lord" Factor

Another consideration in Japanese attitudes toward American business is the Big Brother or "Winning Lord" factor. It is a deeply ingrained characteristic of the Japanese to transfer both their loyalty and dependence to whatever power is in ascendancy or exercises an important degree of influence over their lives. As the victor in the Pacific war, the United States automatically fell heir to the rights, as well as the responsibilities, of a Winning Lord.

Once they discovered they weren't all going to be slaughtered, the Japanese automatically expected the United States to consider them one of the family. The average Japanese were so cooperative and eager to please that Americans were astounded. They also felt the United States was not living up to its obligations when the American government asked Japan to pay for some of the aid extended to the prostrate country during the immediate post-war years. Their attitude was: "What master or older brother would do a younger brother a favor and then demand that he be paid for it?"

But as the years passed and the symbols of American authority disappeared, the Japanese gradually withdrew their familial allegiance. The realities of modern political and business life, plus an emerging nationalism, soon resulted in further weakening these superior-inferior ties. Virtually the last of this feeling disappeared with the Olympic Games held in Tokyo in 1964. Just before the so-called Nixon Shock in 1971 (when President Nixon placed a 10 percent surcharge on imports), it seemed, in fact, as if the Japanese felt that they would soon be in a position to actually switch roles and become the Winning Lord—economically speaking! They continue to deny officially that Japan is further advanced economically than the U.S., but privately they gloat that the roles have indeed been reversed. In any event, they have not resumed and will not resume the inferior position of the loser.

Japan vs. the World

Because of deeply embedded beliefs that they are unique in the world, that no one else can understand them, that they in turn cannot be like other people, the Japanese habitually see themselves as standing alone against the world. This feeling of aloneness helps bind the people together for good and bad. It is one of the primary reasons why they strive to excel in all things. At the same time, it is difficult, if not impossible, for them to put themselves in the other fellow's shoes—to see the world through other than Japanese eyes. Furthermore, it makes them supersensitive and puts them on the defensive. Many times I have had people ask me what I think of Japan, and when I hesitate for a second before answering, they invariably say, "You think we are crazy, don't you!"

The concept of national identity is very strong in Japan, and the people's feeling of facing the world alone is so intense as sometimes to appear neurotic. But at the same time, both of these attitudes provide the Japanese with a tremendously viable cooperative spirit in their pursuit of company and national goals.

The *Samurai* Syndrome

Middle- and high-level Japanese government bureaucrats in particular take the position that their primary responsibility is to protect Japan against inroads by foreign business and foreign capital. The section and department chiefs in the Ministry of International Trade and Industry, the Finance Ministry, the Foreign Office, and so on, are often accused by more internationally minded Japanese of exhibiting a *samurai* syndrome. They appear willing to sacrifice their lives or fight to the death for a cause or a master in their determination to hold all "foreign invaders" at bay for as long as possible.

The upper level of the bureaucracy, particularly the ministers who are appointed, are more often than not very urbane, broad-minded, internationally oriented individuals who are pleasant and cooperative in manner, if not in spirit. But they do not run the bureaus. The lower-level bureaucrats do, and they exercise power by what they do, as well as by what they delay or refuse to do. The foreign businessman who offends one of these fellows is in for a rough time.

A general criticism of American business is that Americans are quick to fire an employee who makes a mistake or is not efficient. There is also a strong suspicion that American firms in Japan are interested only in making a lot of money and then pulling out. What most impresses the Japanese about American firms is how hard American managers work. They point out that this is not generally the case in Japan. Because of differences in the system, Japanese managers often seem to do very little when judged by Western standards. They do not dictate letters, run around checking on people, give orders, or supervise at all in the American sense. However, ordinary Japanese employees generally work very hard. They may not always be efficient by United States or European standards, but on the whole they display a greater dedication to their jobs than is common elsewhere and work many more hours per week than their Western counterparts.

After the "Nixon Shock"

Japanese attitudes toward the United States appeared to undergo a sudden change in 1971, when President Nixon announced his plan to visit Peking, and then one month later placed a surcharge on imports and removed the gold support from the United States dollar. The new economic policy hit the Japanese hard. Fanned by large segments of the press, a wave of near-hysteria swept the country. Headlines in mass-selling weekly magazines proclaimed that "even bonuses," which are so economically and emotionally important to the Japanese, were doomed by Nixon's action. (One school in northern Japan held a scarecrow contest just after the shock wave. A caricature of Nixon won second place.)

The Nixon Shock (also called Dollar Shock) brought Japan to a virtual standstill for a few days. For the first time in nearly a decade, businessmen, bankers, and government leaders looked out at the world without their cherry-blossom glasses on. What they saw sobered some, frightened others, and angered many . A number of top men in business and government admitted that Japan had been traveling first-class on half-fare, and they accepted Nixon's move as a necessary step. But, at the same time, they pointed out that if the United States had exercised control over its runaway wages the problem wouldn't have developed in the first place. Down deep, a great many felt the move by Nixon was motivated by envy of Japan's burgeoning GNP and was intended to keep Japan from becoming number one in the world.

The Japanese have a compelling desire for international acceptance and prestige, which at this stage they equate with economic power. They felt and often said, before Nixon's import surcharge, that their economic success gave them the right to spread their brand of business "harmony" abroad. Following the "shock," this feeling was replaced to some extent by a grudging new realization of the fragility of Japan's economic strength and its dependence on the United States. There was a return to the general feeling among the masses that Japan had been stabbed in the back and that the resentment the Japanese had felt at being defeated and occupied, mostly repressed during the 1950s and 1960s, had been justified all along.

To understand the feelings and attitudes of the Japanese, it is necessary to understand that they do not regard their country as a world power in the American sense. They therefore do not use the same standards as we do when considering their obligations to the United States and other nations. They feel that the idea of economic reciprocity between the huge, rich United States and tiny, "poor" Japan (in area, resources, ability to be self-supporting) is outrageous. The prevailing attitude is that Japan does what it does out of necessity, while American moves are made with either malicious or callous motives.

The "Too-Japanese" Syndrome

Without considerable foreign travel during their early years, it is very difficult for the Japanese to become fully cosmopolitan. It is a truly painful experience for businessmen who are not Westernized to go abroad. Besides the linguistic strain, which they find extraordinarily burdensome, many become quite ill from eating non-Japanese food for several days in a row. Being exposed to Western behavior for several days or weeks also tends to frazzle their nerves and leave them exhausted.

Because of this, many Japanese who travel overseas avoid exposing themselves to the outside world until the last minute by flying Japan Air Lines, staying in Japanese-run hotels, and eating in Japanese restaurants. In 1971, a bank and several other large companies announced plans to build private restaurant-recreational centers for Japanese tourists and businessmen in such cities as Anchorage, Seattle, San Francisco, Los Angeles, New York, London, etc. The centers, according to the announcement, were to be known as Pacific Clubs. Staffed by Japanese, they were to provide a strictly Japanese atmosphere for those going abroad for business or pleasure.

The clubs did not materialize, but other Japanese-owned and operated businesses, from restaurants to clubs, have appeared, and the feeling still exists that such Japanese-operated facilities are needed.

93

Chapter 7

Penetrating the Impenetrable Barrier

"When dealing in two such entirely different languages as English and Japanese, with their corresponding different historical, social, and cultural backgrounds, it is important to realize that communication begins before a word is spoken."
—Sen Nishiyama, In **Meeting with the Japanese.**

The Language Problem

The communications barrier between the Japanese and foreign businessmen visiting or doing business in Japan is a problem of almost unbelievable proportions. "The language problem is the beginning—and end—of almost everything. It acts as a filter through which the foreign businessman views his entire operation. It determines the decisions he makes and eventually his success or failure," noted one of the few foreign businessmen in Japan who is both bilingual and bicultural.

Although the Japanese are habitually lavish in their praise of Westerners who speak even a little of their language, it can harm, rather than help, one's position if the speaker uses it in a non-Japanese way—that is, if he does not or cannot use the accepted tone and vocabulary of respect and humility demanded by the Japanese. The Japanese cannot distinguish between their language and their particular social system and attitudes. The Japanese may also presume that the foreigner knows more than he does, resulting in misunderstanding and problems. Of course, the same situation exists in reverse, and it is far more serious because it is far more common. Usually, it is the Japanese side that makes an attempt to communicate in the foreigner's language.

Since their language has also traditionally served as a defense against outsiders, some Japanese feel a certain amount of antagonism toward Westerners whose language ability gives them access to this final Japanese sanctuary—a situation that they regularly acknowledge in a joking manner.

95

While only a small percentage of the foreign businessmen in Japan speak enough Japanese to conduct their company affairs in the language, many of the Japanese who work for foreign firms as clerks, secretaries, and managers generally speak fair to good English. But the problem goes much deeper than either side's ability to speak the other's language fairly well or even quite well. Said another foreign businessman: "We have a hell of a time getting things across—not words, but concepts. Even when we understand each other's words, communication is often nil."

The problem is not in word communication as much as it is in cultural communication, which is affected by subtle cultural differences that range from personal mannerisms to the deepest and broadest human values. One example of behavior that is typical of American and European men and illustrates this point is their custom of "sizing up" attractive female employees whom they have just met and making what they regard as suitable comments about the feminine charms they have observed. Japanese men appreciate attractive women as much as anyone, but they consider such behavior in an office to be out of place.

To the Japanese, nonverbal communication is often more important than verbal, and this is a level of communication from which even the Japanese-speaking Westerner is essentially barred. This nonverbal communication is based on a deep, inexplicable, visceral feeling, described in Japanese by the word *kan,* which can be translated as "emotional attunement." The Japanese are always reluctant to make a decision or initiate any action until this "gut feeling" is right—and it is based on more than 2,000 years of common cultural experience.

In 1969, there was a new surge of interest in speaking English in the Japanese business world. Hundreds of companies throughout the country began to urge all their employees to study the language. At Sony, it was made company policy that every employee would learn some English. Many companies set up schools for their employees and began conducting seminars in English for senior executives. Other companies retained private organizations, such as the Tokyo English Center, to come in and instruct their employees.

The presidents of companies urging their employees to take up English did not spare themselves. They, too, began crash programs, even though many were in their late 60s and 70s. Said one: "You cannot be a fully effective president of an important company in Japan today if you don't speak English." Others explained that besides traveling abroad regularly, they met as many as three foreign businessmen a day in their own offices. One president said that two or three hours of each of his working days was spent with foreign businessmen and that he was determined to communicate with them directly. "An interpreter is an obstacle to heart-to-heart conversations," he said.

This mass effort by the Japanese to learn English, which is typical of their approach to everything, was only partially successful. Hundreds of thousands of people made some improvement in their ability to understand and speak some English, but still today the overwhelming majority of Japanese businessmen speak little or no English.

Even though virtually all Japanese study English for several years in school, the emphasis has traditionally been on reading rather than speaking. Thus, few people have become fluent in the language without going on to special language schools or studying abroad. All this is now changing, albeit gradually. Jochi (Sophia) University is especially well known for the English language ability of its graduates.

In 1986, Education Minister Masayuki Fujio inaugurated a program to hire an additional 1,000 American language teachers for the Japanese educational system in 1987. He said he wanted to see the number of native English-language teachers in Japan rise to 5,000 or more in the future. There were 79 American English language teachers in the employ of the Education Ministry in 1986, with another 156 employed by the various prefectural governments.

In announcing the new policy, Fujio said that present language differences are blocking the improvement of U.S.-Japan relations in the areas of education, science, and culture, adding that it was vital for Japan to learn about American culture in "American terms."

Because of the pressure on Japan to internationalize its educational system, the Tokyo Metropolitan Government established an international high school, where regular Japanese students are to be mixed with students who have lived abroad and foreign students whose families live in Tokyo.

The purpose of the school is to help equip more young Japanese with "a rich international sense that will allow them to cope with the rapid internationalization of Japanese society." Courses will be taught in both English and Japanese, with emphasis on foreign languages and international understanding. The school is scheduled to open in April 1989.

Confusion from Misuse of Terms

It is estimated that native-born speakers of the same language and culture—even those who are highly educated and effective speakers—cannot achieve more than 80 percent understanding in any conversation dealing with abstractions. It should therefore not be surprising that Japanese and non-Japanese have difficulty communicating with each other. One of the more common areas of confusion between them is the misuse of terms.

In importing Western technology, Japanese businessmen had no choice but to bring in Western terminology, as well, because there were no words in the Japanese language for many of the new foreign concepts. In other cases, traditional Japanese words with related meanings were grafted onto the imported ideas. Because of fundamental cultural differences, however, the average Japanese businessman is incapable of understanding and using Western words as they are understood and used in their country of origin. When he uses his own native terminology to identify and describe new and alien ideas, the loss in meaning and spirit ranges from a few percent to one hundred percent.

An excellent and typical example, in reverse, was observed in the arcade of Tokyo's Okura Hotel. A product display by Matsushita Electric Company featured several sun lamps that bore English-language signs reading "For Water Bugs." Asked to explain what the sign meant, an attendant said: "Used to kill water bugs." A glance at the Japanese sign next to the one in English explained the mystery. The lamps were designed for the treatment of athlete's foot. In Japanese, athlete's foot is *mizu mushi*, which translates literally as "water bug."

Another example, mentioned elsewhere in this book, is the difference in the way Japanese and Westerners use the word "service." To the Japanese, service means a reduction in price or a free gift with a purchase. The same kind of difference is actually the rule, rather than the exception, for practically every abstract word in either language—love, sincerity, obligation, contract, loyalty, courtesy—all have different shades of meaning when translated into or out of Japanese, and all conjure up different images for the cross-lingual users.

When the Japanese businessman talks about management practices, cost accounting, contract responsibility, and a host of other things, he may be using Western words, but he is most likely speaking from a strictly Japanese cultural viewpoint. This is further complicated by the ingrained habit of the Japanese to leave the impression that they understand and agree, when in reality neither may be true. About the only way to avoid or at least minimize the problems arising from this situation is to reduce all agreements, instructions, etc., to their basic components and systematically cover each part—in writing, if understanding still seems doubtful.

How to Use and Not to Use Interpreters

Probably less than five percent of the people regularly employed as interpreters in Japan could be ranked as first-rate. The average is no doubt lower than fifth-rate. In addition, very few, including those whose language ability is more or less adequate, know much about business. They are usually handicapped by an inadequate business vocabulary even though their conversational ability may be excellent. This puts both the foreign businessman and Japanese businessman at a serious disadvantage. Occasions on which interpreters wrongly translate comments or instructions are commonplace.

It is essential, therefore, that foreign businessmen in Japan as residents or visitors take nothing for granted. All interpreters should be thoroughly tested before they are used. Resident businessmen will find it profitable to brief their interpreters before every bilingual conference. It is advisable to set up rigid training courses for interpreters, regardless of the "loss of face" involved.

Most American businessmen in Japan are forced to do business using second-hand information. And when this information comes to them through interpreters and translators whose ability is always questionable, the implications can be frightening. "Some of the old hands in Japan," remarked one observer, "are the least successful of all the foreign businessmen here. They keep themselves isolated from the Japanese community and depend upon what might be called 'foreign gossip' to keep themselves informed. Far too many of the newcomers fall into this crowd."

Bilingual businessmen in Japan estimate that in order to have a fair idea of what is really going on in the country—as opposed to what appears in English for foreign consumption—the foreign businessman would have to read regularly (in Japanese) the *Asahi Shimbun, Nihon Keizai*, the *Asahi Journal, Akahata* (the Japan Communist Party organ), several of the leading entertainment- and leisure-oriented weeklies, proceedings from the Diet, the best-selling political and economic books, press handouts from the Prime Minister's Office and the Economic Planning Agency—as well as listen to various types of television commentary.

Again paraphrasing the very astute Sen Nishiyama, mere fluency in English does not make a good interpreter. An interpreter should also have a highly developed rhetorical ability, quick mental reflexes, and a willingness to concentrate intensely on other people for hours at a time. Not only should he have a thorough understanding of the topic concerned, but he must also have a deep and wide knowledge of all the cultural factors involved. "Above all, he must have a broad enough international goal to motivate a deep commitment to the job of interpreting," adds Mr. Nishiyama. This requirement alone would probably disqualify all but a handful of the interpreters—professional and amateur—in Japan.

One of the reasons why there are very few really professional interpreters in Japan is that the function has no status in the business world. Japanese businessmen (and Westerners, as well) tend to look on the interpreter as they would look on their chauffeur. Americans in particular tend to make do with whatever English-speaking Japanese personnel they happen to have in their offices.

Nishiyama suggests a number of excellent dos and don'ts, besides the obvious ones, for getting the most out of an interpreter. These include: Make sure he is sitting where he can hear everyone. Don't require him to conduct interviews or host meetings and interpret at the same time. Avoid interrupting him when he is listening or talking. Don't get your explanations from him—have him get them from the original source.

If you are working with an interpreter who is less than bilingual and bicultural, it is especially important for you to speak slowly and in very short stretches; to use common words; to write out all large numbers; to give the interpreter time to take notes while you are talking; to explain each point at least twice; not to lose your patience; not to work an interpreter for more than two hours without a break; and to maintain a friendly, calm attitude.

There are many reasons why more foreign businessmen do not speak adequate Japanese, but probably the two most important ones are (1) that it is an exceedingly difficult language, requiring up to two years of intense daily study to master; and (2) that not many people can afford or are willing to invest all this time in studying the language. Both of these factors are influenced by the reluctance of many foreigners to make a career of working in Japan, either because of personal or professional reasons. Some do not wish to subject themselves and their families to a different style and standard of living. Others prefer not to stay abroad too long because they lose touch with top management (which after a few years is apt to regard them as members of a special breed, who can no longer be seriously considered for higher corporate positions).

Another problem that plagues Western businessmen in Japan is the communication between themselves and their head offices. A number of resident foreign businessmen say that the international telephone, the telex, the facsimile, and the jet plane have just about destroyed communications between the Japan managers and their superiors back home. Explained one: "The superior back home assumes that—since he can reach his man in Tokyo by phone, fax, or telex within a few minutes or confer with him personally after a quick jet hop—full, adequate communication, or its potential, exists. This is a fallacy that regularly has serious consequences. The man here cannot communicate clearly or fully what is going on by fax, telex, or phone or even in a brief face-to-face meeting."

The situation is further complicated because Western companies often send over men who are little more than mouthpieces or caretakers. Top brass feel that when anything important comes up they can make the necessary decisions at headquarters and implement them by remote control. This, of course, emphasizes what the company wants and minimizes what the situation demands.

Some Suggestions on Negotiating

The Japanese are superb negotiators, particularly when they are dealing with Americans. The American way is to put all cards on the table and then sit back and wait for the other side to accept or make a counter offer. Thus, in one fell swoop the American negotiator exposes his position. Then, when he gets no clear-cut response—or silence—he starts to repeat himself and often begins to hint at concessions.

In the meantime, the Japanese side remains polite and noncommittal, waiting for its opponent to further extend himself. The more time passes, the more anxious the American becomes for an agreement, and the more likely he is to make many concessions to get only one.

In any dealings with the Japanese, it is essential that the negotiator keep in mind that they are guided by what is possible and expedient—not by principles. The primary negotiation technique of the Japanese is continuously to adapt their strategy to take the fullest possible advantage of their position, on the basis of their opponent's actions. In the meantime, the American negotiator tries to convince the Japanese to accept his proposition by presenting a set of logical reasons. Because his position is basically set and because he generally plays the game according to objective rules, the Japanese team has the advantage.

The American negotiator also tends to assume that the two sides are after the same thing, which may or may not be true. The biggest area of disagreement is usually in the contractual arrangements of how the goal or goals will be achieved. The Japanese do not like detailed contracts in which every possible facet is precisely defined and limited. They prefer—and often insist—that contracts be left loose enough that adjustments can be made to fit changing circumstances. In any event, they usually interpret contracts in this manner.

Despite a friendly, humble exterior and often a manner that the Westerner is likely to take as an expression of naiveté, the Japanese are tough and wily, and they go into negotiations with the attitude that dealing with foreigners is something like eating *fugu,* or globe-fish. *Fugu* is a delicacy in Japan, but it contains a deadly poison. If it is not prepared just right, the poison permeates the flesh of the fish and kills the eater.

In negotiating with foreign businessmen, the Japanese automatically expect the foreign side to present its case first. They will simply keep quiet. Since most Western businessmen, especially Americans, cannot stand vacuums, they begin talking. The Japanese listen and listen. After the foreign side has repeated its presentation from several different angles, the Japanese begin to ask questions. The questions go on and on.

Between sessions, the Japanese discuss the project among themselves, often conferring with other company personnel not attending the meetings. When they are satisfied that they know everything about the project—and this may take days, weeks, or months (and require dozens to hundreds of more questions)—they attempt to reach a consensus.

This process of arriving at a consensus is a gradual one that develops over a period of time, and the Japanese seldom, if ever, announce, "All right, fellows; we have reached a decision." They are more likely to continue asking questions and negotiating right up to the last day or night of the foreign side's scheduled visit, signing (when they do sign) at virtually the last minute.

The foreign businessman who goes to Japan to negotiate an arrangement or contract will usually have allocated a specific number of days for the trip—five or seven or whatever. He will also often give his Japanese contacts his exact travel schedule, expecting that they will speed up the negotiating process if they realize that he is going to be in town for just a few days. This often has a reverse effect, and in virtually every case it seriously handicaps the visiting businessman. Japanese businessmen are well known for dragging out the negotiating process until the last moment in order to put pressure on the foreign businessman to accept their terms.

More often than not, this ploy works because the visiting foreign businessman does not want to go home empty-handed and is under a lot of pressure not to extend his trip—because, for example, the hotel is costing $200 a day.

Foreign businessmen are also often thrown off-track by the custom of Japanese negotiators to remain silent for long periods of time, often leaning back, closing their eyes, and sometimes even appearing to be taking a nap. They are not being rude or demonstrating lack of interest. It is nothing more than traditional behavior. They are giving themselves time to think—and rest, for that matter. The typical American's reaction is to assume that something is wrong and either get angry and break off the meeting or repeat his position, frequently weakening his conditions.

In this situation, the American negotiator should also take a break, consult with his own team, or review the Japanese position and come up with his own set of new questions.

There are a number of other guidelines the foreign side can follow to improve significantly its chances of getting a viable arrangement and at the same time to prevent any of its negotiating members from having a heart attack. Perhaps the most important of these guidelines involves the time factor. You cannot expect a contract to be negotiated and signed within a matter of days. It usually takes weeks and sometimes months. If the matter is an important one and is to cover a long period of time, the American side should not set a deadline on negotiating.

Preparation is certainly next in importance. The Western negotiator should first of all be thoroughly familiar with his own organization, policies, and plans. He should also thoroughly familiarize himself with the Japanese company concerned—its history, group and bank affiliations, its position in the market, its top management, and its "personality." It is just as important that the Japanese you are negotiating with be equally familiar with your company, and you should make sure they are by providing them with printed material in advance.

It is also extremely helpful to learn the names of the people you will be negotiating with and, well in advance, to invite them out to eat and drink or play golf a number of times. If you have "face" in a recognized cabaret, this is the time to use it. On these outings, only the most casual references should be made to the forthcoming negotiations.

When formal negotiations start, assume that the first two or three meetings will be preliminary, and remember that the Japanese do not make decisions individually or during meetings. The Japanese do not negotiate alone, but in groups of three or more. It is usually helpful for the American side to follow this practice and to avoid changing team members in midstream.

At any grouping or meeting of the Japanese, the man who is seated farthest from the door is usually the senior member of the group, and the man who sits closest to the door is the lowest in rank. In meetings, it is invariably the senior man who speaks first and provides the cues for the group's behavior.

In many cases, the best way to negotiate with the Japanese is to use the traditional diplomatic approach. This includes assigning staff to research the Japanese company and prepare reports on all pertinent areas. If the negotiations are likely to be protracted and sensitive, a "second team" should be sent in to engage in preliminary talks on a lower level, to get all the routine matters out of the way, and to lay the groundwork for the chief negotiators to come in at the "right" time.

Another worthwhile practice is to write out in detail (but in nonlegal terms) your proposal and objectives and have them translated into Japanese. In this presentation, it is vital that you discuss your objectives at length, enumerating them one by one. In this manner, you can at least be assured that your proposal is fully understood, and it gives you something to negotiate from.

Do not press for clear, unqualified responses on particular points if the Japanese side shows any hesitation. This is a sign that they have not yet made up their minds. Pressuring them for a reply when they are not ready to give one is dangerous. They may consent to your proposition, but they may not be ready to commit themselves to it. The Japanese also habitually agree to things just to avoid a negative confrontation, with no intention whatsoever of following up. It also generally means no when they are noncommittal or when they look pained and say that something is *muzukashii* (difficult). The negotiator must be very careful to avoid this pitfall. About the only way to do this is not to ask for an unequivocal yes or no before or when the meeting ends, but to have a third party contact the company later and make the crucial inquiry.

It is not smart to play up profits when dealing with Japanese on a very high level. In the Japanese value system, it is far more effective to emphasize growth, market share, and permanent employment for more people—with profit potential tacked on somewhere near the end. Remember also that before they even consider your proposition, they will pass judgment on you as an individual. They will measure you for your sincerity, honesty, humility, and learning and for your attitude toward them and toward Japan.

The Japanese are extremely sensitive, and if they feel that a negotiator dislikes the Japanese they are apt to refuse to do business with him and his company. They are also turned off by attempts to pressure them. They are especially incensed by the threat of being taken to court over a disputed matter. They go to extreme lengths to avoid litigation. The Japanese also dislike arguments. When they feel that they are right and the other side continues to push, they simply stop talking. The Japanese avoid confrontation whenever possible by compromising or withdrawing and taking no action.

In any negotiation with a Japanese company, the Westerner has to keep in mind that the government is always present as a third participant—invisible but nonetheless powerful. Occasionally, a representative of the company's bank will take part in the discussions. In some ways, the government is more important in the negotiations than the Japanese company. In any event, the government is always a convenient excuse if the Japanese company wants to delay the talks or end them altogether.

After a negotiating session ends, it is a good idea to write down what was agreed on and to provide the Japanese negotiators with a copy. This is a convenient way to find out if they have a different view of the agreement.

When negotiations reach an impasse, it is customary for the Japanese to break off the meetings and behave as if they are no longer interested in the proposition. If they are still interested, the purpose of the ploy is to wait until the other party panics and makes an acceptable concession. If you can't wait, you can often find out what is going on by again bringing in a third party who has contacts in the company.

The Japanese regularly present each other with gifts at conferences and business talks. This may be a worthwhile custom for Westerners to follow because it demonstrates both a knowledge and appreciation of the Japanese way, and it does not have to be repeated.

The Importance of Name Cards

Name cards (*meishi*) are important in penetrating the language barrier in Japan because they tell the Japanese who and what you are. Foreign businessmen living in or visiting Japan should by all means have their name cards printed in both Japanese and English. Besides being a very worthwhile courtesy, this assures them that all Japanese to whom they give their card will be able to read and understand it—as well as pronounce their name with reasonable accuracy. Some airlines serving Japan can get bilingual name cards printed for you before your departure.

Presenting name cards in Japan is a formal affair. They should always be presented with a certain amount of ceremony—and to the senior man first. If you have run out of cards or have not yet obtained any, it is good diplomacy to apologize and, if you want to develop an enduring relationship with the person, send him a name card later with a note attached.

The English translations of titles on Japanese name cards are often confusing because there are no universally accepted equivalents of the Japanese titles. If you cannot read an individual's title in Japanese, have someone read it for you. The Japanese title tells you a great deal about the person's age, rank, and position in the company.

Employees usually join large, typical Japanese companies at the age of 23, immediately after finishing college. For the first eight to ten years they generally have no title. Their first title will be that of *kakaricho,* or assistant section chief. The next promotion, another ten or so years later, is to *kacho* or section chief. In some cases, an employee may be given the title of *kacho dairi,* or acting section chief, while he waits for a *kacho* slot to open up.

The next rank in Japanese companies is either *bucho dairi* (deputy general manager of a department or bureau) or *bucho* (general manager or department or bureau chief). Promotion to *bucho* usually takes place when the individual is in his late 40s. Depending on the type and size of the company, it may be the equivalent of a vice presidency in a Western company.

The next step up for favored *bucho* is *torishimariyaku,* which is usually translated as "director." This is followed by *jomu torishimariyaku* (executive managing director), *senmu torishimariyaku* (senior managing director), *fuku shacho* (vice president), *shacho* (president), and *kaicho* (chairman).

Chapter 8

Joint Ventures and Their Special Problems

"All the friction that is liable to occur between Japanese and foreign businessmen is brought to a head in joint ventures."

—Member of a joint venture

The First Mistake

Most Western businessmen coming to Japan to survey some segment of the market or search for a joint venture partner take too many things for granted. As a result, they often do a slipshod, amateurish job. The attitude that allows this to happen is caused by varying degrees of culture shock they undergo once they are out of their home country. Some of the shock is external. The different language, manners, and even the appearance of the Japanese make Western businessmen tend to accept at face value whatever they see and hear. Another part of the shock, however, is internal. The businessmen hypnotize themselves into suspending some of their critical faculties even when there is no outside influence. This stems, perhaps, from an overpowering urge to make a favorable impression on their Japanese contacts by meeting them more than half way.

The foreign businessman is also thrown off balance by the apparent willingness of his Japanese contacts to provide him with any amount of information and help. After several days—or weeks—of collecting brochures, catalogs, and other handouts by the pound, plus being impressed by tours through modern offices, factories, and stores, interspersed with a number of parties, the visiting businessman, who may have a vague idea that something is missing, goes home. Once he starts trying to put his facts together and prepare a report, he generally finds he doesn't have enough definite information to do more than present an inconclusive outline.

The Japanese contacts, official or private, are not necessarily misleading the foreign businessman or purposely withholding information from him. They may not understand completely what he wants or why he wants it. But even if they do understand perfectly, they may not be of much more help because, in many cases, the information desired is not available to them. At the same time, the Japanese are much less open about company affairs than their foreign counterparts are.

Although the visiting businessman may get a good picture of the physical makeup of his field of interest and return home very optimistic, this doesn't mean that he has accomplished his job. If he doesn't also manage to get a good grasp of the personal factors that are the controlling principles in his particular business field, he has only the bones without the meat or spirit.

Whether the foreign businessman wants to deal through an agent, affiliate with a Japanese company in a joint venture, or set up his own operation in Japan, he is faced with unique problems—not the least of which is the Japanese government.

The Strange Bedfellows

Fundamentally, the Japanese government bureaus concerned—the Ministry of International Trade and Industry and the Finance Ministry—are against joint ventures, licensing, or foreign participation in business in Japan in any form. For years, they approved certain tie-ups only because of tremendous pressure and various other inducements from local businessmen who could not get the desired technology or product any other way. Under these circumstances, the government tried to make sure that the advantages were always on the Japanese side, regardless of the type of arrangement. It was not until the liberation moves in August 1971 that the Japanese government seemed to accept the idea that true internationalization was the better part of valor—in principle, if not in practice.

The Fair Trade Commission, which is generally responsible for policing joint ventures and other foreign-affiliated operations in Japan, still does its best to "protect" local industry from foreign capital. Just as the Japanese have always been appalled at the idea of their race becoming mixed through intermarriage, they still tend to regard the idea of Japanese industry becoming mixed as especially dreadful. To Westerners, a joint venture is made because it appears to be a desirable business move. To Japanese bureaucrats, it is more likely to be made as the lesser of several evils.

Despite this attitude and opposition by various ministries of the government, there is overwhelming evidence to show that well over half of all Japanese companies would welcome tie-ups with foreign firms—not only to obtain new technology and new products, but also for market stability. The obvious exceptions are, of course, the companies that are highly successful and still growing and therefore see no advantages in affiliating with a foreign company. By the same token, the opposition of the Japanese government to foreign companies coming into Japan is not entirely capricious. The government recognizes that local companies are at their most vulnerable in the domestic market because they have less experience than Western firms have in mass-merchandising in a competitive market and because they are generally locked into a distribution system that further reduces their ability to compete outside the system.

Most of the larger, more stable Japanese firms that seek and accept licensing agreements with American firms are interested only in new technology and better access to foreign markets—and once they get it they feel absolutely no obligation to the company supplying the knowledge. They are often quite frank in admitting this, much to the surprise of their foreign affiliates. One such firm, for example, pointed out to the American representative that it had no research department and that when the product it was making under license from the American company was outdated, the company would drop it and look for a new licensor. "We save money that way," the spokesman said. Another problem that regularly arises in jointly owned operations is the fallacy that the foreign firm can control the operation of the company if it is the major stockholder. All it can hope to do is to prevent something from being done. If the Japanese side doesn't approve of a request or recommendation, it simply takes no action. In effect, this puts the Japanese in the driver's seat.

One of the typical problems encountered by American managers of joint ventures in Japan concerns directors' meetings. It is customary in Japanese companies that topics to be covered are thoroughly discussed in advance, and all decisions are made before the meetings take place. In some cases, however, the resident foreign manager may not be asked to participate in these preliminary discussions and may therefore be in an awkward position at the actual meeting. (Of course, the foreigner generally doesn't speak or understand Japanese and therefore cannot participate directly in such meetings.) Not only have his Japanese counterparts already made their decisions, he often doesn't know what topics were discussed.

Some companies have gone even further than this and attempted to hold their directors' meetings in such a way that the foreign resident director doesn't realize he's in it. "I know this sounds ridiculous," said one American resident director of a joint company, "but it happened to me twice before I caught on. In any case, I was asked by one of our Japanese directors to stop in at the Grill Room of the Palace Hotel after work for a drink. I did and we had a nice informal chat that I promptly forgot all about. A few days later, I was asked to sign some documents that were in Japanese. I asked for a translation, but it never appeared. The next time this happened, I insisted upon a translation before signing. Sure enough, our most recent chat at the Palace's Grill Room had been another directors' meeting. Now I insist upon having a list of all the subjects our Japanese directors intend to cover before I attend such 'meetings.'"

This man added: "My counterparts on the Japanese side often behave as if the whole thing is a game in which go-slow tactics, sleight-of-hand, and other forms of deception are the necessary skills."

Another incident that is typical of what happens regularly in Japanese firms was recounted by a resident foreign director of another joint venture. In this case, the American side offered to amend its agreement so that the Japanese firm would be able to sell certain products outside Japan. Because it was a relatively minor point, the American company told its Japanese affiliate to decide whether to get the amendment approved by MITI. After four months of discussing the pros and cons of going through MITI, the Japanese firm decided it could avoid a lot of trouble by not seeking the ministry's approval. In the meantime, the foreign director had kept his head office informed as to what was going on. He finally explained that because of the problems of getting government approval for such things the Japanese affiliate had decided just to keep quiet about it.

Shortly afterward, the resident director's boss arrived in Japan on an inspection trip. During a lull at a party one night, the director turned to his Japanese associates and asked them to tell his boss in their own words why they had decided it was best not to get the amendment change approved by MITI. Their reaction: "Oh, we'll get MITI's approval if you want it. There's no problem." Continued the shocked resident director: "Furthermore, they turned around and did just that without any difficulty at all. I was very embarrassed. I knew the Japanese concerned intimately and liked and respected them, but I couldn't explain their behavior. All I could do was look at my boss and shrug my shoulders."

The obvious explanation of this incident is that the Japanese partner was just using the well-known intransigence of the government as an excuse for not taking any official action regarding the amendment. Rather than intending to embarrass the resident director, his Japanese counterparts no doubt felt that a party for his boss was an ideal time to let both of them know that they had changed their minds about getting MITI approval of the amendment.

Handicaps Facing Joint Ventures

A detrimental factor in many joint ventures is that the Japanese executives assigned to the new enterprises may not be chosen on the basis of their ability or how much they might contribute to the affiliation. They are often selected because they are deadwood in the parent company, and the joint venture serves as an excellent place in which to put them out to pasture. Only if the joint venture is regarded as an important project by the parent Japanese firm and such an assignment is prestigious will the Japanese executives be selected on the basis of their overall ability and special talents.

Another weakness of the joint venture is that the Japanese side usually provides or hires the Japanese staff for the foreign side, as well. For one thing, this ensures that their loyalty will be to the Japanese side. A number of Western businessmen concerned with joint ventures recommend that the foreign resident manager at least hire his own private secretary to ensure him of her loyalty. They point out that it is otherwise difficult, if not impossible, to keep certain sensitive matters confidential. This is particularly important, they say, when the staff has been provided by the Japanese side of the affiliation.

In my discussions with resident managers of joint ventures, they emphasized the need for understanding by the home office over and over again. Said one man: "Our head office tends to think of the joint enterprise as a fully controlled subsidiary, completely integrated with the parent firm's operation. In reality, the Japanese side tends to treat the foreign personnel in the joint venture as intruders. Their attitude is one of constant suspicion, and their actions are surreptitious. Of course, when the head office people are in Japan, they present a perfect picture of cooperation and goodwill." Added another joint-venture executive: "The Japanese personnel consider us watchdogs. Anything they can manage to do without us catching them is an accepted part of the game."

Nearly all of the interviewees observed that in dealing with large Japanese firms it is necessary to put pressure on them continually in order to assure that they will abide by their commitments. In a majority of cases, the Japanese will take the path of least resistance in conducting their business. If this path results in complaints, they will ignore the complaints until the volume is so loud that they are forced to act. Without going through such experience themselves, it is hard for the head office people to understand this.

Despite the problems, the number of joint Japanese-foreign business ventures is growing each year, and many of them are very successful. Japanese respect for joint venture contracts (and patents) can also be expected to grow now that they have many such ventures of their own outside Japan. It is still common at this time, however, for them to see foreign patents in particular as a plot against them. It is also still common for companies and individuals to secretly register the names of foreign companies and foreign products so that if and when a registered company wants to do business in Japan it will have to deal with the trademark-holder.

Just as significant as the number of joint ventures in Japan that succeeded is the number that failed or did not get started in the first place. The majority of these failures were the result of "misunderstandings, of incomplete communication," noted the president of a Tokyo-based market research group.

"Many U.S. businessmen coming here have heard about the problems of doing business in Japan, but they don't believe what they hear. They assume that it will be different with them, and they forge ahead almost completely unprepared. When they run into serious obstacles, many of these men opt for a licensing agreement rather than face the problems, thus giving away a product and a market," the market specialist said.

"Before anyone can make a rational decision about whether to come into Japan, he should have an analysis of the market areas, including full information on the distribution patterns in the area and the competition he will face. He should know all about price, credit, rebates, quotas, promotional approaches, media, examples of successes and failures, specific problems, and opportunities. Too often, the American side of a joint venture depends upon the Japanese partner to 'take care' of these details," the specialist added.

What the Foreign Manager Needs to Know

What the Western representative must know before attempting to set up and manage a joint venture in Japan can be summarized in specific points:

(1) He needs to have factual information—and an attitude that will allow him to perceive things as they really are, not as he would like them to be.

(2) He should know a great deal about the character and quality of life in Japan—what it is really going to be like for his wife and children. And if he isn't willing to live under those conditions, he shouldn't come.

(3) He should have intimate insight into his company's principal officers—how they think and what they want. He should also be completely familiar with the structure and operation of his own industry and company, along with its plans and probable future. It is both amazing and sad that many joint-venture representatives arrive in Tokyo knowing little about their own company. The Japanese often know more about the Westerners' affairs than they do, putting the Westerners in a very embarrassing position.

(4) Explicit knowledge of what his job in Japan will entail is also essential for the joint venture manager. It is shocking how many managers arrive in Tokyo knowing practically nothing of what they are supposed to do.

(5) The manager should be thoroughly familiar with the Japanese partner, including personal details about the company's executives—their ages, the schools they attended, their hobbies, their special likes and dislikes, etc.

(6) Before a man is sent to Japan, he should have training in any area of responsibility in which he has not had practical expe-

rience—advertising, accounting, and so on. If the man is not knowledgeable in these areas, he appears to be less than competent to his Japanese staff.

(7) Finally, the new joint venture manager should have considerable knowledge—and some appreciation—of Japan as a whole, including a general familiarity with its history and cultural achievements.

"The most important factor in the success or failure of a foreign company operating in Japan is the man the foreign company sends over here," said Kaz Fujita, Los Angeles-based consultant to several of Japan's leading firms. "He must first of all be receptive enough and flexible enough to be figuratively reborn. He must develop the ability to be genuinely compatible with the Japanese so he can communicate with them in cultural terms and concepts that they understand. Only in this way can he hope to get them to accept and appreciate his goals and influence them honestly to help him try to achieve them. If he is nonreceptive and inflexible and tries to force the Japanese to do everything his way, they will be dishonest and deceptive and will work around him, if not against him," Fujita warned.

It is inexcusable to send a man to Japan who knows nothing about the country or the Japanese system of business. The least a foreign company should do is to send the inexperienced man to Tokyo for several weeks—months would be better—with absolutely no duties other than to study the Japanese scene and become as familiar as possible with it.

Selecting a Joint Venture Partner

Foreign companies are generally severely handicapped when it comes to deciding what Japanese company to approach for a joint venture tie-up or which offer to accept. The foreign side usually knows little or nothing about prospective Japanese partners, and it is very difficult to become familiar with them. Japanese firms keep most of their affairs secret, and in many instances only a few insiders know their company's true role and position in the industry. Meaningful information that has been published about any particular company is usually in Japanese and is not generally available from any one source.

The foreign partner often goes on little more than the name of the company and what he can see of its products, offices, and facilities. When a larger company is concerned, probably the most important factor is its group affiliation. Next is probably its overall position in the trade—not as much its market share as its personal obligations to others. Another factor, regarded by many as the most important, is the management of the company—its attitude, ability, interest, and reputation.

Even when the foreign company finds a potential Japanese partner that appears to suit its purposes and seems willing to enter into an agreement, the marriage may not come off because of opposition from the government. The Japanese government takes the view that no tie-up should disrupt the market—that is, result in a change in the existing market shares of companies already in that field. Because of this, it is sometimes best for the foreign company to tie up with a firm outside the field.

The biggest problem in setting up a joint venture is creating an atmosphere of mutual confidence. Both sides expect to be taken—especially the Japanese. They are much more inclined to look under the bed. They are afraid the foreign company will sometime, somehow take advantage of them.

The second most difficult problem is communication. The typical Japanese company is extremely reticent in English—partly out of fear of misusing the language and thereby committing itself to something it doesn't understand and doesn't want. Often for this reason, a prospective Japanese partner lets letters go unanswered for days and weeks—or fails to answer them at all. Of course, this frequently compounds problems and friction. To be a success in Japan it is necessary for the foreign businessman to use pictures, drawings, graphs, and other visual aids in order to communicate.

Commenting on how to approach a Japanese company for a joint venture tie-up, one American with extensive consulting experience said: "I used to think that if you were concerned with selling technology you should deal with technical people in just that one company. But I have learned that your chances of success are considerably improved if you bring in the company's bank, its suppliers, its customers, its major stockholders, and anyone else it is closely aligned with. The larger and more complicated the project—particularly if you have competition in the market—the more important it is that you include all of these elements in your initial approach. In any event, if your proposal requires a policy decision by the Japanese side, you have to win over all of these important elements."

In setting up a partnership, it is often advisable for the foreign side to retain as much control as possible over marketing and pricing. At the same time, however, the foreign partner cannot act as a dictator in these areas. Several of the more recent joint venture failures in Japan were traced to the insistence of the foreign partner on doing everything its way and completely ignoring the opinions of the Japanese side.

As it happens, the foreign partner is often so relieved to get a joint venture agreement signed that it will neglect to discuss and get general agreement on long-term policies and plans. This frequently results in serious differences of opinion in later years. The long-term objectives of a joint venture should be spelled out and agreed on during the initial negotiating and should be written into the agreement. (Government regulations require that immediate and future activities of any such tie-up be specifically described in the contract.)

Controlling the Joint Venture

Various methods for achieving management control of joint ventures have been described in journals published by the American Chamber of Commerce in Japan. Noting first that the Japanese partner must be willing to relinquish control, the articles then listed several drawbacks to having management responsibility. First, the Japanese may take a short-term view and be interested only in what they can learn. Second, they may resent the arrangement and therefore ruin any possibility of full cooperation with the foreign partner. Third, there may be problems in attracting competent personnel, and the Japanese side may not be willing to assign any of its top people to the enterprise. This suggests also that without the willing support of the Japanese partner the company may have difficulty getting into the market.

The same source enumerated the methods of obtaining control of a joint venture: exerting psychological pressure (from a position of strength and prestige); using administrative devices, such as a confidential side agreement that the real policy-making body will be an operating committee on which the foreign side is in the majority; owning more voting stock than the Japanese partner; and making long-term loans to the Japanese partner.

"Some of the most successful joint ventures in Japan have left management completely up to the Japanese side," said banker Hans Brinckmann, "and it seems to me that the JVs in general are becoming more and more Japanese. Very often, when the foreign partner tries to take the lead, he fails, and the partnership becomes disjointed."

Mitsubishi and the Colonel

The experience of Loy Weston, who negotiated and set up the Mitsubishi/Kentucky Fried Chicken joint venture, makes an enlightening case study, particularly because Mr. Weston (often by intuition rather than design, he admits) did enough things the right way that he succeeded despite many handicaps.

In Loy Weston's words: "The JV contract was prepared by an American lawyer who knew nothing about doing business in Japan. I was told to get it signed unchanged. Naturally Mitsubishi wanted changes. The next nine months were the most trying in my life. I didn't know the true meaning of frustration until that time—and much of this was caused by the home office, which simply wouldn't make decisions when I needed them.

"The Japanese are good negotiators, and they knew what they were talking about. KFC wouldn't give in. I developed a serious pain in my chest and thought I was having heart attacks. I was afraid I was going to drop dead and went to a doctor. He told me it was nerves. After we finally reached agreement and signed a contract, my chest pain went away. But in the meantime, I had ended up talking to myself and swearing.

"Once the contract was signed, Mitsubishi kept sending me old duffers as staff, so I had to go outside to get all of my key personnel. It took a lot of selling, but finally I was able to attract some very good people away from Japanese companies. My Japanese counterpart was old-fashioned in every sense of the word—the pure Japanese type whom you expect to see shuffling around in wooden *geta*. We were both shocked at first sight and grew to loathe each other. But I had to deal with him and he with me. He resisted every suggestion or move I made. It seemed like he was there only to make sure the JV didn't work. I ended up having to blaze all the trails. Each time something came up, their first reaction was 'it can't be done.' I would show them it could be done, and they would take it from there.

"I made a special effort to cultivate personal, friendly relationships with my personnel and colleagues—something I could do because I was a bachelor. A wife would have made that practically impossible. I invited them to my apartment for parties, and they were amazed and pleased that I slept on the traditional *tatami* floor mats and that I collected Japanese art. I asked them to please help me do a good job so I wouldn't get into trouble with my home office and get fired.

"I found that if you have or can make an opportunity to do something personal for a Japanese employee, associate, or client, it is very wise to do it. I visited a guy in the hospital, and it taught me a lesson. The dividends have been out of all proportion.

"Finally, the day arrived when something really crucial came up. I just had to have it. I sprung it on my Japanese opposite, and to my amazement he agreed. We started working as a team for the first time. We still had absolutely nothing in common personally or professionally, but we accommodated each other."

The first KFC shop opened in Osaka in 1970 on the first day of Osaka Expo. Sales were approximately $8,000, which wasn't too bad. Later in the year a second shop was opened in Nagoya as a "cultural adventure," according to Shinsuke Okawa, who was manager of the shop and is now president of KFC Japan, Ltd.

"We had high hopes but few customers," Okawa said. "Our third shop had the same problem. A year after our first opening we were almost bankrupt."

The Japanese side insisted that the American plan of opening shops along highways outside of cities be scrapped in favor of outlets in busy downtown areas. It has been onward and upward ever since.

Another reason for the success of KFC Japan, adds Okawa, is that Colonel Harlan Sanders' sacred recipe of 13 herbs and spices was Japanized—with a measure of shoyu sauce.

Even Fox Bagel, Ltd., a small enterprise started in Tokyo by American George Fox, had to change the size of the "standard" bagel to fit Japanese eyes and stomachs. And the Japanese don't like them as hard, either. Dunkin' Donuts had to close 50 stores before they realized that the American store layout plan did not work in Japan. After converting the floor plan and changing to a "coffee shop" environment, the popularity of the shops boomed.

Weston said that if he had it to do all over again for some other company he would do it differently. "I would first of all insist on being involved in drawing up the initial contract so that I would have intimate knowledge of each point and how flexible I could be in trying to get it signed. I would make sure that the United States side was better informed about business conditions in Japan, and I would say to the president of the company: "Every time I ask for a decision I am going to attach a deadline. If the decision isn't forthcoming within the specified time, I am going to make it myself."

Weston also said that he would spend more time finding living quarters and that, if possible, he would take an intensive course in Japanese prior to going to Japan.

Analyzing why home offices are often slow in responding to requests from Japan, Weston enumerated several possible points: "(1) They have other problems; (2) there is nobody at the home office fighting for the Japan operation; (3) the home office thinks the man over here has it made and doesn't need fast decisions; (4) companies that are new to the field of foreign business are usually guided by a manager mentality instead of the entrepreneur mentality."

Among the dos and don'ts Weston suggested for foreign companies involved in joint ventures in Japan are providing the manager with a special contract covering his salary, housing allowance, tax provisions, home leave, etc.; not sending anyone out who is not at least in his late 30s; making it an ironclad rule to bring the manager back to the home office every six months for at least two weeks; keeping VIP visits to a minimum ("many of them regard Japan as a kind of toy—they like to play with it"); and never sending employee "rejects" to Japan unless they are mavericks with special talent ("it takes a special kind of cat to be a success in Japan").

Weston also advised Western managers to study the personal background of the Japanese they are working with and to send them copies of letters going to the home office so that they will appreciate the idea of being fully accepted employees and members of a team. "It also works wonders if you can get your head office to send copies of all correspondence to your Japanese associates," he added. "The main thing," he continued, "is to take every feasible opportunity to demonstrate to them that they are recognized members of the team and are appreciated—that they are on the inside." The joint venture manager himself should be the type who doesn't take no for an answer, and is ingenious and able to innovate, Weston said.

Weston also cautioned foreign companies about taking Japanese employees to the home office for training and, while there, briefing them on the salaries that foreign workers receive. "This can turn into a serious morale problem when they return to Japan," he said.

It goes without saying (to use the common Japanese preamble again), any foreign company planning to go into Japan should assess its own strengths and weaknesses, do the same with the Japanese market, and then, with the help of experts in the field, tailor its own individual approach—making sure that this approach doesn't contravene any laws of the country, which in all cases have to be obeyed.

Entry via Acquisition

The most difficult way of all for foreign companies to enter the Japanese market is through the acquisition of a Japanese firm, according to Walter L. Ames and David N. Roberts in a report prepared for the American Chamber of Commerce in Japan. Calling the acquisition of a Japanese company "hurdling the ultimate barrier," Ames and Roberts noted that the obstacles to acquisition are government regulations, the structure of Japanese companies, and Japanese culture and traditions.

The most typically Japanese of these barriers are the ones that have to do with structure and culture. As Ames and Roberts noted, Japanese scholars argue that there are few acquisitions in Japan because Japanese business "is not capitalistic" and that the Japanese "hate" capitalism. The scholars are referring to the fact that the shareholders who "own" Japanese companies generally exercise no control over them. More often than not, control is exercised by a strong chairman or president who may own only a few or no shares at all, or by some other company or companies or group of executives.

Ames and Roberts added that large companies in particular seem to exist for their workers and that this is the reason Japanese companies spend so much money on their employees, much of it in the form of entertainment and often exceeding shareholder dividends. They further explain that managers are also regarded as workers; that directors do not come from the outside to represent shareholders' interests, but are appointed from among the company's managers; and that corporate profitability is sought to preserve the organization rather than benefit the owners.

"Thus, Japanese companies are seen as collections of people, not assets—and, of course, one does not sell people. In this paternalistic milieu, management that sells a company is likely to be seen as a failure, and would lose face unbearably," they add.

The Japanese terms used in referring to hostile acquisition attempts are *nottori*, meaning "hijack," and *baishu*, meaning "bribery," which gives a pretty good idea of what people think of them.

Finally, Ames and Roberts said that the successful acquisition of a Japanese company by a foreign firm requires throwing all preconceived notions out the window, doing a great deal of research, having infinite patience, using a trusted and respected go-between, and doing everything possible to help the Japanese company avoid losing face, such as talking in terms of cooperation and merger rather than acquisition, keeping the negotiations totally secret, and not talking about money until there has been verbal agreement that the deal is going through, etc.

In discussing his own introduction to doing business in Japan, Edward W. Rogers, president of Dow Chemical Japan Ltd., said that when he was asked to go to Japan to head up Dow's operation he knew virtually nothing about the country and had many mistaken ideas about it. "When I agreed to move to Japan, Bob Lundeen, Dow's Chairman of the Board, stopped by my house with a carton of books to start my education. I read most of them and they were very helpful."

Rogers added that every foreign businessman needs to know and solve for himself his perceptions of the mysteries of Japan, like basic business practices, the distribution system, Japanese concern about reliability of supply, dedication to quality, and philosophy about contracts, "to name just a few."

Rogers added that one of his real insights into doing business in Japan came when one of his managers told him, "Sign a contract with a Western company and the trouble begins, but sign a contract with another Japanese company and better relationships begin."

Rogers went on to say that most Japanese businessmen are primarily motivated by the survival instinct and that they are acutely sensitive to the marketplace—and plan accordingly. He noted that the corporate obligations of the typical CEO in Japan were different from the priorities of the Western businessman and that this difference was a key to understanding the Japanese way of doing business and successfully competing in Japan. He listed the corporate obligations of Japanese CEOs as (1) their employees, (2) their customers, (3) their government, (4) their bankers, and (5) their shareholders.

Another point that Rogers emphasized: "Japanese managers' emphasis on people is no myth. People are their most important resource—basically their only resource—and managers appreciate the employee as valuable to himself and to the community. Respect for the person and the group ideally leads to higher participation by all employees in working toward the success of the company. The one million quality circles in Japan are a partial outfall of this tradition."

Rogers also made another valuable point: The international company manager must have the power to independently manage the business in Japan, based on good communication and mutual trust. He added: "Problems with headquarters management are legendary and despite being nearly endemic and well-diagnosed, the disease is alive and flourishing." All too often, he said, the attitude of the top executive at corporate headquarters is "Of course, I understand that things are different in Japan, but do it my way anyway!"

Rogers capsulized his recommendations for success in Japan under five P's: Planning, Product, Personnel, Power, and Patience. The foreign businessman must have knowledge about the market and the competition. His company must be offering a product or service that the Japanese want and that has some advantage in the marketplace. Finding and keeping good middle-management Japanese employees to handle negotiating, marketing, and labor relations is vital. Rogers is also strongly in favor of expatriate managers, but emphasizes that they must be carefully chosen.

Finally, patience, he says, is perhaps the most vital resource any company can bring to Japan to ensure its success.

Uniforms May Help

Foreign businesses operating in many service areas in Japan will find that smartly designed uniforms for their employees are very important—not only for their advertising and public relations benefits, but also for employee convenience and morale. After centuries of conditioning, the Japanese like to wear apparel that identifies them as members of specific groups (although most university students have given up the practice). This includes virtually everybody from employees of hamburger shops to golfers and even members of Japan's organized crime gangs.

Uniforms are in fact big business in Japan. There are more than 1,000 manufacturers, with total annual sales of approximately $2 billion. The largest makers include Kashiyama Company (Onward label) and Oriental Kiko Corporation, which was founded by designer Kiko Nakahara, reputedly the only fashion designer who specializes in uniforms.

There are three types of uniforms in Japan: working wear (for factory workers); service wear (for hotel, airline, and restaurant employees); and institutional wear, which includes school uniforms and uniforms worn by employees of banks and various government agencies.

Many companies now have their uniforms designed by some of Japan's top apparel designers.

The Ideal Resident Manager

Taking into consideration the various factors that determine the attitudes and behavior of the Japanese, which in turn are the source of many of the problems encountered by foreign businessmen representing joint ventures in Japan, it is possible to draw up a composite picture of the type of person who would have the best chance of success as the resident manager of a joint firm.

First of all, he should be at least in his late 30s. This, more than any amount of experience or ability, would assure him of some of the automatic respect that is so essential in dealing with the Japanese on any level. Second, his title should be as impressive as possible. A man without a title in Japan is like a man without a country. Third, the man should be high enough and respected enough in his own company that the head office will accept what he says without wondering if he has gone native or taken on more than he can handle. Fourth, the man should be reserved and fairly aloof in his manner. The fast-talking salesman type rubs the Japanese the wrong way.

Fifth, the man should have already made his mark in the business world and be above petty infighting and nose-grinding. He should be able to ignore small, relatively unimportant irritations and forget all about the company after five o'clock. Sixth, he should have the infinite patience and strong but calm reserve that helps make a good chess player. If he delights in quietly matching wits with an unknown and unpredictable adversary, so much the better. He may not only survive, but thrive on it.

Chapter 9

Finding, Hiring, and Keeping Employees

"The Japanese hiring system generally weeds out anyone who does not fit the 'typical employee' mold."

—Paul Maruoka
Banker

Recruiting from Schools

Since the 1950s, the primary characteristic of labor recruiting by larger Japanese companies has been the practice of hiring only once a year, directly from schools. Blue collar workers are recruited from junior and senior high schools; white collar workers and managerial candidates from universities.

For several years during the 1970s, there were not enough graduating students to fill the job openings. With the slowdown in Japan's growth rate in 1973 and again in the late 1970s and early 1980s, this situation was reversed, and for the first time in two decades there was a surplus of graduating students.

The system of recruiting from schools still prevails, but there have been a number of fundamental changes. In prosperous times, personnel recruiters fan out over Japan, visiting local employment agencies, junior and senior high schools, and the homes of graduating students in all the remote corners of the islands. The recruiters stage very sophisticated campaigns to persuade the young people to join their companies—including such gambits as flying them to Tokyo or offering their parents free roundtrips to Tokyo. So fierce is the competition that some of the recruiters resort to less than honest practices.

Competition for the graduates from certain universities can be especially severe. In the past, many companies have resorted to hiring students while they were in their third year, and some companies have put students on their payrolls months before they actually reported for work.

When such conditions prevail, university students tend to become much more selective in the companies they are willing to work for. The Japan Recruiting Center says that basic manufacturing companies have lost their appeal and that college students today prefer such "glamorous" industries as the airline business, the huge trading companies, the ranking newspapers, and the top advertising agencies. Others listed as popular with graduating students were major whiskey and cosmetic companies.

The system of once-a-year recruitment resulted in serious competition among firms for the most desirable employees from the best schools, leading to a "gentleman's agreement" among most of the country's larger companies that no firm would begin interviewing last-year students before October 1. This agreement was regularly breached by a number of firms and virtually broke down in 1986, when many companies, led by banks and securities firms, began recruiting as early as May.

This led to a new agreement among corporate executives that student interviews would hereafter begin on August 20 instead of October 1. The problem has really not been resolved, however, since many companies are not included in the agreement, causing considerable confusion among each annual crop of eligible recruits.

Nowadays, engineering graduates are among the most in demand, and, says one of them, getting a job is easy. Actually, in the case of students from engineering and other technical schools, there is little or no recruiting. The students' professors give them letters of introduction to companies where the professors have good connections. Thereafter, it is pretty much routine "unless you are mentally unstable," adds one student.

The level of education also still determines whether the new employee becomes a factory worker or office worker, and, once established, this category is not likely to change during the individual's lifetime, at least as far as the current system is concerned.

New employees recruited from school graduating classes go to work en masse on April 1.

Recruiting from the Open Market

Because of growth of the knowledge industries and heavy demand for trained people in such fields as science and computer technology, a number of large Japanese companies began hiring from the open labor market in the late 1960s, on a very limited, selective basis. What was even more unusual, some companies with joint ventures or other close relations with foreign firms began placing classified ads in Tokyo's English-language newspapers for secretaries, interpreters, and translators. Such hiring is still only a minor part of recruitment by larger firms.

The smaller the company, the more difficulty it has in competing with larger firms for labor from both schools and the open market. The tiniest enterprises depend almost entirely on family labor and close personal connections, often of a family type, for the extra personnel they need. The next larger categories of companies also depend on family and personal connections and whatever is left over after the largest firms have their pick.

Most foreign firms in Japan depend primarily on the open market or on their local partner for their Japanese personnel. But by the late 1960s and early 1970s, a few foreign companies had reached the point at which they were able to compete with ranking Japanese firms in recruiting directly from schools. Faster promotion possibilities, overseas assignments, and less overtime work are among the chief attractions of foreign companies. The last point counts heavily with young, unmarried women.

IBM (Japan) is now so well integrated into the Japanese system that in 1986 it was ranked the third most desirable employer in the country among graduating students from major universities.

The Lifetime Employment System

The lifetime employment system for which Japan is noted has deep historical roots but is characteristic only of the medium-size and larger firms. As an industrywide phenomenon, it actually dates only from the years immediately following the Pacific war. At that time, discharging a man was virtually a starvation sentence for him and his family. Promoted by the unions and public opinion, this system of employment spread rapidly throughout the 25 percent of Japan's enterprises that are incorporated. (In prewar years, there had been a great deal of labor mobility except among the *zaibatsu* firms and government offices.)

Because the larger Japanese firm hires for life, special care is taken in the screening process. The more desirable companies and government bureaus hold examinations each year at schools of their choice. Students who score sufficiently high on these examinations are then interviewed by senior personnel executives of the company. From this point on, the emphasis is not on academic learning but on personal character and attitude, along with any family connections the student may have with the company, the social status of the family, its health record, and recommendations by professors of standing. Sony's Akio Morita once said that in evaluating a student for employment, the personnel officer is guided as much by a "sixth sense" as by the applicant's school records.

It is also at this point that the system weeds out anyone whom the Japanese typically describe as a *kuse ga aruhito*, which literally means "a person who has habits," but by extension means anyone who is opinionated, individualistic, conspicuously aggressive, or nonconformist in his manner of speaking or dress. (At the same time, Japanese companies often make use of aggressive behavior in negotiation or selling. One member of the company will adopt a *kuse ga aruhito* pose, go in first and hit hard, and then be followed by a second person who uses the soft approach, sympathizes with the customer or client, and clinches the deal.)

Larger Japanese companies still generally do not hire new graduates with specific jobs in mind. Like the army, they recruit "raw material," put new employees through an indoctrination course first, and then farm them out into the various sections and departments for on-the-job training.

Students who are hired at the university level automatically go into administrative categories (*jimu-kei*) if they majored in literature, law, or the social sciences; and into technical departments (*gijutsu-kei*) if they studied engineering, physics, or one of the other sciences. New employees, thus divided, generally remain in these categories for life—which is the reason why technically trained people are seldom found in sales departments.

Once hired, the employee of a larger firm knows he will not be laid off or fired except under extremely rare circumstances. He knows also that his performance will not be measured on a day-to-day or job-by-job basis and that what will count in the long run is his cooperative spirit and his loyalty to the company.

While the permanent employment system has a number of obvious weaknesses, it also has a number of equally impressive advantages. One of the most significant of these advantages is that creates a situation in which the executives of the company, in particular, can think and plan on a long-range basis. Furthermore, since their entire working lives are to be spent with one company, employees can be counted on to have a deep interest in the future of their company.

The Temporary Employee System

Temporary employees play an important role in the unique Japanese business system. Unlike permanent employees who, practically speaking, cannot be laid off or fired, temporary workers can be hired on a daily, weekly, monthly, or seasonal basis, depending on the needs of the employer. Furthermore, the temporary employee can be dismissed at any time, even if he was originally hired for a specific period. The only legal requirement (besides the provisions of the Labor Standards Law) is that the temporary employee not be hired for a period longer than one year!

Wages are paid to temporary employees on a daily basis. They do not receive bonuses, they are generally not eligible for retirement pensions, and about the only fringe benefit they receive is a commuting allowance.

It is estimated that about 30 percent of all Japanese firms with 30 or more employees use temporary workers, the vast majority of whom (90 percent) are women. The practice is especially prevalent in the retail, service, electrical, automobile, cement, and construction industries. One significant reason for the continuation of the temporary employment system is that when business is slack these workers can be let go without any complaints from unions or the government. A number of foreign companies operating in Japan also make use of temporary employees.

Part-time work, both temporary and permanent, is also growing in importance in the overall labor scene, particularly involving women in the manufacturing and selling industries and farmers during the winter in the construction and automobile industries.

Hiring Prejudices in Japan

The Japanese readily admit that they are still "allergic" to foreigners, including Japanese who have been educated abroad. There are still many major corporations in Japan where both foreigners and foreign-educated Japanese are unofficially barred from employment.

The taboo against hiring Japanese who have studied abroad was so strong in Japan that it was not until 1985 that the first graduate of a foreign university was hired by the Ministry of Foreign Trade and Industry—after he had been turned down by 10 out of the 12 private companies he approached because he had gone to school abroad.

When Masahiro Hayafuji, an honors graduate of Brown University, was accepted by MITI, it made national headlines in Japan. The problem, Hayafuji said, is that Japanese companies still tend to hire people who fit specific traditional categories rather than individuals. Japanese who go to school abroad do not have the vital relationships with accepted schools and with professors who are in a position to recommend them to various companies and government ministries.

The need for rapid internationalization and competition from foreign companies is forcing a change in this age-old Japanese attitude, however, and a growing number of Japanese companies are slowly but surely opening a slight crack in their closed-door hiring policies. As limited as it is now and will probably continue to be for the foreseeable future, this new development will add to the competitive ability of Japanese companies.

The stock excuse given by Japanese companies for not hiring graduates of foreign universities is that having been influenced by foreign attitudes they would no longer fit into the harmonious team-approach demanded by Japanese management.

Many Japanese companies still maintain a strict policy of not hiring anyone of Chinese or Korean ethnic backgrounds, even though their families may have been in Japan for generations.

The first employment of non-Japanese in Japan by a major Japanese company on a full-time, regular basis did not occur until 1982, when the Seibu Department Store chain broke through the official and unofficial barriers after a protracted and sometimes bitter confrontation with the Ministries of Justice and Labor. Finally, the government relented and informed Seibu that foreigners could be hired if their numbers were less than one percent of annual recruits. Prior to that, there were government regulations strictly limiting the entry of foreign workers into Japan to a few specialist categories.

There are presently fewer than 15,000 foreign workers in Japan. Over half of these are employed by foreign companies operating in Japan. About one-third of them work for Japanese companies, and the remainder are specialists, such as foreign language teachers and hotel chefs.

On a personal level, the Japanese attitude toward foreigners is one of courteous, if not friendly, interest, but when it comes to officially welcoming foreigners to the country as employees of Japanese companies, residents, or new citizens, the traditional xenophobia of the Japanese still prevails.

Taking Advantage of Japanese Discrimination

Foreign companies wanting to do business in Japan and not able or willing to invest the time and money to train present employees can take advantage of the Japanese preference for "pure Japanese" employees by hiring Japanese students who have independently completed several years of university-level education overseas.

Approximately four percent of the foreign students studying in the U.S., for example, are Japanese, which means there are some 13,000 Japanese students now at American colleges and universities.

A recent survey shows that most of these students are in California, Oregon, New York, Ohio, Washington, Texas, Illinois, Hawaii, Massachusetts, and Minnesota. The schools in the states with the largest enrollment of Japanese students are the University of Hawaii, the University of Michigan-Ann Arbor, MIT, Stanford, UCLA, the University of Pennsylvania, the University of Illinois-Urbana, Harvard, the University of Oregon, the University of Washington, and San Francisco University.

American managers in Japan say that it is best to work with professional headhunters to recruit Japanese personnel from American schools, that employers must be aware of the cultural shock these U.S.-educated students will experience when they return to Japan for employment in a foreign company, and that special efforts must be made to help them adjust and fit in with other Japanese personnel in the office.

It is further recommended that American companies interested in this approach to gaining Japanese language and cultural expertise should recruit the student a year or more before they are due to graduate in order to guide their studies and give them a chance to become familiar with the American company while they are still in school.

Temporary Staff Services

The first temporary worker service company established in Japan was the U.S.'s Manpower, in the mid 1960s. Now there are over 300 such companies in Tokyo alone, with more than 100,000 registered part-time workers available. Such companies began snowballing in the early 1970s, when the oil crisis led many companies to reduce their annual hiring of permanent employees.

How Employees Are Paid

Employee compensation in Japan is fairly complicated. It is usually divided into a monthly basic wage, the twice-a-year bonuses, regular fringe benefits, overtime, incentive wages, retirement allowances, and a number of other miscellaneous categories. The starting salary (*shonin-kyu*) of a new employee entering a Japanese company is determined by his educational level. While this basic wage of an individual can be increased at any time, the prevailing practice is for the base wage of all employees to be increased once a year in conjunction with the annual Spring Offensive by the national labor federations.

The second most important part of the employee's income is the two seasonal bonuses, paid in June and December. Each of these bonuses amounts to the equivalent of two, three, four, or more month's basic wages. As a result of pressure brought by the unions, these annual bonuses are now "officially" called seasonal allowances—the reason being that the unions have no intention of letting management continue to think of the bonuses as unearned extras.

Next are the "statutory" fringe benefits, which include health and other insurance, and the "nonstatutory" benefits, which include housing or housing allowances, family allowances, health services, payment in kind, cultural and recreational services, and various other benefits. Then come such things as position allowances (extra pay for rank), incentive allowances, shift allowances, commuting allowances, regional allowances, and overtime. Under this "lifetime cost of living approach," the worker's income increases with his seniority and the size of his family. Finally comes the retirement allowance, which is usually paid in a lump sum.

Overtime is still an important part of the total compensation of most Japanese workers, amounting to about five percent of the annual income received in larger companies and more for those who work for smaller enterprises. The minimum overtime rate is 125 percent of the hourly basic wage, as calculated from the monthly base wage.

Japanese law requires that all firms with more than five employees provide statutory fringe benefits, health insurance, welfare pension insurance, unemployment insurance, and workmen's compensation insurance. Retirement and severance benefits are not compulsory under law, but the custom is so strong that it has the force of law.

The pay of top executives follows the basic system of salaries, allowances, and bonuses. The lowest ranking director usually receives about half of what the president receives. Bonuses paid to executives, however, are to some extent based on profits. Ordinarily, executives receive bonuses amounting to about six months' salary. If the company is doing poorly, this may be postponed or reduced.

Except for top management positions, most of the foreign companies operating in Japan use the Japanese system for paying wages. The reasons for this are obvious. Japanese employees often prefer it, and foreign employers also find it expedient. The expected bonuses and retirement allowances are usually based on monthly salaries, and these extras would be exorbitant if they were based on a flat, high monthly income. There is thus a tendency for foreign companies that started out paying flat salaries, without all the allowances common in the Japanese system, to change gradually over to the local system.

Many foreign companies pay their top Japanese managers salaries more or less equivalent to what they pay foreign nationals—but without the numerous fringe benefits that are characteristic of the Japanese wage system.

The Retirement System

The retirement allowance is based on the last monthly basic wage multiplied by the number of years of service, plus an additional factor that increases it by as much as 30 percent. In the late 1960s, annuity-type pension schemes gained in popularity, often in addition to—or as an alternative to—lump-sum retirement benefits.

Japanese executives normally receive what amounts to two retirement allowances. One is for the years before they were promoted into the top executive bracket and another for the years they served as director or high officer. The retiring president of a major corporation may receive as much as $750,000. The president of a small company may receive as little as $50,000. In large, successful Japanese companies, it is also fairly common for leading executives to be given shares in their companies well before they retire.

In most Japanese companies, retirement is compulsory at age 55. Some companies have extended the retirement age to 57 or 58. Other companies still require employees below the rank of director to retire at 55, at which time they are paid their retirement allowance. In some cases they are then rehired as temporary employees at reduced salaries for two, three, or more years. Many companies have by-laws specifying that the company president will retire at 65, the managing director at 63, and other directors at 60. But these regulations are seldom enforced.

The reason for the early retirement of those below director level is that it helps keep costs down by getting rid of employees whose salaries have increased with the length of their service. The system also provides more promotion opportunities for younger employees. In larger companies, rehired employees who have reached management level are often placed in affiliated subcontracting firms for "second careers."

Those Famous Expense Accounts

The law allows a company in Japan to deduct a generous portion of its gross income as entertainment expenses, on the basis of a three-step formula. Under the first step, each company is allowed an automatic deduction of ¥4 million for entertainment. In addition to this, each company can deduct the equivalent of 0.25 percent of its capital as entertainment expense; and finally, 30 percent of any additional amount spent on entertainment is deductible. It is said that many companies somehow manage to spend a great deal more on entertainment than the law allows without paying taxes on it. In any event, the expense account is a very important part of the income of all company executives, and the larger and more prosperous the company, the more generous the expense accounts are likely to be.

There are several categories of expense accounts. The two most important are the one that is used for entertaining customers and the one that top executives use for their own private purposes.

These expense accounts may be classified as "special service funds" (*kimitsu-hi*) and "social expense funds" (*kosaihi*). Managers, executives, and sometimes salesmen are authorized to spend so much on a daily or monthly basis. The amount varies, with many executives of larger firms receiving as much as $5,000 a month for entertainment. In some cases, these expense accounts are "paid" to the recipients whether they are used or not. In other cases, the users have arranged with certain restaurants and cabarets that they patronize regularly to "overcharge" them and then kick back the difference, which is then put to personal use.

When Japanese businessmen entertain in cabarets or restaurants, the bills are generally sent directly to their companies, which pay them on a monthly basis, the same way they pay other suppliers.

Compensation for Salesmen

Not many Japanese salesmen are willing to work on commissions alone. Most prefer a fixed salary that is at least enough to provide for their basic needs. The news media report that only about three percent of all automobile salesmen are on commissions alone, while in the insurance industry eight percent receive only commissions. Since these are two areas in which commissions are perhaps the most common, these low figures are a good indication of the unpopularity of the straight commission job in Japan.

There are numerous examples in other industries, however, of salary-plus-commission arrangements that are apparently quite successful. The foreign employer interested in using a commission method of compensation is well advised to keep it flexible and to make sure that the employees concerned throughly understand and accept it.

The Cash-Wage Syndrome

Most Japanese employees continue to insist that their wages be paid in cash. There are several reasons for this. Historically, the Japanese have never used checks as a means of making payment, and they are therefore not familiar with their use. It is also natural for the Japanese to equate checks to some degree with *tegata*, the deferred payment notes used by practically every business in the country, which cannot be "cashed" at par value for 90 days to nine months.

On the personal side, employees say it would be an extraordinary inconvenience in many cases for them to have to take their check to a bank each month before they could get cash for their household and other daily expenses. Finally, virtually all male employees strongly resent and resist the idea because it would make it more difficult for them to withhold any of their salary from their wives—a practice that is solidly entrenched.

This situation also applies to most foreign companies in Japan. Several companies well known to the writer have attempted to switch from cash to check or bank transfer payment. None of them succeeded. The only exception, pointed out by one of the companies, involves employees who are in distant parts of the country, where there is no practical alternative to payment by bank transfer.

The situation is changing, however, and it is now common for companies to pay many of their bills by bank transfer. This will surely continue to spread into other areas, including wages.

The Growing Mobility of Labor

Despite the continued existence and strength of the lifetime employment system in Japan's business world, Japanese labor is far from immobile. In just the first six months of last year, some 2.5 million workers—or one of every 16 wage earners in the country—left their jobs to seek or take employment elsewhere, according to a Labor Ministry survey. During the same period, of the 3.2 million newly employed persons, 48 percent had worked elsewhere. Another interesting revelation: More and more middle-aged women are entering Japan's labor force for the first time. The bulk of this movement is among small and medium-size firms.

Another type of movement that is also gaining momentum involves young professionals, such as computer programmers, planners, researchers, and others with special scientific skills—especially in larger firms. Young employees who are in the clerk and "operative" class are also beginning to move from firm to firm.

Finally, older executives and professionals who work for large firms are beginning to become slightly mobile. This is obvious from the existence and experience of over 20 executive recruiting agencies in the country, the first of which was not approved until 1964. One of these firms, Cambridge Research Institute-Japan (CRI), received resumés from over 10,000 people interested in changing jobs during its first four years of operation. Out of this number, 13.5 percent were employed in companies with over 3,000 employees, and 19.1 percent were working for companies with between 1,000 and 3,000 employees. "In other words," comments CRI's Masaaki Imai, "one out of every three persons worked for a company employing over 1,000 people."

In the late 1960s, leading Japanese companies scrambled to hire professional talent. A number of them, for the first time in their histories, resorted to advertising in the local and national press. The first genuine public recruiting campaigns occurred in early 1970 and were carried out by such companies as Sony, Toray, and Teijin.

Imai said that when he first became active in executive recruiting, the majority of applicants were from small firms, and most of them were unemployed at the time. Now, 84 percent of the applicants are employed. They want to change jobs because they want either a more rewarding or a more challenging occupation. Imai predicts that by the end of the 1980s, major enterprises may be placing equal emphasis on the old once-a-year recruiting from schools and interim recruiting from the open market. At present, however, most large Japanese companies hiring from the open labor market "impose unfavorable conditions" on new employees unless they are professionals specifically recruited by the firms.

With leading Japanese companies also competing on the open labor market for professionals and often paying salaries that are substantial, even by American standards, foreign firms operating in Japan must be prepared to offer more than just money—unless it is a stupendous amount. On the encouraging side, Imai said that from his experience, many of the objections that qualified Japanese traditionally had against working for foreign companies have diminished considerably over the years, and should continue to dissipate as time goes by. In any event, said Imai, the days are gone when a Japanese company can select the employees it wants just because it is big. Besides the long-range future offered by the company and the actual take-home pay, young people today are also interested in the job they will be doing and in the personality and attitude of the company's top management.

IMC, another of the personnel recruiting agencies with a good reputation, recruits in Japan for both foreign and Japanese firms.

Through its affiliates, IMC recruits foreign personnel for Japanese companies setting up affiliates overseas. This agency also places Westerners who are in Japan seeking work with Japanese organizations.

Quitting Isn't Easy

It is sometimes as difficult to quit a job with a large Japanese company as it is to get one. There are usually provisions for resigning from a company in the rules of employment (*shugyo kisoku*). These rules specify such requirements as an advance notice of two to four weeks and a written letter of resignation. In some cases, the rules say that a resignation is effective when management "accepts" it (in which case, the employee may mail in his resignation, getting a document from the post office certifying the contents of the letter and its delivery).

In any event, when a person makes known his desire to leave a large company, he is often subjected to several kinds of pressure and delays. The company may send several people to the employee's home to talk to his wife. His own associates are instructed to try to persuade him to change his mind. His superior may refuse to send the resignation to the personnel department or tear it up and announce that he can't quit because the company needs him.

Sometimes a company will not acknowledge an employee's resignation even after he has left and is working somewhere else. There was one publicized case in which the former employer continued sending salary to the individual for several months after he started working at a new company. Since the number of people who are willing to go through the agony of leaving a company is increasing each year, it seems likely that *ten-shoku* (job-changing) will inevitably become more and more common in Japan.

Small enterprises are naturally more susceptible to labor mobility because they cannot afford to match the pay scale, allowances, or retirement benefits of the larger companies. The critical period begins after workers have been with a small company for ten or so years, particularly if they have had two or three children in the meantime. Then many look for work at companies that can afford to pay more. Others open their own business.

Two other types of labor mobility in Japan have been common for years. The most common of these (as far as volume is concerned) is called *shukko,* or "transfer," and refers to parent companies sending executives, young and old, to subsidiaries or affiliated firms, such as joint ventures. In some cases, such transfers are made just to get rid of less talented managers who are bunching up at the top of the promotion escalator. In other cases, the transfer may be intended to help an ailing company, to keep an eye on its fiscal practices, or to give young executives a broader background of business experience.

The other type of labor mobility is known as *amakudari,* or "descending from heaven," which is a poetic (if sarcastic) way of describing the movement of high-ranking government officials into private industry when they retire. A law states that a national government official cannot accept employment in a company closely connected to the office he held until he has been retired for two years. But each year the National Personnel Authority turns around and grants exemptions to practically every official who retires. As a result, most of them immediately move into director, managing director, vice president, or chairman positions with banks, automobile manufacturers, pharmaceutical companies, or construction firms, etc., depending on whether they were with the Finance Ministry, the Transportation Ministry, the Ministry of Welfare, or the Ministry of Construction.

Executive Recruiting Agencies

In 1987, there were several dozen executive recruiting agencies operating in Japan and playing an increasingly important role in helping companies locate and hire talented management personnel. Some of these firms offer only employee recruiting service. Others offer a wide range of preemployment and postemployment services to the client, including identifying the requirements of the position, as well as general consulting and market research.

The law authorizing executive recruiting agencies dates only from 1964 and restricts the service fees the agencies can charge. Since these fees are fixed and relatively low, a number of the agencies insist upon rendering related services, plus charging a consulting fee, in order to get around the government limit on fees. The fees for finding and placing an English-speaking candidate are higher than when only the Japanese language is required.

The recruiting firms attract candidates by advertising and by personal contact. One firm reports using a system of scouting whereby employees in various companies help the agency locate qualified persons in specific fields who might be interested in changing jobs.

The clientele of some of the recruiting agencies is primarily medium-size Japanese companies. Other firms handle mostly foreign clients and specialize in helping staff joint venture companies. The American Chamber of Commerce in Japan (Tokyo) keeps track of the agencies catering primarily to foreign operations and can advise the newcomer on which one to go to for what.

Who Wants to Work for a Foreign Company?

"The foreign businessman in Japan should have no false illusions. The cream of the annual labor crop still goes to the large Japanese corporations. No matter how big or how well known the foreign firm, it gets no better than second or third choice. Foreign firms cannot compete with the Japanese in either outright benefits or the special tolerance that is shown toward employees by Japanese organizations," observed the resident manager of a big foreign operation. "In a large Japanese company," he continued, "an employee may be sick for several years and not only continue to draw full salary and other benefits, but upon returning to work be assured that he has not lost seniority and has been automatically moved up in the company hierarchy.

"In Japanese firms, the employee can automatically take hundreds of other things for granted. He knows the system and psychology of the company and can blend in. In the foreign company, however, he is never sure of himself, of anyone around him or the firm, and is in a constant state of mental trepidation. He also knows that he can never reach the higher executive levels. His school ties lose much of their meaning. For these reasons, recruitment of personnel for foreign firms is difficult. But," the resident manager went on, "too many foreigners allow themselves to be impressed by a certain amount of English-language ability and have more or less come to depend upon this as the only qualification required in their Japanese employees. We have often been surprised to discover that one of our most valuable workers turned out to be a man whose foreign language ability was limited or nil and who made a very poor initial personal impression."

Pursuing the same subject, another Western executive said: "Only a certain type of Japanese will work for foreign firms, even the large, internationally famous ones. Part of the reluctance to do so stems from the very strong idea that no foreign company in Japan is permanent. Much of the original pool of Japanese who went to work for foreign firms in Japan in the 1950s and 1960s were ex-occupation employees. In most cases, they worked for foreign companies for two reasons: They got used to higher basic incomes than what Japanese firms paid; also, the fact that they once worked for foreigners automatically made them persona non grata to major Japanese companies. But now," he added, "young people who are more interested in immediate returns than in pension 35 years from now are entering this pool."

A Harvard-educated Japanese who has worked for both Japanese and American firms said: "The good man doesn't like to work for a foreign firm. He is afraid he might be fired and thereby disgraced, without any choice of turning to a first-rank Japanese company. Because of this sense of insecurity, the Japanese who do work for foreign companies have very little incentive to be loyal. They stay on first of all because they have no other place to go. Secondary considerations are more money and a chance to go abroad. Many young girls who have studied English or English literature just want to be near foreigners."

While these opinions about the reluctance of Japanese to work for foreign companies are generally true, it should be emphasized that there are exceptions and that they apply more to women than to men. In fact, Japanese girls and women are apt to develop strong loyalty to a foreign company because they feel more secure and wanted in a foreign company, and their opportunities for advancement are better. In Japanese companies, women are expected—and in many cases required—to resign when they marry. Few ever achieve even the lowest rank of management in Japanese firms.

The implementation of the Equal Opportunity Law in April 1986, however, emphasized the growing power and importance of women in business and public affairs in Japan. The same month saw the founding of the Japan Association of Female Executives (JAFE) by Noriko Nakamura, a successful businesswoman, who said such an organization was needed by women to help them compensate for not having *sempai* (higher level alumni/mentors) to look out for them and guarantee their rise in the managerial hierarchy—the powerful networking system that is one of the main ingredients of the male-dominated business world.

Nakamura said JAFE was designed specifically to create networks of female executives, to conduct seminars on management and other topics that relate to women, and to conduct monthly personal development programs, including public speaking and beauty and fashion information. Nakamura made the point that attractive women should emphasize their looks in order to advance their professional careers, instead of trying to appear sexless in order to compete with men.

JAFE has an advisory board of persons in positions of power, including several men, to give members advice and help them expand their networks into all types of enterprises.

Getting a Nose Job First

Competition among graduating female students in Japan for desirable jobs is so fierce that thousands of them resort to cosmetic surgery to make themselves more attractive—knowing full well that male recruiters will react more positively to physically attractive women.

The director of the Kawai Clinic in Tokyo's Chiyoda Ward says that until the latter 1970s most of his patients were single women seeking to improve their looks prior to marriage but that the majority now are job-hunting university students. The most popular forms of cosmetic surgery are doubling the eyelids and heightening noses.

One of the strongest attractions foreign companies have for Japanese workers is faster promotion. Promotion in Japanese companies is slow. When the newly employed university graduate takes his place on the crowded first floor of the company hierarchy, he knows that it will take him the standard seven and a half years to reach *kakaricho* (literally "someone in charge," often translated as "chief clerk"), which is something like an officer candidate becoming a second lieutenant. The next jump to *kacho,* or section chief, takes eight to ten more years. An additional seven to ten years is required for promotion to *bucho* (division chief). Only a chosen few go beyond this level.

A factor that discourages Japanese from working for foreign companies, however, is fewer titles and other symbols of prestige and authority. As one Japanese management consultant put it: "There is no middle echelon in any except top-ranked foreign firms—just Japanese clerks and foreign managers. If foreign businessmen want to gain the loyalty and the complete cooperation of their Japanese employees, this will have to change."

The foreign manager of a major Canadian company expressed the opinion that foreign firms should hire only local staff who have studied abroad or have had extensive experience with foreign firms in Japan. "Otherwise," he said, "you get nothing but bodies." He added: "One of the biggest obstacles facing a new foreign company coming into Japan is the problem of finding really competent bilingual secretaries. There are only a few hundred in all the country. I recently interviewed around 700 girls and found that less than ten could converse in English. The ones who could had all studied abroad for at least one year. The others just didn't have the right mental attitude. They couldn't deviate from conditioned patterns of thinking, and they naturally had a negative attitude about everything. They were not able to project themselves or put the other person at ease and inspire confidence. Much of the wasted motion they go through is honest effort, but it is misdirected. These may be small things, but when added together they affect the overall image and efficiency of a company."

Commenting on the ability of Japanese who work for foreign firms, a foreign-educated Japanese who works for 3M said: "Most Japanese who work for foreign companies are too domesticated . . . that is, they cannot or will not contribute any original thinking to problems." A Siber Hegner vice president, speaking on the same problem, said: "It is difficult to get our Japanese coworkers and managers to accept the idea that ours is a type of partnership—that we want them to participate in management decisions and planning. The most that we can expect now is that when something goes wrong, one of our staff may mention casually that he expected something like that to happen all along. It is also left up to the foreign employer to know if his staff is satisfied or if any of them have any problems that are detrimental to their own performance or to the overall activity of the company. If you approach them, they will say, 'Yes, I thought something was wrong, but I wasn't sure.' You have to keep on the alert for this, or it infects the whole organization, and may eventually get to the point where only radical surgery is effective." He added: "We make a considerable effort to foster team spirit among our Japanese staff, particularly our salesmen, but it is often a one-sided conversation. The foreign staff does all the talking. Only rarely will one of the Japanese salesmen speak up."

Another complaint frequently voiced by foreign businessmen in smaller companies is that it is necessary personally to check every last detail on any job, no matter how trivial, that is done by the Japanese staff. Said one such manager: "The Japanese are great at handling mechanical routine work, but they appear never to question the validity or accuracy of anything they do. A clerk will add up a set of figures and get an answer that obviously could not be correct and will do nothing about it. The staff won't ask questions when they have a problem. They just sit at their desks until you happen to notice their predicament, or else they let whatever it is go through, knowing that it is probably wrong. When you ask for an explanation of how a mistake was made, you get embarrassed silence."

An American banker in Tokyo has a different view of the quality of Japanese workers. Said he: "Japanese office personnel are among the best anywhere. Their dedication, accuracy, and diligence are exemplary—provided they are motivated to bring out these good traits. Most foreign managers cannot motivate Japanese workers. They must rely on Japanese managers for this, and for such Japanese managers to be successful in this task they must be given a great deal of authority, and they must never be overruled or criticized in the presence of subordinates.

"If I were to set up a new branch now in Japan, I would staff it with a few highly paid Japanese managers recently rehired (after their early forced retirement) and a small army of female high school and college graduates to assist them. The Japanese managers' first task would be to interview a number of male college students scheduled to graduate the following spring and hire the good ones. Repeating this process for five years would produce a strong, homogeneous, key staff—very young but guided by the aging seniors.

"In 10 to 15 years, there would be no need to hire any more 'retired' Japanese managers—you would have developed your own. The only effective personnel management policy in Japan is the Japanese one—at least in the business of banking."

146

Efficiency is, of course, primarily a function of motivation. The Western manager in Japan often fails in his efforts to motivate his Japanese employees because he is either not familiar with their values or does not fully appreciate the fact that these values cannot be changed by pep talks.

The Law of Effect works just as well—if not better—in Japan as it does elsewhere when it is presented in Japanese terms. The solution to the problem of efficiency in Japan is to keep both the problem and the rewards for effective behavior in a strictly Japanese context. This generally means the Western manager must work through competent Japanese assistants who know what to say and how and when to say it.

Alternatives for Foreign Firms

As a result of the various problems involved in hiring personnel in Japan, different companies have different solutions. One European company manager said: "We try to employ only fresh, untrained personnel direct from schools. Once the Japanese have been trained in Japanese methods, it is hard to change them. If you catch them early enough, they are as flexible and adaptable as can be expected of any man. Once you reach a balanced compromise between the Western and Japanese way of doing business, things are easier here than in many Western countries. On an individual, personal basis, I find the Japanese more diligent than Western employees."

An American executive in charge of a large buying operation said: "We have hired from schools, but our hiring is usually on a more personal basis. We advertise in newspapers, or someone introduces a prospect to us. There is still tacit agreement among large trading firms like C. Itoh and Mitsui that they will not raid each other's staff, and we feel it is best to honor this."

Most foreign businessmen advertise in local newspapers whenever they want to hire Japanese personnel. Response to Help Wanted ads placed in the English-language dailies is usually effective. Those who respond generally have had some experience with foreign companies or the United States military forces or have studied abroad. There is, however, a fairly large group of misfits and beachcomber-types that use the English-language papers for leads, and these have to be sifted through.

One of the more chronic labor shortages in Tokyo, mentioned earlier, is for highly skilled female secretaries in the American mold. There are tens of thousands of pretty, charming, well-mannered girls available for office work. Some of them speak English fairly well and some can type, but highly skilled, responsible secretaries who can function as a foreign manager's assistant are rare.

Reprimanding Japanese personnel is another serious problem facing foreign businessmen. Most foreigners delegate this responsibility to ranking Japanese in their employ. Others, unwisely, take the burden upon themselves. No matter how justified the reprimand, Japanese employees resent being admonished by foreigners. When it is done by a Japanese manager, they are able to accept it as the natural order of things. One Japanese manager who commented on this point said he tried to anticipate when his foreign boss was about ready to chew someone out and took care of the problem before it was brought up. "This seems to be working out all right," the manager said. Many Japanese business executives regularly humiliate their subordinates to remind them of their relative position. This may be upsetting to the bilingual foreign businessman who observes it, but he is advised not to interfere unless he is prepared to accept a complete breakdown in the authority and influence of his Japanese managers. At the same time, any foreign executive who humiliates his Japanese employees for any reason and in any way is making a serious mistake.

An area of irritation that generally escapes the notice of Western managers in Japan is the impression their Japanese female receptionists, secretaries, and telephone operators make on Japanese businessmen. For the most part, the Japanese callers or visitors consider them ill-mannered and obnoxious because they have become Westernized to some degree and no longer behave in the way Japanese men expect of Japanese women. Said one Japanese executive: "These Americanized employees do an incalculable amount of harm. Foreign businessmen here should hire for such positions only (pure) Japanese girls who have been graduated from women's colleges and are recommended by their teachers."

Foreign employers should have their Japanese employees sign "articles" stating the conditions of their employment. These articles should be very detailed, and a copy should be provided to each employee for his own reference. This would help prevent many of the small irritations that eventually build up into major problems.

Renting Your Japan Staff

There are now a dozen or more companies in Tokyo offering office-away-from-home services to foreign businessmen who do not want to go to the considerable expense of opening and staffing their own offices in Japan. A number of these companies operate on a membership basis, with annual fees ranging from $1,000 to $2,000 a year.

Membership in one of the groups covers an office address in Japan for mail, phone and fax messages at no additional charge. Mail and message-forwarding, secretarial service, the use of office facilities while the businessman is in Japan, staff assistance in making appointments, interpreters, transportation, hotel bookings, etc., are available for additional fees.

Among the better known of these services are Tokyo Base (Kabuto-cho Yachiyo Bldg., 20-5 Kabuto-cho, Nihonbashi, Chuo-ku, Tokyo 103, Japan—tel 661-2661; fax 639-5927); and Idea Bank Inc., (Shinjuku NS Bldg., 18th fl., 2-4-1 Nishi Shinjuku, Shinjuku-ku, Tokyo, Japan—tel 348-3711; fax 348-7625).

These new businesses have a way of coming and going, however, and there is no doubt that some of them will fall by the wayside. One of the more substantial is the Jardine Business Centre-Tokyo, established in the fall of 1986 by the Japan affiliate of the famed British trading group. The JBC offers all the usual business services, from bilingual staff and personalized telephones, to facsimiles, conference rooms, consulting, and assistance from foreign and Japanese management staff. The JBC is located in the ABS Building, 2-4-16, Kudan Minami, Chiyoda-ku, Tokyo 102, Japan—tel 239-2811; fax 239-2817; telex J32384.

Chapter 10

Peculiarities of Japanese Unions

"Many foreign companies in Japan are plagued by union problems because they ignore the Japanese way of doing things."
—A labor consultant

The Enterprise Union System

Unions in Japan are unique, and it behooves the outsider doing business here or wanting to do business here to inform himself fully of the various labor laws and the peculiar characteristics of Japanese unions.

To begin with, Japanese unions are "enterprise" unions, not trade, industry, or occupation unions. That is, each individual union is made up only of the employees of one company. Further, in a Japanese enterprise union, everybody in the company up to and including younger management members (section managers and department managers) are members of the union. In addition to this, most company managers are sincere supporters of their firms' unions. Konosuke Matsushita, legendary founder of the huge Matsushita empire, once suggested to his company union that it call a strike, so everybody concerned would have personal experience of what a strike can do to a company and its employees.

The key to the character and behavior of the Japanese company union is that all members of the union, including the union leaders, are company employees. Second, all are permanent employees under the lifetime employment system and, for the most part, expect to remain with the same company for their entire working life. All participate in the benefits of the highly paternalistic Japanese company system and know that as long as the company survives and grows, their annual income will go up automatically under the seniority system.

151

It thus happens that the primary aim of most enterprise unions in Japan is to protect the rights of the workers, which most often means fighting any attempt to change the established system.

Mutuality of Interests and Ongoing Negotiations

Overall, union leaders and management in Japanese companies cooperate closely to maintain harmony (*wa*) within the firm. Both sides are motivated by a very strong desire to avoid conflict. To this end, there are built-in systems for revealing and resolving problems, usually through third or neutral parties, on a day-to-day basis. Special care is taken to avoid putting any person—union member or manager—on the spot and letting or causing him or her to lose "face."

Important matters, such as overtime and benefits, are extensively discussed on an informal basis before formal "negotiations" begin, so that generally at formal meetings previously made agreements become official. When a consensus cannot be reached or when the union members want to emphasize a point, the leaders may form strike committees and vote to stage parades, refuse overtime work, slow work down or, in extreme cases, even stop work altogether—for anywhere from one to 24 hours. Few strikes ever go beyond 24 hours. When they do, the employees wear armbands and headbands, wave red flags (which are not Communist flags), and usually do a lot of singing of martial-sounding songs.

These strikes are quite often scheduled well in advance, with the time of their beginning and ending well publicized. The purpose is not to force management to take action while the strike is going on, but to emphasize the employee's opposition to some issue and the fact that *wa* (harmony) within the company has broken down.

If company management still refuses to work out an agreement with its employees following a strike, and no acceptable solution appears possible, the union or management will appeal to the Labor Relations Commission, which provides conciliation, mediation, and arbitration services.

The Japanese employee is generally too closely and intimately bound to his company to take a really antagonistic, destructive attitude toward the firm. Since neither pay nor status is determined by job assignment, there is no reason for a union to concern itself about jobs or procedures. Besides, personnel are continuously rotating from one job to another.

Japanese unions are just as concerned about how to increase production, improve safety, and upgrade quality, as they are with job security and higher wages.

At this time, less than 30 percent of Japan's work force is unionized. The ratio has been decreasing at about one percent a year. Generally speaking, larger companies are unionized; small ones are not. The percentage may stabilize soon because it is unlikely that the thousands of firms with under 30 but over nine employees will become unionized. (By law, unions can be established only in enterprises with ten or more employees.)

The National Union Federations

The other primary characteristic of unionism in Japan is that most of the individual company unions are affiliated with one or the other of four large national trade union centers or federations or with one of the other 90-some smaller federations. The largest of the Big Four federations is *Sohyo* (The General Council of Trade Unions of Japan), which has five million members and is dominated by left-wing political radicals. *Domei* (Japan Confederation of Labor) is second in size, with about two million members, and is regarded as politically moderate. Third is *Churitsuroren* (Federation of Industrial Unions), with a little over one million members; and fourth is the *Shinsanbetsu*, which has fewer than 70,000 members. Several dozen others have a total of some four and a half million members. The *Zenmin Rokyo* (Private Sector Trade Unions Council, founded in 1982) overlaps the other federations and has around five million members.

Sohyo usually supports the Japan Socialist Party (which so far hasn't done either *Sohyo* or the JSP much good); and *Domei* usually backs the Democratic Socialist party.

It often seems that the only worthwhile effort the national union federations engage in is the annual Spring Offensive (*Shunki Chinage Kyodo Toso*—or *Shunto*, for short), which is spearheaded by Sohyo and aims at bringing about the highest possible annual wage increase across the board in Japan. By influencing many of the larger organizations to make negotiated settlements on basic wage increases, the union federations know this will have a tendency to set the pattern for the rest of the country (because of competition for labor, as well as "face").

The Spring Offensives begin in early spring and usually end in April. They are characterized by short strikes, numerous demonstrations and parades, and a great deal of singing and flag-waving. Wage increases take effect in April.

In larger Japanese companies, it is the overall Japanese management system—not union membership—that provides job and position security to managers, allowing them to devote their lives to one company and to be interested in and accept responsibility for the operation of the company as a whole. They know absolutely that no ambitious younger or newer employee is going to come up under them or behind them and threaten their job or their seniority. They know they are not going to be replaced by someone who is more capable or works harder. Their job is safe.

Being a member of a company union doesn't help you get another job if you are laid off or fired or if you quit. There is no connection among company unions. The power of the national federations is also limited because most union dues are paid into the coffers of the individual company unions, not to the federations.

The only union in Japan that is described as similar to the typical American union is the All-Japan Seaman's Union. Unions are rare in Japanese companies with under 100 employees.

Foreign Firms and Japanese Unions

Virtually all foreign companies of any size in Japan are unionized, and many have had very serious problems with their unions—problems that were far more serious than those that usually arise in purely Japanese companies. There are several reasons why foreign companies are prone to have more union problems than Japanese companies are. One is that the foreign firm is most likely to try to institute "foreign" management practices of which the Japanese employees do not approve. Another is that the foreign firm is more likely to offend its employees by not following Japanese customs closely enough or, in some cases, by actually breaking a labor law (either from ignorance or disrespect).

Yet another problem (which seems to apply more to smaller firms than to larger ones) is that agitators might attempt to infiltrate the foreign company, disrupt its operation, and bring about bankruptcy or closure by the frustrated owners. These professional agitators are sometimes Communist-oriented. Once a foreign company comes under union fire in such circumstances, the union usually resists everything that management proposes. The union may also demand the prerogative to set the amount of the annual wage increase and the twice-a-year bonuses, as well as other benefits.

In these extreme but fairly common cases, most of the union resistance can be traced to one or two individuals. Usually, the only way the company can get rid of these troublemakers is to win the support of all the other employees in the company and get them all to agree that they will no longer cooperate with, be friendly to, help, and in some instances even speak to the agitators. Completely frozen out of the company family, the troublemakers often find that they cannot take the pressure and quit.

It is of the utmost importance that any foreign company setting up an operation in Japan bring in a labor consultant to help write its employment contract, structure pay scales, and hire staff. There are simply too many rules—too many ways even the experienced businessman can make mistakes or fail to anticipate future problems—for a company to attempt to go it alone.

If you have more than ten full-time employees, you must have Work Rules and submit them to the Labor Standard Office. Once you have established your Work Rules, they can be very difficult to change, especially if your workers have a union. When you are dealing with unionized labor, it is essential that you consult with union leaders before making any changes in the Work Rules.

Unions have more rights and prerogatives than employers have and it can be anywhere from difficult to impossible to fire someone unless you have very specific, very detailed Work Rules that cover when and how someone can be dismissed.

Regular employees in Japan do not have work contracts, but they have the most protection under Japanese labor laws. When foreign employers take labor disputes to court in Japan, they almost always lose, regardless of the circumstances, because the courts tend to favor Japanese workers over foreign management.

One of the biggest mistakes foreign employers can make in Japan is to attempt to treat workers the way they do in their home country, even though such treatment may appear to be more enlightened and more favorable to the employees. A number of such foreign companies have been hit by employee rebellions, and they were shocked when they discovered how unhappy the workers were.

How to Do Business with the Japanese

Most foreign businessmen who hire Japanese employees fail to look beyond their resumés. Foreign labor consultants with extensive experience in Japan agree that it is very important to do as the Japanese do and employ the services of a *koshinjo*, or investigative agency, to check the backgrounds of employee applicants. This can be of vital importance to foreign employers because they are almost always severely handicapped in evaluating the ability and character of Japanese applicants.

Some of the most common mistakes foreign businessmen make in Japan include not taking the time and effort to qualify employee prospects; hiring and firing too quickly; favoring employees who speak English; failing to communicate regularly and fully with their employees; trying to cover things up; not offering the employees any opportunity to participate in management; promoting employees too quickly; ignoring the seniority of older staff; appearing uncaring, unfair, or insincere; being too direct; and singling out individuals for special praise.

Chapter 11

The Makeup of Japan's Consumer Market

"Women make most of the buying decisions in Japan."

—A marketer

Shopping in the *Shotengai*

Still today, a majority of Japan's 40 million housewives go grocery shopping every day, on foot, as they have done since community life began. There were and still are many reasons for this: lack of means or space to store and keep perishable foods, a strong preference for fresh foods, and lack of or inconvenient transportation. As a result, small "shopping streets" (*shotengai*) have traditionally been an integral part of every neighborhood, and remain the basic pattern today.

In large Japanese cities, there is one shopping street for every 10,000 persons, each street serving an area within a radius of some 500 meters. Each shopping center has from several dozen to 200 stores, which, on the average, are quite small. On the shopping street are two or more stores selling rice, fish, vegetables, meat, bread, drugs, clothing, electrical appliances, furniture, confections, milk products, kitchen and household goods, cosmetics, shoes, and so on. There are also service shops—such as barbershops, beauty parlors, photo shops, and tailor shops—a tiny convenience market, and maybe a "supermarket" or two. Some of these shops carry imported lines.

The housewife, with shopping basket on her arm (or on the handlebars of a bicycle), usually goes to market in the late afternoon to buy the daily perishables and any incidental items she may need. She naturally buys in very small quantities and is extremely sensitive to the slightest change in the shape, color, or texture of the perishables she buys. These neighborhood shopping centers are sometimes referred to as "daily cycle" *shotengai* because their customers patronize them daily.

157

Another distinctive characteristic of retailing in the food industry is the amount of manufacturing, processing, and packaging that takes place at the wholesale and retail levels. As is well known, the Japanese eat a lot of fish, one of the most popular of which is *maguro*, or tuna. The steps involved in getting *maguro* to the consumer is an excellent example of how complicated distribution can be in Japan. First of all, there are 11 different kinds of fish called *maguro*. Each has its own flavor, which the Japanese recognize and distinguish. The fish are brought into the local central fish market very early in the morning and laid out for viewing. Brokers inspect the fish and then bid for them one by one. Then each individual fish is cut into three parts—the tail part, the back, and the middle. A price is set on each of these different pieces because the demand differs.

Then the original brokers who bought the fish from the fishing coop auction the different pieces of fish to fish wholesalers. The wholesalers then add their markup and sell the fish cuts to subwholesalers or directly to retailers, who buy whatever cuts they know their customers prefer. For other types of fish, the retailer does all the cutting.

The distribution of goods to food shops is in the hands of subwholesalers who are usually supplied by secondary wholesalers. Wholesaler control over vegetables and fish is said to be particularly strong—because it is a hereditary business dating back to ancient times. Most of these shops are thus family businesses. Some that do not have a steady flow of customers are taken care of by the wife or old grandmother with the after-school help of young girls in the family.

While there is a definite trend for some of these shops to amalgamate, expand their size, and take on the appearance of supermarkets, there is no indication that the overall number or importance of such shops will change markedly in the next several years. They will therefore continue to exert considerable influence on any distribution pattern to be developed.

Central Shopping Districts and Specialty Shops

In addition to the ubiquitous neighborhood shopping areas in Japan, a tradition that has remained more or less the same for centuries, there is also a large number of central shopping districts in each city or town of any size. These centers have grown up in the last several decades, primarily around major local transportation terminals. In Tokyo, for example, there are more than a hundred local train stations, and many are nuclei for large and important shopping centers. Some, like Shibuya, Shinjuku, Ikebukuro, and Asakusa, constitute large-scale cities within themselves and boast one or more giant department stores—which usually devote one or more floors to foodstuffs.

In addition to a complex of theatres, restaurants, bars, and cabarets, these central shopping districts are made up of hundreds of specialty shops dealing in every type of commodity produced in Japan. While some of them are tiny, unpretentious stores similar to those in the neighborhood centers, most are modern, sophisticated businesses that would not be out of place in the newest American shopping center. Some deal in cheap merchandise; others, in the best available. Some of these shops also carry selections of imported goods. Most of them belong to some type of association, usually based on location rather than type of merchandise handled. The most important functions of the associations are to promote the areas as shopping centers, represent the individual stores in ward and city affairs, and exercise some degree of control over the opening of any new shop in the area.

In the case of certain products, retailers in these areas are able to maintain complete monopolistic control. One such example is phonograph records. Retail outlets in this field are strictly limited to the already existing 1,800 dealers. "If anyone else tries to get in, suppliers, who are forced to cooperate with the monopoly, will boycott them, and they can't possibly be successful if they are not able to stock all labels," said a leading importer of records.

The most famous of Japan's hundreds of well-known central shopping districts is the Ginza in Tokyo's Chuo Ward. About half a mile long and a quarter of a mile wide, this thickly populated area boasts six of the world's largest and best department stores, plus several hundred of the top specialty shops in the country. A colorful, fascinating place to Japanese and foreigners alike, the Ginza draws millions of shoppers and visitors every year. As one of Japan's best retail locations, real estate in key areas of the Ginza is fantastically expensive, the southwest Ginza 4-chrome corner being officially valued at thousands of dollars per square foot. A majority of the specialty shops on the Ginza deal in ready-made clothing, fabrics, accessories, and tourist-type souvenir items, such as pearls, binoculars, transistor radios, and cameras.

Department Stores

Department stores in Japan are unique in many ways and never fail to impress—perhaps shock would be more exact—foreign visitors. In addition to being one of the most important retail outlets in the country, they play a dominant role in fields ranging from fashions to fine arts.

A department store is a special category in Japan and comes under the Department Store Law. Under this law, any store that has 3,000 or more square meters of sales floor space and is located in Tokyo, Osaka, Kobe, Kyoto, Nagoya, Yokohama, or Kitakyushu is classified as a department store. A store that has from 1,500 to 3,000 square meters of floor space and is located in any other city in Japan is also legally registered as a department store. Government permission is required (from the Ministry of International Trade and Industry) before a department store can be expanded or a new one opened. The law also requires that department stores close by 6:00 P.M. (they open at 10:00 A.M.), that the big city stores close for a minimum of four days each month, and that the smaller ones close two days a month.

In addition to independent stores, there are 20 department store chains in Japan—including Mitsukoshi, Daimaru, Takashimaya, Tokyu, Hankyu, Meitetsu, and Seibu. Nationwide, they account for some ten percent of all retail sales; in urban areas, up to 17 percent. While the establishing of new department stores and the expansion of those already in existence is controlled by law—to help protect small retail shops—the number of department stores has almost doubled since 1953, and both floor and counter space are expanding steadily.

Mitsukoshi is both the largest and oldest department store in Japan and is therefore the "senior" in the field. As a result, it is said to be unofficially understood that no other department store would think of surpassing Mitsukoshi in floor space. This attitude, however, has not prevented several other stores from opening branches under different names, thereby surpassing Mitsukoshi in sales.

The largest item in department store sales is clothing, which accounts for about 41 percent of the total. This is followed by foodstuffs (17.4 percent), home furnishings (15.9 percent), small sundries (13.4 percent), and accessories (7.8 percent).*

Japanese department stores operate differently from those in the United States and Europe. For one thing, they buy less than 20 percent of their merchandise directly from manufacturers. When they do buy direct, the makers from which they buy are usually completely owned subsidiaries or otherwise closely affiliated firms. "Wholesalers generally have exclusive agent rights from all independent manufacturers; so we cannot buy directly," said a spokesman for Takashimaya's Research Department. "In many cases, the wholesaler has become a manufacturer, thereby controlling both functions," he added.

For the most part, Japanese department stores carry very little or no inventory. Stock turnover is therefore very rapid and wholesaler service is geared to making deliveries in a matter of minutes to hours. Despite the fact that they do not have to go to the expense and trouble of warehousing merchandise, however, the markup in Japanese department stores is from 25 to 40 percent (in contrast to the 35 to 40 percent in American department stores). The price of most of the merchandise sold in Japanese department stores is set by the supplier, not the store. The department stores have full return privileges; so it is not their problem if merchandise doesn't sell.

There are two types of department stores in Japan: the relatively new so-called mass stores, and the old "class" stores. The second type, which includes Takashimaya, Mitsukoshi, and Matsuzakaya, developed from drapery dealers whose origins go all the way back to early Tokugawa days (1603–1868). The new mass stores, like Seibu, Tokyu, Hankyu, and Meitetsu, were started by private railway companies at transportation crossroads. These stores originally specialized in convenience goods in the lower price ranges. But beginning in the 1960s, they began trading up, and this distinction is not always as important as some of the older prestige and class stores would like to believe.

Interestingly, the initial reason that the private railway firms went into the department store business was to get more passengers to use their transportation facilities rather than to compete with the old-line stores. They surmised—and rightly so—that people by the hundreds of thousands would move into the areas

*Source: Department Store Association.

161

their trains served, forming important residential districts around each of their local stations. They quickly became important retail outlets in themselves.

Some merchandise in Japanese department stores, such as curios, antiques, cameras, fresh fruit, juices, and art crafts, is on a consignment basis, but the overall percentage is low. In the past, some department stores have made a practice of giving discounts on special occasions or to special customers. There is now a growing tendency among these stores to discount on a wider basis in order to compete with outside discount stores. Some department stores have inaugurated self-service on a small scale, and the practice is expected to grow rapidly from now on.

At present, Japanese department stores have from 20 to 30 percent more employees than their American counterparts have, with the proportion of men to women running about the same in Japanese stores. Personnel costs in Japanese department stores average about seven percent, as compared to about 18 percent in the United States.

The present system of no inventory, fast turnover, free delivery, cultural exhibits, and other public services has begun to show signs of change, and part of it seems doomed to an early death. Until the early 1970s, free delivery cost Takashimaya one percent of gross sales, but the expense has been spiraling upward since. As a result, the store now offers free delivery only within Tokyo. "In the foreseeable future we will have to reduce this service further," a spokesman said. "The first changes will probably be to stop completely delivery of such items as beer, which has a low, controlled price, preventing a higher markup and restricting all delivery to a certain minimum purchase value."

Japanese department stores are being forced to change their system of buying in very small quantities from wholesalers and getting delivery on a moment's notice. Strangely enough, the biggest factor in this change is traffic congestion, which has considerably increased the time it takes for the wholesalers' delivery trucks to get to and from the stores. In many cases, stores are already having to allow wholesalers 24 hours or more delivery time. "Before long, they will have to build warehouses and stockrooms," said a member of the Department Store Association. All of Japan's department stores realize that the present system of buying from wholesalers on a piecemeal basis is a luxury that can't last, and they have begun subtle maneuvers to eliminate the bulk of the wholesalers standing between them and the manufacturers. Takashimaya has a central buying office for its stores and buys about 50 percent of its merchandise centrally. It does not expect to go much further than this because the individual stores need considerable leeway to account for differences in demand. Other department stores with branches buy varying percentages of their stock jointly.

Japanese department stores sell "everything except coffins." Most of them feature several restaurants, snack bars, ice cream and soft drink parlors, beauty shops, barbershops, pet departments (which stock such animals as parrots, monkeys, and baby alligators), travel and stock market offices. They also have small nursery rooms where mothers can take their babies for changing, feeding, and napping. The Osaka branch of Takashimaya includes an elaborate wedding hall with a number of adjoining reception rooms. The Odakyu Department Store in Tokyo's Shinjuku Ward offers just about everything except swimming pools.*

All of the independent department stores are active in other fields of business. Takashimaya owns 14 subsidiary companies, including two taxi companies, a real estate agency, an advertising and display agency, and a trading company. In 1960, all the leading department stores in Japan entered into tie-ups with banks to initiate credit sales. Shortly thereafter, the stores not already aligned with trading companies affiliated with one or more of the huge trading houses and began using them as suppliers of both domestic and imported goods. In the latter part of the 1960s, department stores also began affiliating with local general merchandise stores "as a means of protecting themselves against invasion by foreign department stores," noted a spokesman for the Department Store Association.

One of the biggest disadvantages of Japanese department stores is that they stock nothing in depth. The have one or two units of just about everything that is available in the country. But if they don't happen by coincidence to have your size and preference in

---

*Other businesses besides department stores also emphasize free customer service. A bank in Osaka, for example, offers depositors and visitors such services as free orange juice, color TV, and a large selection of books and magazines to read while waiting. A Fuji Bank branch in Tokyo features a lending library and a large children's playpen equipped with toys.

color, you cannot be served without special ordering. Furthermore, no one in the stores knows whether what you want is being made without checking with several wholesalers. Under the best of circumstances, this will require an hour or so and may take several days. Not many customers bother to have such inquiries made because they have learned from experience that manufacturers make the narrowest range possible and that there is practically no chance that it will be available.

There is one area in which Japanese department stores are world leaders. In a nation that is noted for its cultural consciousness, Japanese department stores are among the chief disseminators of culture. All of them devote large areas of two or three floors to permanent exhibition space and have up to six shows going at a time on a daily and weekly basis. Exhibits include ceramic masterpieces, folk arts, sculptures, paintings, and photographs, plus newly designed home products. The department stores support hundreds of the country's leading artists and craftsmen by displaying and selling their work and often purchasing it directly for their own use.

Supermarkets and Chain Stores

There were several dozen self-service stores in operation in Japan by the mid-1950s, but Tokyo's Kinokuniya, which opened in 1958, claims to have been the first supermarket. By 1971, there were well over 7,000 chain supermarkets throughout the country, with the number increasing at a rate of several dozen a month. The majority of these stores were members of one of 17 large chains, most of which are tied in financially with one or the other of the large trading companies—notably Mitsubishi, Mitsui, Marubeni, and C. Itoh.

Among the largest of the retail store chains are Daiei (classified as a supermarket), Ito Yokado, Seiyu, Jusco, Nichii, and Yuny. There are also several smaller chains.

Besides these chain supermarkets, there are stores that have affiliated themselves into voluntary chains in order to get better terms from manufacturers. These stores have contracts (nonexclusive) with manufacturers that allow the latter to exercise considerable control over the stores by the stores' stocking their own products and as far as payment is concerned. But the shops can stock merchandise from other manufacturers, as well.

Sales in supermarkets and convenience stores surpassed department store sales for the first time in 1972, and by 1979 these stores claimed 15 percent of the total retail sales market in the country, as compared to some ten percent held by department stores. Since then, the department stores have regained some of the ground they lost.

To qualify as a supermarket under MITI standards, a store must have a sales area larger than 100 square meters, and over half of this must be devoted to self-service. According to a recent survey by the Hakuhodo Advertising Agency, the chain supermarkets sell from 30 percent to 80 percent of the following product lines: detergents, hair oil, face soap, shampoo, toothpaste, canned fruit juice, canned fish, canned meat, instant coffee, black tea, synthetic seasonings, salad oil, butter, catsup, mayonnaise, chocolate, crackers, cake mix, macaroni, and pudding.

Some of the problems faced by the supermarkets in their early years (and overcome) were a limited supply of many products, items needing additional processing and packaging, undependable consumer buying patterns, and few officially inspected and graded products.

Supermarkets that emphasize the sale of food items must generally be near large commuter stations or on shopping streets because few shoppers shop in cars even when they have them. Because of this, many supermarkets concentrate on nonfood items.

In comparison with supermarkets in the U.S., Japanese stores are smaller in size, operate on a much higher profit margin, provide more customer service, sell less food, often display distressed merchandise as bargains, and in general have lower turnover.

Superstores and department stores now dominate the retail industry in Japan, as far as sales are concerned. Eighteen of Japan's retail chain stores have sales in excess of $1 billion a year, and the six largest have annual sales of over $2 billion each.

The early 1980s saw something of a revolution in Japan's retail industry as the department stores, chain stores, specialty stores, and convenience markets scrambled to keep or increase their shares of the trade. This revolution included the massive renovations of stores, which resulted in a virtual face-lift for the entire industry, the implementation of point-of-sale systems, the introduction of house brands, the streamlining of store staffs, and a strong move to cater to the new consumer demand for private, exclusive labels, with less emphasis on national brand names.

This revolution grew out of the maturation of the Japanese as consumers. They stopped buying things just because everybody else had them or because they were made by a nationally famous company and became much more discriminating in what they bought and where they shopped.

The Japanese now spend their money on education, household utilities, medical care, transportation and communication, reading and recreation, housing, furniture and household goods, other living expenditures, and food, in that order.

The "ceremonial events" in the lives of the Japanese usually determine when they make large expenditures. These events are the naming ceremony shortly after a child is born; the first birthday; at age three or four, when the child enters kindergarten; at the three, five, and seven children's festivals; at six, when they enter elementary school; at 12, when they enter junior high school; at 15, when they enter senior high school; at 18, upon entering college; at 20, when they become legal adults; at 22, when they finish college and enter a company; at 25 or 26, when they get married; at 27, when they have their first child; and between the ages of 55 and 60, when they retire.

During the 1960s and 1970s, the Japanese were obsessively brand conscious. Now they are the most demanding of the world's consumers when it comes to quality, reliability, durability, and exclusivity. The typical American-made product, for example, often does not sell in Japan because it has a scratch on it or because there are loose threads somewhere or because the back or bottom or interior of a product (which normally can't be seen) isn't finished.

The Japanese generally pay more for what they buy in real money terms, and they expect more—a lot more.

The Japanese are also extraordinarily fashion-conscious and swing from one fad to another, often within a period of a few months. Hundreds of the new products introduced into Japan each year have a lifetime of a year or less, or they are quickly imitated, and the market becomes diluted.

Another factor that foreign marketers must take into consideration is the color consciousness of the Japanese. These color values are derived from the use of sand, stone, plaster, straw, and natural woods in the traditional Japanese home and for the use of bright colors to complement these natural tones. Color preference is also linked with age. As a person grows older his or her choice of color in apparel and other things becomes more subtle and more conservative and tends toward neutral tones.

Young people generally pick subtle tones that blend well with their black hair and swarthy complexion or very bright primary colors for their leisure and recreational activities.

The Importance of "Detailers"

One of the keys to succeeding in the mass market in Japan is the effective use of "detailers" employed by manufacturers. Since most sales are made on a consignment basis, and retailers have the right to return unsold merchandise, it is necessary for makers to develop and maintain close relationships with both wholesalers and retailers in order to encourage and help them sell their goods—as well as to maintain a close watch on the volume of inventory on the retail level and keep manufacturers informed on the percentage that is likely to be returned.

These detail forces act as free consultants to both wholesale and retail levels, providing them with extra product information and, particularly where smaller retailers are concerned, making sure that the shops display their products to the best advantage. The detail men see that retailers who do an especially good job get special rebates.

The number of retailers in Japan remains a primary factor in any marketing program. In the apparel industry alone, there are some 67,000 retailers, of which over 80 percent have four or fewer employees and account for only about half of the sales. Department stores have about 20 percent of the apparel market in Japan, followed by superstores, with about 19 percent. Large apparel-specialty stores have about four percent of the market.

Retail outlets operate under one or more systems. They buy the goods outright from makers and wholesalers, receive them on consignment, or rent a portion of their stores out to wholesalers or makers for a commission on sales. This latter system is especially common among department stores, particularly where men's suits are concerned. Makers and wholesalers using this approach generally assign some of their own sales staff to work in these department stores.

Discovering the Female Market

It was not until the early 1980s that Japanese manufacturers and marketing experts began to accept the fact that their major domestic market was female—not male—and to direct their marketing efforts toward women. It is now estimated that somewhere around 80 percent of all private consumption expenditures in Japan are made by women, and this has brought on a new retail marketing strategy that, according to Hakuhodo Consumer Research Institute, consists of "fiction, female, and feeling."

To succeed in Japan today, most products have to be designed to please women, including many that are for men, because women make most of the buying decisions. A recent survey of department stores and apparel shops revealed that the wife makes the final decision of which suit or tie the husband buys. The same goes for major appliances, even for cars. Several of Japan's car makers now produce models especially designed for women. One, the Alto, made by Suzuki Motor Company, has a swivel driver's seat to make it easier for women wearing dresses or skirts to get in and out.

One of the most courted segments of the Japanese market are young, unmarried women who are working but still living at home and have substantial amounts of money to spend for clothing, accessories, gifts, and travel.

"Reading" the Japanese Market

Among the many attributes that foreign businessmen must have in order to succeed in Japan, two of the most important are flexibility and consistency. The businessman must be flexible enough to start over again when it comes to "reading" the Japanese market. It is not enough to accept the idea that the Japanese have different cultural values. The businessman must often be able to redesign his product, as well as his approach to marketing. And he must be determined and consistent. He must stop looking at quality on a cost-risk basis. To the Japanese, deliberately making a low-quality product is not only immoral, it is bad business.

The demand for high quality in both products and packaging is perhaps at its highest in prestige cosmetics. Reiko Lyster, founder and president of Elle International, which imports and retails the French line, Orlane, said: "The trait of appreciation for 'fineness' that is rooted in the Japanese consumer has not received proper attention from foreign manufacturers. There have been numerous instances of quality, prestige products losing out in the market simply because the packaging did not measure up to the standards expected of prestige products.

"This attention to detail is even more severely demanding when it comes to the marketing of prestige cosmetics. Golden-colored caps are expected to stay gold, without chipping or discoloring. Edges of a compact should have a delicate smoothness to the touch of fingers. Plastic compacts of blushers or eye shadows must be made to last even beyond the life of the product itself. Mirrors installed inside the compact should be of high quality."

There are some 450 medium-size to large cosmetic manufacturers in Japan and hundreds of smaller firms operating on the fringes of the market—not to mention the dozens of foreign brands that are sold in the marketplace. To keep its 30 percent share of the market, Shiseido makes 1,800 different products and sends its own specially trained cadre of 8,400 *biyobu-in* (beauty specialists) to the larger of the company's 25,000 storefront dealers to help in counter sales.

Besides its own beauty specialists, Shiseido runs a school at its head office at which selected employees from its 25,000 dealers are trained in how to apply and sell its cosmetics. In addition to this school, Shiseido operates an ¥850 million training facility in the hot spring resort city of Ito, 70 miles south of Tokyo, where it trains 20,000 sales people each year at a cost of well over ¥100 million annually.

Market Is Still "Japanese"

While cultural values in Japan *are* changing rapidly, and these changes are having a direct impact on the market, the market is still very much *Japanese* despite a surface patina of Westernization. Almost nothing can be taken for granted just because it "looks" American or Western. There is always a Japanese nuance that must be considered.

George Fields, the bilingual, bicultural chairman of the board of ASI Studies Inc., and a recognized authority on marketing in Japan, lists eight cultural influences that are at work in the consumer market in Japan: the dependency syndrome (the continued importance of authoritative brands/makers); groupism (which results in booms and busts in the marketplace); the tendency for young spenders to be mavericks until they join the adult work force as a *Shakai jin* (literally "society person"); the growing mobility in the work force, which will tend to level out market segmentation; the growing influence of consumer taste; the increasing importance of the role of the housewife as a money manager, as well as a money earner; a gradual rationalization of the clanlike ties that bind retailer and wholesaler relationships; and, finally, the revolution in housing in Japan (from traditionally styled houses and apartments to Western-style housing).

Fields added that despite all the changes occurring in Japan now and that are likely to occur in the future, the one constant will be the basic cultural values of the Japanese—and the foreign marketer must be familiar with these values to succeed in Japan.

A Case in Point

Mattel's entry into Japan with its phenomenally successful Barbie Doll is a classic case in point. Mattel had sold over 200 million of the dolls in some 60 countries before it approached the Japanese market. Mattel licensed Takara and Company, a leading Japanese dollmaker, to sell Barbie and Ken in Japan. They went over like lead balloons. Mattel was shocked. How could the doll be so successful in so many other countries and fall flat in Japan? How could five-year-old Japanese girls be so different from other girls of the same age?

Mattel asked Takara about the problem and was told that even five-year-olds in Japan have a strong cultural bias, and that Barbie and Ken were "too foreign" for the tastes of Japanese children.

Showing extraordinary acumen, Mattel Japanized Barbie by changing her blue eyes to brown, mussed her hair up, reduced her bra size, shortened her curvy legs, and then rechristened her Rikka-chan, a very Japanese name for a cute doll. Rikka-chan was an immediate hit. In fact, not only was Rikka-chan a big hit in Japan, *it became a collectors' item in the U.S.*

So much for the belief that children are children, even if they are Japanese.

Still, opportunities for entrepreneurial types, both Japanese and foreign, are growing rapidly in Japan. Examples of successes by individuals and small companies range from marketing household products and manufacturing bagels to franchising ice cream shops by a California company started in 1982.

In the case of the ice cream shops, company representative Ranji Wakwella said: "Winning in business in Japan is a matter of perseverance and flexibility. We decided to go with Junichi Matsumoto, an entrepreneur whom we think has a future. He is a young, energetic man who is open to work with us and develop the market with us. He is one of the young, new generation in Japan who can move fast. The reason we didn't choose a major corporation is because of the endless power struggles, decisions by committees, meetings, etc. With Matsumoto, we established ourselves in a relatively short period of time."

Enduring Traditions

Despite the Western facade that much of Japan now presents to the world, there are many things that have not changed in essence for hundreds of years. Toyama-Do medicine, for example, is symbolic of the tradition-bound aspect of product distribution in Japan.

In 1690, when Shigehiro Itakura, the lord of what is now Fukushima Prefecture, was in Edo (Tokyo) to take his turn at the *shogun's* court, he came down with a severe stomachache. One of his fellow Lords, Masatoshi Maeda, from the fief of Toyama, happened to have some medicine he had bought from a *ronin* (masterless) *samurai*, who had picked it up in Nagasaki. Maeda gave some of the medicine to Itakura.

The concoction worked, and Itakura was lavish in his thanks. When Maeda returned to his own domain, he ordered his retainers to set up a factory to produce the medicine in volume and to develop a system for selling it all over the country. Maeda's retainers hired peddlers to sell the medicine door to door, carrying their supply in backpacks. Each peddler had an established route that he covered on foot, once or twice a year. On the first visit to a home, he left a box of the medicines. On the next visit, he collected payment for any of the medicines that had been used.

Over the following decades, Toyama-Do medicine became a standard household item throughout Japan, making Maeda one of the richest domains in the country.

Toyama-Do medicine is still peddled door to door and office to office throughout Japan exactly the same way it was some 300 years ago. Instead of walking their routes, however, Toyama-Do

derstand and use the essentials of Western art. However, the rate of improvement among unusually progressive firms and by the larger advertising agencies soon accelerated to the point of becoming increasingly visible year by year and is now generally excellent.

Product Displays

The tradesman's traditional concept of displaying merchandise was to show everything he had. This idea still clings in Japan. Every conceivable bit of space—often including the ceiling—is used, making many of the shops appear like overcrowded bat caves. Department stores are also strongly influenced by the urge to show samples of everything they are able to supply. The resulting profusion of goods is very impressive, particularly to foreign visitors who are used to more open space and less colorful exhibits.

On the average, the Japanese are better at arranging attractive—even though crowded—displays than Westerners are. This is the result of the tremendous amount of aesthetic training experienced by all Japanese, both formally and informally. The ordinary clerk is very often capable of developing and presenting a good product display without previous experience and with very little direction. This gives Japanese merchants an advantage over their Western counterparts.

Chapter 12

Japan's Distribution Labyrinth

*"An important factor that troubles many
American marketing men sent to Japan is that the
size and importance of their company in the United
States means nothing in the Japanese market."*
—A market research executive

Ties That Bind

Many categories of product distribution in Japan are complicated and difficult for the foreign marketer to understand, appreciate, and work with. The process is simple when it is put into words because the terms are the same ones commonly used in the West. But the similarity tends to end with the words. As could be expected, the most important factors determining the nature of distribution are traditional; they are a direct inheritance from the Tokugawa (1603—1868) period: (1) the feudalistic relationships that exist between the people involved; (2) the peculiar role of the still-powerful wholesalers; and (3) the fact that there are so many retail outlets in the country. In the Tokyo area alone, for example, there are over 20,000 retailers handling soap products.

The first factor, in addition to incorporating all the inconsistencies and handicaps resulting from interpersonal rather than objective business relationships, also functions as a tremendous barrier to change and the implementation of modern merchandising techniques. Because the distribution system in Japan is generally based on complicated personal relations, the foreign businessman cannot simply walk in and expect to use the same approach or techniques that he uses in the U.S. or Europe.

Max Factor's success in Japan is said to be due in considerable degree to the fact that it "ignored the mechanism but not the underlying principles" of the traditional system and established its own. Certainly, if the foreign firm is able to set up its own system,

175

It is hard for the Westerner, particularly the American, to understand and appreciate this aspect of business in Japan. Occasions when the Japanese businessman's sense of obligation overrides his business sense are daily occurrences. This state of affairs often reduces the foreign businessman to a mass of frustrated impulses and values. Unless the foreigner dealing with Japan understands this factor for what it is, it is difficult, if not impossible, for him to adjust his views to the point where a workable arrangement can be made.

Direct Sales Outlets

Manufacturers in several fields in Japan—notably fabrics, confections, and home electrical appliances—own varying numbers of retail outlets, which are called *chokubai-ten,* or literally "direct sales shops." In the case of fabric manufacturers, these company-owned shops sell only material, not made-up goods. In other fields, the shops sell a complete line of finished goods. All of the shops are located in major population centers. Fujiya Confectionery, for example, owns several hundred stores throughout Japan and runs them on a chain-store basis. Japan's largest confectionery manufacturer, Meiji Seika, owns and operates a number of coffee shops but no actual retail shops. Toshiba, Hitachi, Matsushita, and the other large electrical appliance makers also operate their own retail shops.

Exclusive Franchise Shops

In addition to the *chokubai-ten,* or completely owned direct sales shops, the large manufacturers in most consumer fields in Japan also use what are known as *semmon-ten,* or "specialty shops," which handle products or material from one maker only. *Semmon-ten* first began to appear in about 1957. They are privately owned and function as exclusive agent outlets. Generally, these shops purchase outright from their manufacturer-supplier on 30- to 90-day credit. But where a new product or material is concerned, the maker gives it to the shop on a consignment basis for a predetermined test period. Toyo Rayon, for example, now utilizes several hundred *semmon-ten.*

The big advantage of the exclusive specialty shop is that it stocks a much wider range of styles and sizes than ordinary retailers or department stores do. The large manufacturers supplying these shops also do a considerable amount of advertising for them. As a result, the small general retailer—already suffering from department store and chain store competition—operates at a very low profit margin. No one will say that they are disappearing, but they are not increasing in number. Some are amalgamating and becoming miniature department stores.

Directly Owned Sales Shops

Many of the larger manufacturers in most fields in Japan have wholly owned separate firms responsible for domestic consumer sales. In the case of Tokyo Shibaura Electric Company (Toshiba), for example, sales are handled by Toshiba Shoji (Trading) Company, which has nine major branches and 70 subbranches throughout the country. Under these 70 subbranches are some 600 franchised wholesalers who distribute to retailers. Around 200 of the 600 wholesalers handle only Toshiba products. The others handle competing lines, as well. A second distribution system used by Toshiba consists of nine wholly owned *geppu-semmon-sha*, or "credit specialty firms," which buy on cash terms from Toshiba Shoji and distribute to selected dealers on a consignment basis.*

Hitachi's sales organization, known as Hitachi Katei Denki (Hitachi Electrical Home Products Distributor), differs slightly from Toshiba Shoji in that most of its wholesale agents are exclusive. Matsushita Denki (National Products) owns most of the stock in its chain of some 50 wholesalers, which function as sole agents. Sony has its own wholesale distribution network. So far, all the other firms in this field sell directly to wholesalers. Meiji Seika, in addition to being Japan's largest manufacturer of confections, is also a large producer of sugar, bread, milk, and pharmaceuticals. Sales of all the Meiji group, except for milk, are handled by Meiji Shoji, which has six branches in the main population centers of the country and 80 subbranches in the secondary areas. From the subbranches, the merchandise goes both to wholesalers and directly to retailers. The wholesalers often have two more subwholesalers under them.

*Cash terms in Japan usually mean promissory notes up to 180 days.

Meiji Seika and Meiji Shoji set prices jointly. "We set two prices, one for primary wholesalers and one for retailers. We don't care how many secondary or tertiary wholesalers may be used—our price doesn't change," a company spokesman said. If one of their wholesalers sells above a certain volume, he gets a rebate from the buying price. Shoji buys from Seika on 60 days' credit. When sales are direct to retailers, credit terms are usually 30 days. "We prefer that the retail price of our merchandise be the same for all types of outlets, but there is some discounting by supermarkets," the spokesman continued. "Also, many of the largest wholesalers in the confectionery field specialize in selling to thousands of *pachinko* (pin ball) shops, which give the merchandise away as prizes. Then brokers buy the prizes from the winners at 60 to 70 percent of their wholesale value and sell them back to the *pachinko* shops— which are usually controlled by gangs, and have hired thugs around to watch over things. We don't approve of this, but it represents such an important percentage of our business that we can't afford to cut it out." Meiji Shoji gets 60 days' credit for foods and confections, 90 days for medicines. The average retailer purchases twice a month. Coffee, tea, and juices are bought in large volume over longer periods.

Fujiya, third largest of the big four confectionery manufacturers, with hundreds of retail stores throughout Japan, has no sales company and relies on wholesalers. Morinaga, number two in total sales last year, and Glico, smallest of the Big Four, have the same system as Meiji Seika. Under the Big Four are several hundred small firms, all of which specialize in one particular line. Lotte, for example, is the largest manufacturer of chewing gum in Japan. The makers of traditional Japanese-type confections (sweetened bean paste, etc.) are family groups and number in the thousands.

Primary Wholesalers

Altogether, there are approximately 230,000 registered primary wholesalers in Japan and several thousand unregistered ones. At the top of this heap are several hundred firms generally referred to as class A wholesalers. These include all the giant trading companies, which are involved in such products as steel and heavy machinery. Their main function is to buy merchandise in large volume directly from manufacturers, which they then sell to other wholesalers. Most of these primary wholesalers are relatively old firms; they have very strong personal ties with their manufacturers that transcend purely business considerations.

In the case of the pharmaceutical industry, however, makers have their own salesmen calling on retailers, and they deliver merchandise directly to dealers. But in most cases, there are at least two wholesalers between the manufacturer and retailer who process the paper work involved in each transaction and tack on a considerable markup for themselves.

Japan's primary wholesalers owe their powerful position both to feudalistic ties that exist between them and their sources and to their traditional function as financiers to the manufacturing trade. They have been able to maintain almost complete control over their suppliers because until recently most of the makers concerned were small in size and couldn't perform the distribution function themselves. Examples of primary wholesalers who in the last few decades have branched out and become large general trading companies include C. Itoh, Marubeni-Iida, Toyo Menka, Nichimen Jitsugyo, and Gosho.

Secondary Wholesalers

Beneath the primary wholesalers, which generally function as manufacturers' exclusive agents, is a much larger number of so-called secondary wholesalers, who buy from the primary wholesalers. These secondary wholesalers, in turn, sell both to large retail outlets and to a vast network of subwholesalers who service the thousands of tiny shops and stalls located throughout the country. Many of the secondary wholesalers are large, complex organizations, often completely overshadowing the primary wholesalers from whom they buy. Most would prefer to buy directly from manufacturers but are prevented from doing so by the exclusive rights of the primary wholesalers.

Tertiary Wholesalers

There are no exact figures for the number of tertiary wholesalers in Japan. If both registered and unregistered operations were included, the total number would probably be well over 300,000. A big majority of these are run by one man with from one to half a dozen helpers. Transportation ranges from bicycles to small trucks.

The number of outlets a manufacturer must have to achieve adequate distribution of consumer products in Japan is often enormous, as this extraordinary proliferation of retailers and wholesalers indicates. Billing is usually to the primary wholesalers, but the merchandise is just as often shipped directly to secondary or tertiary wholesalers.

Trade practices generally permit retailers and wholesalers to return anything at any time for full credit. Rebates in cash and kind are the rule, and terms of payment are often adjusted on a case-by-case basis, with sales personnel wheeling and dealing with considerable latitude, depending on the outlet's size and importance.

"Market Shock" and American Companies in Japan

It is frequently observed by old-timers in Japan that most of the frustration suffered by Americans trying to establish a foothold in the Japanese market results from the fact that the market is different from what they expect it to be, and they can't easily readjust their thinking. Another important factor that troubles many American marketing men sent to Japan is that the size and importance of their company in the United States means nothing to the Japanese market. They have to start at the bottom and work up, keeping in mind that all phases of business in Japan—particularly the marketing phase—are based on personal relations, trust, and obligations that have been building anywhere from decades to generations.

Before he can adapt the distribution system in Japan to fit his own needs, the foreign marketer first has to understand how the Japanese system works. "Several of the marketing failures that have occurred in Japan happened because the foreign marketing men felt that they were selling one thing, while the Japanese felt they were buying another," said Fred Perry, bilingual director of Pacific Marketing (Japan), a research company. "The marketer must know not only how his product is inherently perceived, but also how it is viewed economically and emotionally, as well as from the viewpoint of its newness, uniqueness, and any previous history in Japan."

The marketing man must also know his competition—the products in the same field, as well as the Japanese marketing men handling them. What they may lack in American technical marketing experience, they make up for with their intimate knowledge of the market, their trade ties, and by having few, if any, communications problems with their management. In most cases, the foreign company must be willing to invest heavily in advertising and public relations to get a foothold in the Japanese market.

It is possible but tricky to change a distribution channel once it has been set up. In order to avoid making enemies, you should get as much compliance and acceptance as possible from all parties concerned each step of the way.

Complexity in the Food Business

The distribution system in the food business is especially complex. There are over 400,000 wholesalers, most of which are tied in very closely with networks of retailers that they either finance or support in some way. The personal nature of the business in Japan makes it extremely difficult for an outsider to break in to the system. Commenting on the system, H. W. Allen Sweeney, Executive Vice President of Yamazaki-Nabisco, said that it was not a distribution system but a social system and that anyone who ignored that essential fact was in for serious trouble.

In addition to the huge number of retail outlets, many of which are minuscule in size, with very limited shelf and storage space, and the closed nature of the distribution system, there is also the payment problem. Payment is usually in cash, 60 days or more after invoice, and must be collected in person by cadres of salesmen.

Virtually all foreign food products sold in Japan must first be reformulated to suit Japanese tastes, with specific consideration given to the fact that the Japanese perceive sweetness and saltiness differently than most Westerners do.

Redesigning the packaging of foreign food products being sold in Japan is just as important as Japanizing the taste. Once again, the Japanese have been conditioned over the centuries to a very sophisticated level of package design that verges on fine art. Their packaging may be overdesigned from the Western viewpoint, but it is an undeniable fact of business life in Japan, and anyone who ignores it will pay the price.

Besides the art quality of packaging in Japan, there are many other factors that must be taken into consideration—the size and shape, weight, plastic containers versus glass, and so on.

Because there are so many new products introduced into the Japanese market in many categories, especially processed foods and clothing, there is often a system in which retailers can return unsold goods for full credit. In the processed food industry, it is the manufacturer who accepts this risk. In the clothing industry it is intermediate wholesalers.

The Apparel Industry

There are some 10,000 apparel wholesalers in Japan, classified as primary, secondary, or tertiary wholesalers. The primary wholesalers, also known as "origin" wholesalers, buy apparel from one or more makers and sell to secondary wholesalers, as well as large retail outlets. The largest of the primary wholesalers are in Tokyo, Kyoto, and Osaka, and some of them are known as *shusanchi*, or "maker wholesalers," since they have large numbers of cottage-level makers working under them as commissioned makers, in addition to distributing.

Most secondary apparel wholesalers sell to retailers outside of the major metropolitan areas, but their role is gradually being usurped by primary wholesalers because leading retailers prefer to go directly to the major trading companies and *shusanchi* wholesalers. One of the reasons for the tenacity of the secondary wholesalers is that they often provide financing for retailers.

The tertiary wholesalers service the thousands of tiny retail shops throughout the country, but they, too, are gradually losing out to the larger wholesale firms.

Because of the role of wholesalers in Japan, Japanese retail prices are four to five times higher than wholesale prices—as compared to two times in the U.S. and Western Europe. Because there are additional costs in importing goods into Japan, most of them are priced far higher than competing domestic goods by the time they reach the retail level.

Direct-mail marketing is growing relatively rapidly, but still makes up only a fraction of the retail sales in Japan. One of the major obstacles to the development of DM marketing in Japan is the high postage rates, but there are predictions that it will be one of the growth industries of the next two or three decades.

Direct marketing specialists say there are several factors that will contribute to the expansion of the industry in Japan: the shifting of urban population to suburban bedroom communities, women having less time for shopping because more and more of them are staying in the workforce after marriage and rejoining the workforce after their children are raised, the highly competitive retail situation in Japan, and a growing demand for specialized products and services that lend themselves to direct marketing.

The Japan Direct-Mail Association has some 135 member companies, and they account for over 80 percent of the direct-mail sales in the country. Several of these companies are Japan-American joint ventures. The largest direct-mail firm in Japan is Fuji Sankei Living Service, which produces a 500-page catalog of 3,000 items three times a year.

Chapter 13

How the Japanese Sell

"Selling in Japan is a humiliating experience."
—N. Mizumura President
Mizumura Company

The Japanese Philosophy of Selling

Salesmanship, as the term is understood and used in the United States, is still exceptional in Japan—despite the extraordinary economic success achieved in the past several decades. Buying and selling among manufacturers, wholesalers, and retailers are primarily based on personal connections, liberal applications of obligation-building entertainment, and the old-fashioned rebate.

Following industrialization in the 1870s and 1880s, most businessmen continued the same pattern of selling that had prevailed for centuries. As the economy grew in size, various factors continued to work against the development of Western-type merchandising, including the appearance of vast numbers of tiny factories and equally tiny wholesalers and retail shops.

Japanese management did not begin to look seriously at the Western art of selling until the 1960s, when it became impossible to ignore the success of some of the foreign firms selling in Japan—and the threat that other foreign firms would soon be competing with Japanese companies in their own market.

The traditional Japanese method of merchandising remains especially strong in the industrial goods sector of business. Few contracts exist. The participants are linked together by ties far more binding than written documents. The relationships between the makers, wholesalers, and retailers in this field are also characterized by what we consider to be an extraordinary willingness to be flexible in pricing, sales terms, and other marketing factors.

Salesmanship in the hundreds of thousands of "Mom and Pop" shops throughout the country also remains practically nonexistent. In most such shops, family members spend their time in the living quarters in the rear when there is no one in the store. Customers are expected to call out when they enter or when they find whatever they want.

Selling in Department Stores

Clerks in Japanese department stores (except for those in the basement food departments, and those assigned to the store by manufacturers introducing a new product or sponsoring a special sale) are instructed not to try to sell anything to anybody. The philosophy behind this is that people come to department stores to enjoy themselves, as well as shop—to avail themselves of such department store services as restaurants, coffee parlors, cultural exhibits, and rooftop recreational facilities. "Probably more than 60 percent of the people who enter Japanese department stores have no intention whatsoever of buying anything, even though they remain in the store half a day. If our sales clerks should approach these people they would be embarrassed and offended," said a spokesman for a leading department store. "Since it is virtually impossible to distinguish between a visitor who is just passing time and someone who actually wants to make a purchase, our clerks are told to wait for them to make the first move."

As a result of this policy, it often seems that clerks in department stores are hiding in an attempt to avoid seeing the shopper, and it is often necessary to go to extremes to get their attention. The more negative the approach, the better they impress potential customers, in the opinion of the management. "If a store like Macy's set up in Tokyo and kept its American attitudes and sales techniques, it would fail. By and large, Japanese customers don't like American-type selling," added another department store executive.

One of the more conspicuous exceptions to the nonselling in department stores are the cosmetic "beauty bars" set up periodically in the stores by cosmetic manufacturers to introduce new products. The pretty girls who staff these beauty bars are employees of the cosmetic companies rather than the department stores. They have been taught to sell aggressively—and effectively!

Another important factor in many department stores, particularly on weekends, holidays, and other heavy shopping days, is the fantastic crowding—especially in the terminal or "mass" department stores. On such days, these stores are frequently so packed with people that one can move about in the aisles only with the greatest difficulty. To even approach providing this mass with good service would require a clerk for every square meter of floor space. But then it would be so crowded nobody could move.

Selling in Specialty Shops

Despite the department store policy, the buying behavior in Japan is changing among the younger people. They don't expect or want the negative etiquette preferred by their parents. Their time values are different also, and they want faster service. Some department stores recognize this new factor and admit that there is a need for two sales approaches—one for the older generation and one for the younger. "Our clerks will have to develop the ability to judge which approach to use on a customer," a spokesman said.

Positive selling on a retail level has, in fact, already gained a firm foothold in Japan in specialty shops, particularly those employing young clerks or operated by younger owner-managers. This phenomenon is most commonly found in fashion and cosmetic shops. The recent experience of the wife of a friend emphasizes the development. She went to a cosmetic store specifically to buy some Ban deodorant. The young female clerk recommended a deodorant made by Shiseido. My friend's wife replied that she preferred Ban. The clerk persisted, and finally the customer agreed to take the Shiseido product to avoid an argument. There is every reason to believe that this type of aggressive selling will continue to expand.

Door-to-Door and Direct-Mail Selling

Despite the cultural obstacles, door-to-door selling in Japan is also growing in importance. Pioneered on a large scale by Pola Cosmetics Company in the 1950s (in a takeoff on Avon), there are now many companies that engage in this type of selling, including some of the automobile sales companies.

Door-to-door selling in Japan would no doubt develop at an even more rapid pace if it were not for a Gangster Prevention Ordinance, which was passed in 1961. This law is primarily aimed at protecting Japan's easily intimidated population from a large gangster element, but it also covers high-pressure selling. The second clause of Article Six states that a person will be punished if he displays sales articles, sits down, or does not leave the premises immediately when his sales or other offer is turned down. Several door-to-door sales companies, including Pola and Encyclopaedia Britannica, have run afoul of this law.

While there are no huge mail-order houses in Japan at this point, the volume of direct-mail selling is also increasing significantly. Among the most active in this area are department stores, publishing houses, and textile manufacturers.

Changing the Salesman's Image

In the 1960s, an effort was made by several leading Japanese firms to overcome the almost pariah-like stigma that was attached to outside salesmen. Prior to that, a few movies and a number of TV programs had taken up the "untouchable" status of sales personnel in Japan, but there had been no planned effort by business to improve the image of salesmen. The leader in this new attempt was a securities firm. The campaign consisted of a series of television commercials that showed the company's salesmen as handsome, well-groomed young men who were an instant success with the younger children of prospective clients, with the parents, and finally with their attractive, eligible daughters. Once acceptance on this personal level had been established, the commercials implied that the sale was a foregone conclusion.

But salesmen in Japan still have a hard time of it, particularly those who call on the large retail firms. As a very Westernized Japanese sales executive presented the problem: "To Americans, buying and selling are both formally accepted areas of business. In Japan, this is not so. Being a buyer here makes you king; being a seller makes you a beggar. The various American techniques of selling are generally useless. In the United States, the product talks. If you have a good product you can walk in and show it to a purchasing agent. He may not buy it, but at least he can automatically be expected to treat you as a human being. Here, if you don't have the proper type of introduction, you generally can't get into the batter's box. Every business call has to be preceded by careful and intricate planning, keeping in mind not only the common Japanese attitudes about business transactions, but also the personal idiosyncrasies of each individual concerned. Even a simple sales call requires subtle diplomacy and often intrigue of the highest order. This puts a serious strain on the salesman in Japan that few foreigners take into account. In addition to having the right connections," he went on, "the reception that can be expected by the salesman representing foreign products here also depends on whether or not his product line is known. Quality and price don't enter into it."

Going in Headfirst

Selling without an introduction in Japan is known as *tobi-komi*, which means "jump in" or plunge in headfirst (the connotation being that you may bump your head on a stone). There is some selling of this type now, and it is becoming more common, but the very frequent use of this word indicates that it is still not accepted. In Japan, one doesn't rush in and talk about product benefits.

Not all of the comments on outside selling in Japan were critical. One American, a graduate of Harvard Business School who eventually succeeded in establishing a consulting-market research operation in Japan, got his most important account by walking in without an appointment and without knowing anyone in the firm. "I've had more than my share of disappointments in attempting to sell Japanese companies, but there is no hard and fast rule," he said. He added that "maintaining personal-company relations in Japan after making a sale is a nerve-wracking, frustrating thing."

Another American in Japan for a year said: "Much of the way we do business in Japan is forced upon us by what other foreign companies do and the advice we get from businessmen who have been here for some time. When I first arrived, everyone told me I'd never be able to get a Japanese company to buy our services by making personal calls on them. But I've been very successful, and 60 percent of our accounts were signed up on my first visit." This man continued: "I've been selling here for over a year now, making an average of four calls a day and have yet to meet another American salesman on the road. There are a few, but most foreign businessmen in Japan don't sell. They direct a group of Japanese salesmen—telling them how to sell a market they themselves don't know."

Purchasing agents, in Japanese department stores particularly, are described as arrogant toward salesmen. "Even when they want your line, they will not deal with you if you don't approach them through 'proper' channels," said one salesman. Another salesman for a Japanese company recounted his efforts to sell a certain product to a leading Tokyo department store. The only connection he could establish within the store was with a man in the Foreign Department. On the basis that an introduction from the Foreign Department was better than none, he got in to see the purchasing agent of the proper department. The purchasing agent was very frank with him. "I like your product, but your introduction from our own Foreign Department doesn't warrant my doing any business with you," he told the salesman.

Every sales call requires an entirely new plan of approach and a new campaign. The man who introduces you must have weight equal to or heavier than the man you want to deal with. The Japanese have no compunctions about handing out introductions, even to relative strangers, but the ritual of presentation is very formal, indeed. One Japanese businessman confided: "Using the American system is time-consuming, and the probability of success is slim, even though our system is perceptibly changing. My advice to the foreign firm is to use the Japanese system where it is expected if you want quick results."

Rebates and "Service"

Sales in Japan are predicated on rebates and are tied very closely to what the Japanese refer to as "service." But "service" in Japan is not related to service in the United States. It has nothing to do with efficiency during the buying process or with aftermarket service. It relates, instead, to catering to the personal desires and interests of the people involved in business transactions. This includes entertaining and feeding them, giving them gifts, and/or making yourself available to perform other types of personal favors. This is what the Japanese call "service without reward"—something that they regularly say "you foreigners can't understand."

There are very few Japanese businessmen who understand and use the word "service" as Americans do. This applies to the so-called service industries, as well as to product makers. Japanese banks, for example, don't return cancelled checks or issue periodic statements as American banks do. The large appliance makers, although they are making some progress, sometimes give terrible service. They may lack parts for repairs because they try to make everything themselves and sometimes end up with limited quantities of replacement parts. In Japan, getting "service" also means getting a lower price in the form of a discount or rebate.

Rebates cause salesmen a great deal of trouble. They take many forms. In the freight-forwarding business, for example, one firm literally buys its accounts by giving a ten percent kickback on a contract basis. A type of kickback practiced by other forwarders is to undermark the weight of the shipment. Larger forwarders put their own men in the shippers' offices on a full-time basis to handle all the paper work.

Another of the problems facing salesmen calling on Japanese firms is the budgeting system. Budgets are established twice a year for forthcoming expenses. Unless the case is exceptional, you cannot go in and expect to sell anything for which they are not budgeted. It is therefore sometimes necessary to wait up to six months for a sale that might otherwise be accomplished in a matter of hours.

A number of years ago, one of the biggest problems of salesmen in Japan was getting someone to look at their samples. Said one salesman: "Japanese businessmen used to have the idea that if they looked at a salesman's sample, they were obligated to buy it. They are now a lot more sophisticated. They have seen all the competing products in our line; so it is necessary to sell them with auxiliary aids. Young people are more willing to look at the samples we carry."

Learning a Lesson

One of the factors that has held manufacturers back in their sales efforts is the custom of using the same agents their competitors use for both sales and service. Because of this system, they build up little or no product identification or loyalty among either dealers or consumers, both of whom are swayed only by whoever gives them the best credit terms. This has been adequate for domestic business, but it doesn't work in international trade because no one else does it. Another drawback that applies to the machinery field is the custom of sending out as salesmen ordinary engineers instead of sales engineers. As a result, their representatives don't know financing or any other of the several important factors involved in closing a sale.

After they had been on the mass production merry-go-round for several years, Japan's large manufacturers recognized the necessity of creating markets for their goods. Among the most active in this field were the large appliance makers, particularly Matsushita, Hitachi, and Toshiba, which account for more than 15 percent of the total production in the industry.

Hitachi's approach consisted of organizing family centers and women's clubs for the purpose of familiarizing members with Hitachi products. Each of these clubs and centers is equipped with a music hall and an auditorium, which members are invited to use free. Hitachi also has a panel of PR advisors made up of prominent people who are asked to criticize the company's sales promotion and publicity activities and offer suggestions to improve them. As a result of these programs, Hitachi controls a network of 20,000 dealers throughout the country. Toshiba and Matsushita, on the other hand, each have more than 40,000 retailers handling their products.

Toshiba's hard-sell system consists of a tape-recorded correspondence course for its dealers. Set up in cooperation with Toshiba Trading Company, the course, called Home Study Course in Technical Service, is aimed at improving the technical knowledge of the owners and employees of shops acting as exclusive Toshiba dealers. In addition, Toshiba has a chain of cooking schools in various parts of the country, the idea being that every woman who attends the school and learns how to use Toshiba appliances to her best advantage will be likely to buy them. Toshiba also sponsors meetings that feature cultural lectures and cooking lessons. These are known as Toshiba Home Life Circles.

Matsushita, often a maverick in Japan's business world, goes about its hard sell in a different way. It has a Factory Visitors' Section, which attempts to get a million people a year to visit its factories in different parts of the country. Matsushita has also arranged with sightseeing bus companies to include its factories in their tours. In inviting people to tour its plants, Matsushita puts special emphasis on getting the following groups in this order: housewives, PTA officers, school teachers, students, its dealers, the dealer's best customers, and, finally, foreign tourists.

It Can Be Done!

A growing number of successful marketing operations in Japan that have been developed outside the established distribution networks emphasize the fact that firms going into the market for the first time do not necessarily have to follow existing patterns of distribution or selling.

It is critical, however, that any company wanting to develop its own distribution system in the Japanese market make a thorough study of all the factors involved and work closely with local experts to develop the necessary network of personal connections in all levels of the trade.

Chapter 14

The Japanese Way of Advertising

"Advertising as it is done in Japan today is not the right way or the wrong way; but the Japanese way."

—Kaz Fujita
Advertising and marketing consultant

The Postwar Background

Assessing advertising in Japan in 1946, the late Hideo Yoshida (then executive director of Dentsu, the nation's largest advertising agency) said it was 50 years behind that of the United States. The growth of advertising was complicated by the fact that, as late as 1948, a newsprint shortage and other handicaps limited newspapers to four-page editions twice a week. Magazines had ceased to exist as an advertising medium. Under such circumstances, the small amount of advertising was understandable.

Even the small amount of advertising that was available shortly after the end of the Pacific war in 1945 was more than double what could have been accepted. When space rates were decontrolled from wartime regulations in 1947, the printing media market for advertising was firmly entrenched, and a series of high-rate increases followed immediately.

The reappearance and growth of advertising agencies in postwar Japan kept pace with the nation's economic recovery. In 1947, there were five large agencies and dozens of smaller ones. Except for a number of structural reforms by Dentsu and Hakuhodo (the second largest agency), these postwar agencies were identical with their prewar predecessors, which had functioned more as space brokers than advertising agencies in the Western sense. Both Dentsu and Hakuhodo, however, made rapid progress in adopting some facets of the American agency format and, for the first time, began to display some interest in learning what American-style

197

advertising was all about. Half a dozen or so of the lesser Japanese agencies (Daiko, Sanshodo, Standard, Nitto, and Mannensha) also began modernizing both their facilities and systems.

Commenting on this period of Japan's advertising history, Kaz Fujita, an American advertising and marketing consultant associated with Nitto Agency, said: "Advertising didn't have the same meaning or importance in Japan as it had in the United States. Japan's economy boomed after 1945 because there was such a tremendous demand for goods of all kinds. Manufacturers could sell anything they made. There was no need for product advertising. The only promotional effect made by companies was to display their name before the public, emphasizing their size and long history. During these years, Japan was a seller's market."

Advertising in Japan Today

Advertising came of age in Japan in about 1967. Many of the policies and practices that characterized the advertising world in Japan during its early years and on into the 1950s and early 1960s still exist, however. That is, advertising is still done in the Japanese way. But it has grown up, become sophisticated, and is now one of the most powerful social and economic influences in the country.

Japan is one of the world's most difficult markets to sell, but it is also one of the most profitable for those who succeed. The Japanese are far more advertising-oriented than are consumers in many other countries. It is therefore necessary for a company that wants to maintain or increase its market share to advertise continuously and more heavily than is usually the case elsewhere—in as many media as possible.

Warned one American employee of a top Japanese agency: "To be a success in the Japanese market, the foreign advertiser must have three things: money, time, and patience. The Japanese do not respond to the American fireball approach. They do not get excited. Everything must be done step by step. And for the foreign company, the very first step is to decide how much the Japanese market is worth."

One facet of advertising in Japan that tends to upset foreign businessmen is that the well-known American rule of one-agency, one-product is not observed by the Japanese agencies. Japanese companies are obligated by tradition and deep personal commitments to divide their accounts among several agencies—although a few companies do give all their business to one agency. This is further complicated by the strongly entrenched custom of splitting accounts in terms of media rather than product lines.

It is Dentsu's opinion that the one-agency, one-product rule will not be feasible for Japan any time in the near future. Dentsu spokesmen also question its merit in the United States. Their point is that the application of this rule would reduce the billings of all the agencies to the point where they could not offer full service if they wanted to. In an effort to forestall objections by its foreign accounts, Dentsu has what is described as a "series of vertical subdivisions" in its planning and creative departments, which are designed to keep competing products apart.

There is a lot more speculation in the agency business in Japan than there is in the United States. Japanese firms divide their ad budget by medium. Several agencies make up to four separate presentations each in an effort to get just a small share of a firm's budget for only one medium. Half a dozen different agencies end up getting a share of the budget for one product—the size of their share depending on the medium they represent. The agency placing an advertisement in one of the larger media has to sign a contract—which the medium can unilaterally break—and make a deposit on the contracted space. If the agency subsequently does anything the medium disapproves of, it may cancel the contract without further ado. Since Japanese advertisers don't usually pay within the customary 30 days, agencies must have a large amount of operating capital.

Generally, only the larger advertising agencies in Japan can place ads in all of the major newspapers. Newspaper space is still at a premium, and the papers will accept ads only from agencies that have been "appointed" by them. Further, the larger agencies prebuy space in the newspapers, guaranteeing that it cannot be used by other agencies. Smaller advertising agencies, therefore, often have to go through one of the larger agencies to place advertising for an account.

This problem is compounded by the advertisers' practice of delaying payment of bills for up to six months. Some advertisers won't pay at all unless pressured regularly. Regardless of the size of an advertiser, a company wanting to launch a new product in Japan cannot by itself determine the amount of advertising space it is going to use or when it is going to use it. This has to be negotiated between the agency and the media. Japanese agencies also regularly buy space in certain media solely to contribute to the maintenance of good relations with those media.

Agency commissions are often negotiable with both the client and the media. An agency may get as much as 30 percent off from a medium and then pass 15 percent of this on to the client. "This kind of shakes United States-trained ad men," said an American ad man. The Japanese custom of rotating personnel from one department to another, irrespective of the activities of the department or their previous experience, also upsets both foreign clients and foreign staff. "The individual is often not in one section or department long enough to become really good or expert at anything. This contributes to a continuing high level of incompetence in too many cases," said one foreign client.

Another of the differences between American and Japanese advertising agencies is that in the United States, creativity is usually ranked first. In Japan, creativity is fifth or sixth in importance, well below influence with the media and ability to finance. A second very important difference is that in Japan the media buyer, especially in the case of newspapers, has to court the media—the reason, again, being the limited amount of newspaper advertising space.

Advertising agencies and large Japanese advertisers have considerable influence on the editorial content of media. And in their role as guardians of Japan, Inc., the media sometimes go overboard in their efforts to reduce the effectiveness of foreign marketing operations. When the cyclamate scare came along, national TV channels jumped at the opportunity to hit Coca-Cola. Following an announcement that cyclamates cause cancer, the stations then showed a close-up of a bottle of Coca-Cola, followed by the statement: "Coca-Cola contains cyclamates."

As strange as it may sound, one of Japan's major agencies has more than once refused to accept a foreign advertising account because it was not at least half-owned by Japanese. Commenting on the future growth of his agency a few years ago, a key executive said that thereafter most growth would be abroad, where Japanese businessmen were setting up Japanese-owned companies. "Because, as you know," he added, "we Japanese do not like to do business with foreigners if we can avoid it."

Recent reports indicate, however, that more and more Japanese multinationals are placing their advertising through foreign agencies, not through the overseas branches of Japanese agencies, because the foreign agencies are more familiar with the market and produce more creative—and presumably more effective—ads.

English-Language Advertising

The men in charge of English-language advertising in many Japanese companies do not speak English; yet they commonly assume the right to make changes in advertisements prepared for them by foreign copywriters. Even when a major Japanese firm places advertising through a top agency in which there are professional foreign copywriters, non-English-speaking personnel in the advertising department of the company generally have the final say on all copy. The results of the situation are usually frustration for the foreign copywriter and very often advertising for the Japanese company that ranges from ineffective to hilarious.

Although the whole concept of advertising in Japan has changed from "after-the-fact" advertising—thanking people for buying their product or service—to selling, the Japanese still do not like competitive advertising. Newspapers will usually refuse to accept ads knocking competing products or making unfavorable comparisons.

New Magazines Proliferate

Dozens of new magazines were inaugurated from 1969 on, most of them either in the comic category or aimed at teenage girls and young men and emphasizing explicit sexual material. The ubiquitous weekly magazines began to cater more exclusively to specialized categories of readers, thus enhancing their value as advertising media. They also began to emphasize full-color ads and to promote the versatility of magazine advertising in such areas as multiple and tie-in ads.

Japanese ad agencies also stepped up their introduction of English words and phrases into popular usage to an extent that is staggering. The words are given Japanese pronunciation (Ritz crackers becomes *Ri-tsu ku-ra-ka-su*), but the meaning remains the same. Brand names and single words are usually used for their exotic, foreign appeal (or, in the case of brand names, because the foreign manufacturer insists on it). Whole phrases are being introduced because Japanese does not lend itself to short, crisp, pungent messages. Not only is the range of nuances very limited in Japanese, but there are many brief ad-type messages that cannot be adequately expressed. The practice is especially common in advertisements for clothing and cosmetics.

The New Low-Posture Image

Probably the most significant change of all in Japanese advertising occurred in 1970. This was an abrupt change of the creative character of the ads brought about by a build-up of consumer protests against price discrimination, a new awareness of defects in cars and other merchandise, and the growing dangers of industrial pollution. Almost in concert, advertisements changed from hard sell to soft sell. Human values, peace, quiet, and return to nature became the overriding themes.

Not as conspicuous, but perhaps as significant a change occurred when Japanese companies that in the past had been virtually obsessed with promoting their bigness, their importance, and their growing power all at once began to soft-pedal, to take a "low" rather than "high" posture. To top it off, JETRO, the trade promotion arm of the government, announced in 1971 that it would henceforth change its image so as not to attract criticism from those who were beginning to be disturbed by Japan's economic inroads abroad.

All at once, it seemed that the Japanese became aware that the Western world was looking at them as a strictly materialistic society made up of "economic animals" whose only goal in life was to develop the world's highest GNP. Explained one American advertising executive: "Many young Japanese were highly embarrassed by Expo 70, regarding it as a materialistic orgy. They felt they were had by the Japanese Establishment. Being very sensitive to national sentiment, the ad agencies picked up on this theme."

The Japanese have always been very visually oriented, and mood ads are preferred to hard-sell ads. The borrowed-interest technique is now even more of a favorite with ad men because it is especially appropriate for the new Japanese cultural pattern.

"Mood advertising" was pioneered in Japan by Parco, a commercial-cultural complex created by the Seibu Group, a huge conglomerate that owns department stores, hotels, railroads, and a baseball team. The first Parco shopping-entertainment center, founded in 1969, included fashion boutiques, bookstores, theaters, gourmet restaurants, art galleries, and so on—all under one roof.

Tsuji Masuda, director of Parco, decided to go with an entirely new kind of advertising, one that would appeal to the sentiments and dreams of the young—without making any reference at all to the products or services provided by the giant complex. The resulting ads were both shocking and provocative—completely off-the-wall as far as Western consumers as well as Western advertising experts were concerned. The graphics used in the ads ranged from nudes to African women nursing their babies. Some of the ad headlines: "Don't stare at the nude: be nude"; "Men! Be beautiful for women!"; "Girls be ambitious!"

The ads were done in a spontaneous, sensual, visually explosive manner. Masuda readily admitted that it was impossible for anyone to understand the ads or to connect them with Parco unless they saw them all and then thought deep and long about their meaning—which was to change the Japanese way of thinking and trigger rapid social changes.

The ads probably would not have worked anywhere else in the world, but in Japan they became famous and they worked. The ads reflected feminist preoccupations, and the dreams and yearnings of the younger generation, which was infatuated with the West, with themselves, with avant-garde art, jazz, third-world culture—a fantasy world that the young lived in during their leisure time. Not surprisingly, the young soon made an adjective out of Parco (which is Italian for "park")—*parkoteki*, by which they meant "something quirky and difficult to understand."

Parco now has ten such centers, and is still growing rapidly.

Japanese advertising agencies and their clients were surprised and mystified by the Parco ads when they first began to appear, but in typical Japanese fashion they soon began following Masuda's lead.

The Almighty Dentsu

"We are a very important social, economic, and ecological force in Japan—far more so than advertising agencies in the United States. We cannot really be compared with any other advertising agency in the world." This statement by a Dentsu executive is quite literally true. Dentsu, which refers to itself as a "marketing agency," accounts for about one-fourth of all the advertising expenditures in Japan, with billings over three times that of its nearest Japanese competitor and nearly nine times the combined billing of all foreign or foreign-affiliated agencies in the country.

Dentsu places approximately half of all television advertising appearing on the major networks during prime time and over half the advertising that goes into the nation's major printed media. Through a number of large, wholly owned affiliated companies, Dentsu also provides clients with a wide range of other services. The most important of the affiliated companies are the Dentsu Research Company, which plans and executes recurring and client-requested market research; the Dentsu PR Center, which is associated with Ruder and Finn in New York; and the Video Research Company, which is a leading audience-survey firm. In the Tsukiji head-office building of Dentsu are consumer rooms for pre- and post-testing marketing concepts and products. The testers use such sophisticated equipment as the tachistoscope, polygraph, and eye camera.

In addition to the services offered by these companies, Dentsu also conducts management seminars, retail sales seminars, and general educational programs to help win acceptance for a client's products. Where foreign clients are concerned, the agency also functions as a consultant and a go-between in helping to set up distribution systems.

To operate these facilities, Dentsu has its pick of some of the brightest minds in the country. In a typical year, over 2,000 university students apply for employment with Dentsu and take the company's entrance examinations. After careful screening, perhaps 100 are selected. Once accepted by Dentsu, young employees are sent to a company training center, staffed by full-time instructors, where they are prepared for middle-management responsibilities. This is followed by on-the-job training that continues for years.

"We see ourselves as serving industry per se, rather than a large list of individual clients," said a spokesman.

Dentsu does not insist that an internationally known company change a brand name that has great prestige abroad, even though it is unknown in Japan and is difficult to render into Japanese. "If the client is strongly opposed to a change, we develop a campaign that overcomes the weakness or handicap of a difficult name. When it comes to slogans, however, there is just no way some English-language slogans can be translated into Japanese, and others are completely unacceptable for various reasons. We must be allowed to use a purely Japanese market approach," the Dentsu man said. "If we do come up against a client who has a slogan that won't translate into Japanese and yet he won't give it up, we compromise with a political solution—we put it into the ad in English in very small type down in the corner somewhere," he added.

The creative originality and presentation of the best ads that Dentsu produces for both Japanese and foreign clients is good—so good that some of them are startling. Nothing better is being done anywhere.

Getting into the Spirit

The foreign advertiser must accept the fact that in most cases, English-language copy cannot be literally translated into Japanese without coming out strange. It is possible, of course, to make the same points, but usually the ad has to be completely rewritten in Japanese. This is when it pays to deal with one of the larger agencies, where the staff can at least be expected to be highly professional.

No matter how professional the agency and its staff, however, it is very important that any slogan or copy translated from English be tested before it is released. The foreign advertiser sometimes has to agree to having the name of his product changed because there are some terms that simply cannot be rendered into Japanese—which means they would be unpronounceable in their English form. Other brand names are too long for convenient use and expression in Japan, and these are subject to being shortened.

The foreign advertiser must contend with the fact that there are four ways of writing Japanese, and each has an entirely different image and effect. These four ways are the *kanji*, or the multi-stroke Chinese ideograms; the *hiragana* and *katakana*, which are simplified one- or two-stroke methods of representing the sounds of Japanese syllables; and *romaji*, which is Roman letters used to spell out Japanized English (bread for example becomes *bu-re-do*; milk is *mi-ru-ku*; pants are *pa-n-tsu*). English as it is used in Japanese-language advertising should also be looked at (by the foreign reader) as a "foreign" language.

Kanji gives a rather formal, stiff impression, and if it is overused it can kill an ad. *Hiragana* is a soft, intimate style of writing that imparts a delicate and often feminine mood. It is much used in advertising aimed at women. *Katakana* is used to express foreign words that have been Japanized in pronunciation. This style of writing imparts a foreign, crisp, direct feeling to the ad copy. English, which is not necessarily used in Japanese ads for meaning, gives a foreign, exotic flavor.

Because the Japanese are exceedingly sensitive to the different nuances imparted by these styles of writing, their mixture is very important and invariably can only be done by a very experienced Japanese advertising man.

Another thing the foreign advertiser has to get used to is the layout of Japanese ads. Ads may be laid out to be read vertically or horizontally. If the layout is vertical, the copy may read from right to left. If it is horizontal, copy reads "Western style" or from left to right. The foreign advertiser is also often disturbed by the Japanese practice of breaking sentences and words up into two, three, or more sections or blocks, without apparent regard for readability, for the sake of aesthetic balance. Obviously, the Japanese do not find this custom disconcerting.

Japanese ad copy reflects the manners and attitudes of the Japanese. What is appropriate in English or some other language is often ineffective, incomprehensible, or offensive in Japanese. And just like American advertising, the style and tone of the ad copy differs with the market, whether it is aimed at teenagers, married women, salarymen, or company executives—all facets that the foreign advertiser is prone to forget when he sees and hears what has been done to his company's slogan or favorite piece of copy.

Besides all the cultural nuances pertaining to advertising in Japan, advertisers and copywriters are not free to write any kind of copy they want. All copy is subject to various regulations imposed by the Fair Trade Commission, trade associations, the Ministry of Public Welfare, and the major media.

If the visitor in Japan were concerned only with packaging, he might very well get the idea that he was still in the United States. There is some English on virtually all packaging, and in numerous instances there is nothing but English. The visitor must not fall into the trap of reading the English as English, however. For the most part, it is just a part of the design and is not meant to be read at all. Its purpose is to give the product a foreign image.

Media and Presentations

There are some 180 newspapers in Japan. The three largest have a daily circulation of more than 23 million. The other 177-plus papers reach more than 40 million readers. There are about 100 important weekly magazines in the country, with a combined circulation of more than one billion, and approximately 2,000 monthly magazines, with total circulations of more than 2 billion. With more than 99 percent of adult Japanese literate and this extraordinary selection of reading material, print advertising in Japan has a potentially broader reach than in any other country.

There are some 1,500 VHF television stations and more than 9,450 UHF TV stations in Japan. The Japan Broadcasting Corporation owns 1,113 of the VHF stations. Japan has more than 1,000 radio stations.

Despite the increase in the number of pages of leading daily newspapers in 1969 and 1970, newspaper space is still scarce and therefore expensive. Also, despite the fact that the shortage has been chronic since the early 1950s, magazines did not really begin to capitalize on the available advertising demand until the end of the 1960s. Television time is also at a premium. The density of TV spots in Tokyo, for example, is about three times that of New York. A 30-second spot on one of Tokyo's several local channels during "A" or "Golden Time" (7:00 P.M. to 9:30 P.M.) costs many thousands of dollars—much to the surprise of first-time advertisers.

In addition to the Japanese-language print media, there are several English-language newspapers published in Tokyo and Osaka and several dozen English-language magazines.

In terms of total expenditures, the most popular advertising media in Japan are newspapers first, followed by television, outdoor signs, magazines, radio, and direct mail. The largest advertisers for the last several years have been machinery and tool manufacturers, food producers, finance and insurance companies, cosmetic companies, and publishing houses. The total amount of money spent for advertising in Japan doubled between 1966 and 1970, going from $1 billion to more than $2 billion, and has continued to rise rapidly.

Japan's Audit Bureau of Circulation was founded in 1953 at the instistence of Dentsu's late president Hideo Yoshida, but it was not until 1958 that he could get all the major newspapers to join it. Actual ABC auditing did not begin until 1961, and for several years there was still no guarantee that the results were more than token.

The bureau has made progress. Said an advertising agency spokesman: "Publishers are frequently astounded by the thoroughness of the auditors' check-up, which is going a long way toward elucidating the whole subject of the relationship of newspaper circulation to advertising in Japan."

The officially announced circulation figures of English-language magazines in Japan remain deceptive. The true figures may be no more than half (or less) of the "official circulation," which is used when magazines sell advertising space.

The Captive Audience

Transit advertising is one of the most important forms of advertising in Japan. With its extensive public transportation systems utilized daily by millions of commuters, advertising via posters and placards on buses, subways, and trains is a vital part of the marketing of thousands of firms. Each year Japan's railways alone have some 20 billion passengers, and the average daily commuting time for people on all forms of public transportation is well over an hour, giving advertisers a huge captive audience that can avoid their ads only by closing their eyes.

The cost of transit advertising is based on the average number of daily passengers, the number of posters per bus or coach, whether the posters are placed on the side-walls of the cars or hung down from the ceiling over the passengers' heads, and the type of advertising.

On Tokyo's popular Chuo Line, it presently costs approximately ¥600,000 to have 1,840 posters (one poster for each car) displayed for two days.

The biggest users of transit advertising in Japan include department stores, supermarkets, cosmetic manufacturers, pharmaceutical companies, hotels, restaurants, magazines, newspapers, and English-language schools.

One interesting advertising insight pointed out by the Japan manager of a tobacco company: In Japan, advertising that appeals to the machismo of males is redundant because if you are a male you are, by definition, macho. Another factor of importance to foreign marketers in Japan is the role of "in-channel" trade advertising. Because of the huge number of small wholesalers and retailers in Japan, companies wanting to reach most or all of them generally develop major in-channel, as well as consumer, advertising programs. The importance of advertising to these segments of the trade varies with the product and its distribution. The more widespread your distribution and the more wholesalers and retailers handling your product, the more promotion you may have to do to motivate them to get your product out and on display.

In-channel promotions include margins, rebates, various types of in-store promotions, and other services, such as free trips and entertainment provided to the retailers. Margins vary with the type of product, the volume of sales, whether a product is new, and so on. Rebates to wholesalers vary according to the level of the wholesaler and a number of other factors.

There are no legislative restrictions on the levels of rebates that can be granted in Japan, but retailers are controlled on the percentage the posted price can be above the planned discount price of an item. There are also limitaitons on rebates in the form of other products given to retailers by producers.

Market Research

In early 1987, there were 100 market research companies in Japan. Of this number, only a dozen or so are of any real importance in the trade. The largest and most active of the organizations include Marketing Intelligence Corporation; the Institute of Marketing Research and Statistics; Marketing Research Service; Audience Studies (Japan) Inc. (better known as ASI); A. C. Nielsen Company (Japan); Dentsu Research Ltd.; Marketing Center; Japan Marketing Research; Central Research Services Inc.; International Marketing Services; Japan Market Research Bureau; and Fuji National Consulting Corporation. Some of the smaller, highly specialized organizations include Asia Marketing Group, Cambridge Research Institute (Japan), and Pacific Projects Ltd. In addition to these independents, there are several agencies affiliated with specific firms or industries that are primarily statistics-gathering services.

Commenting on the state of marketing research in Japan today, a leading American MR executive based in Tokyo said: "As far as most Japanese manufacturers are concerned, market research is still in its development stage. Many studies seldom go beyond demographic statistics. The main problem is still a lack of capable analysts. Instead of producing clear facts, Japanese market research is slanted toward showing 'impressions,' and it is left up to the MR staff to use their 'Japanese knowledge' and intuition to make the desired marketing decisions."

Many firms carry out different types of surveys and do random sampling, but only a few use outside agencies. The firms that do carry on market research use their own personnel, who have had little or no formal training in the modern techniques of MR. A number of the firms know how to employ high-level techniques, but only a few large clients are sold on the idea and are willing to invest money in marketing research in the real sense of the word. This is especially true of medium- and small-size enterprises that are always notoriously short of money in the first place. Also, companies are afraid to engage an outside research organization for fear that company secrets will leak out. The moral code that controls this factor in the United States is not firmly established in Japan.

Because they are afraid to bring in an outside agency, many Japanese companies divide their surveys into a dozen or more sections and then pass the parts out to unrelated sources for information, attempting to correlate the results themselves. Market research firms that are subsidiaries of foreign companies have a certain advantage in this regard because Japanese firms are much more prone to trust them than they are a strictly Japanese agency.

As competition increases in Japan, individual firms are finding it more and more desirable to have the exclusive benefit of independent market research surveys. But many such firms still consider MR too expensive. Some firms also tend to believe that once a survey is conducted it is not necessary to do it again. This hinders the growth of the industry in that it prevents clients from benefitting fully from the advantage of sustained marketing intelligence.

Marketing research activities conducted by ad agencies are similar to what the independent firms do in method, but the independents do not consider the ad agencies to be competitors in a direct sense. In the past, manufacturers have asked agencies like Dentsu to do market research, but such efforts "tend to allow secrets to get out," so firms are reluctant to engage ad agencies. They lean toward independent agencies when they lean at all.

Dentsu and Hakuhodo, Japan's two largest advertising agencies, both maintain large research departments that engage in market research for agency clients. Dentsu's research department engages in media research, copy testing, radio and TV research, consumer panel studies, motivational research, advertising statistical research, and market research. Dentsu also conducts a monthly consumer panel survey in the Tokyo and Osaka areas covering daily necessities, cosmetics, and textiles. A nationwide retail store survey is regularly conducted on pharmaceuticals. Yoron Kagaku Kyokai (Public Opinion Research Association) undertakes market surveys on request.

Except for statistical information made public by the government, there is very little prepared market data available to the foreign businessman in Japan. Japanese firms, particularly trading companies and wholesalers, have a phobia about keeping the details of their operations secret and generally refuse to give out any meaningful information. They make a pretense of cooperating by passing out pounds of brochures and catalogs, but these contain only the most general information and are usually of no more value than the yellow pages of a telephone book.

It is apparent that a shortage of personnel experienced in market research, plus some inadequacies that show up in present techniques as applied in Japan, are serious shortcomings. One of the problems that the research firm has to overcome is that many wholesalers and retailers systematically garble or destroy their sales records as a regular policy to keep them out of the hands of the Tax Office.

Foreign companies operating in or interested in Japan invariably go to one or more of the several foreign or joint-venture research firms offering specialized services that for the most part are non-competing and complementary. These firms include Audience Studies (Japan) Inc., Marplan, the A. C. Nielsen Company (Japan), Fuji National Consulting Corporation (which absorbed CORAL in 1971), and the Japan Marketing Research Bureau, a division of J. Walter Thompson (Japan).

Foreign marketing men should keep the following points in mind. First, ad agencies that offer to do MR at below going rates expect to make up for it in advertising commissions. Second, if an individual or company offers to do a piece of research for a price that is "ridiculously" low, the quality of the results is likely to be the same. (Depending on the case, a research project in Japan usually costs from 10 percent to 20 percent less than it would cost in the United States.) Third, strictly Japanese MR agencies are often handicapped in dealing with foreign clients because of the language barrier.

211

Overall, the market research industry in Japan still suffers from lack of credibility, and there is a tendency for companies to ignore the relationship between cost and credibility. Advances in the use of sophisticated computers and software packages are having a profound effect that is greatly benefiting the industry.

The biggest users of market research in Japan are advertising agencies, food manufacturers, and textile/chemical companies. Some 40 market research firms are affiliated with the Japan Marketing Research Association.

Chapter 15

The Importance of Good Public Relations

"Lack of effective public relations is Japan's biggest bottleneck in both business and diplomacy."

—Dr. Yoshitaka Horiuchi
Economist

"Who Needs It?"

American-style public relations is still a relatively new concept in Japan, and even though it is growing there is some doubt that after it matures any American PR practitioner would recognize it. The Japanese see little difference between PR, advertising, and publicity, and they often use the words interchangeably. "The present stage of the public relations business in Japan, when compared with that in the United States, is somewhere in the Middle Ages," said the director of one of the few independent agencies in Japan that has been succcessful. "Most executives here have no idea what public relations in the modern sense is and automatically equate us with the men in their own general affairs section who arrange company outings and that sort of thing. Their reaction is: 'Why should we pay an outsider to do what our own people have been doing successfully for years?' As a result of this attitude, it is impossible to get Japanese companies to use our services in a straightforward business approach," he added.

Japanese companies split their public relations accounts among several agencies, just as they do in advertising. And even more than in advertising, they prefer to maintain control of not only the creative process, but the execution of all activities, as well. The idea of depending on an outside agency for its image is regarded by the typical Japanese company as absurd. Futhermore, agencies face the usual problems in dealing with a Japanese client—few individuals can take a stand or approve of anything on their own, making it necessary to submit things to committees and put up with long delays.

From the American viewpoint, Japanese PR agencies are also hindered by internal problems that are typical, beginning with insufficient cooperation between departments. "The degree of jealousy and noncooperation even within departments is hard to imagine," said a foreign employee of a major agency. "A copywriter, for example, is told to write so many words on a particular subject but may be given no opportunity to coordinate the project with the layout artist simply because of professional jealousy."

"While purely Japanese PR agencies are effective and often do outstanding work in the Japanese market—for both foreign and Japanese clients—they are generally less successful when working in English. As a result, the foreign-managed and joint venture PR agencies in Japan attract most of the foreign firms, along with a number of Japanese companies that have come to realize the importance of presenting an acceptable image abroad.

It is especially important for foreign firms operating in Japan to have good public relations—not only to help overcome the basic antagonism the government and certain associations exhibit toward outside companies, but also to establish and maintain a desirable image among the people at large. Some foreign companies operating in Japan are well known for their success in this area; others are notorious for their failures.

The key seems to be that the foreign manager must first of all recognize the importance of effective PR and then follow through with the effort and budget to mount and maintain a good program. The rewards for success are substantial—improved relations with the government, fewer employee recruiting problems, less employee turnover, and better acceptance in the marketplace.

Types of PR Agencies

There are two types of public relations organs in Japan: independent agencies and those established by and operating within the larger advertising agencies. Most of the independents are associated to some degree with foreign public relations agencies and offer the usual range of services in both English and Japanese. The most important ad agency PR organs are Dentsu's PR Center and

Hakuhodo's PR Department. Both are strictly internal organs, catering to company clients.

All of the Japanese public relations agencies depend on political patronage and personal connections to procure clients. Some time ago, one small agency, whose advisor was an ex-baron, managed to get a former prime minister to put in an appearance at a reception staged for a client. As can be imagined, this impressed the attending press corps. The next day, an American PR man in Tokyo got a call from one of his clients asking why he couldn't get ex-premiers to attend his receptions!

Tyranny of the Reporter Clubs

One of the first things the foreign company interested in PR in Japan must learn is how the Japanese press works. The huge Japanese press (one newspaper will send as many as 50 reporters to cover a major story) is an integral part of the Japanese Establishment and Japan, Inc., and assumes the role of both censor and instructor for its reading public.

The Japanese press is not necessarily directed by any feeling that the people have a right to know all the news. Individual editors and reporters often take it upon themselves to decide which news should be printed on the basis of whether they think it is "in the best interests of Japan." By the same token, the press often does the public relations and propaganda work of both business and the political establishment—in a highly nationalistic, often anti-United States manner.

This stance of the press stems from its self-appointed role as the first line of defense against undesirable political and economic influence "invading" the country. By "undesirable," the press means anything that lessens Japanese control of the economy or reduces its political options. The press thus contributes to the problems many American businesses experience in operating, or trying to operate, in Japan—problems that can be reduced or overcome only by continuous public efforts on a broad scale.

The most unusual feature of the press in Japan, however, is the so-called press clubs. These are exclusive groups of reporters that have been assigned or have assigned themselves to all of the usual news sources, including all government agencies on a national and prefectural level, political parties, industrial organizations, social organizations, and labor unions. There is a club for each of these sources made up of reporters from selected media. A reporter from a business publication, for example, is not allowed under any circumstances into the club covering political news emanating from the Prime Minister's Office—or to attend a press conference arranged for the political reporters' club.

The clubs are so powerful that it is difficult, if not impossible, for a news source to get news to the public except through the club that has attached itself to that particular news source. The clubs zealously protect their exclusivity, and woe be it to the news source that tries to go around them—or to the outsider who tries to sit in on a news conference by their source.

A story that makes world headlines may not appear at all in Japanese newspapers if the concerned reporters' club decides that it should not be printed. These clubs strongly resent the printing of any information about Japan that is critical in any way. (One example of information that is deliberately withheld from the Japanese at large: American investments in Japanese companies.) Because of the power of the reporter clubs, the various news sources, particularly the political sources, are compelled to cooperate with them and to cater to them through gifts and other "fringe" benefits, as well as provide them, lavishly, with the communications and other facilities they need.

The news media represented by these clubs do not as a general policy accept news from other sources; thus, most of the domestic news printed in Japan comes through the clubs. The reporter clubs can make or break any politician or businessman they want to, as far as his public relations are concerned. At a press conference concerned with general news, the PR agency (or the news source) can invite only members of the general news club, and it is necessary to invite them all. If an outsider succeeds in getting in, the worthy members of the club will halt the proceedings and demand that he or she leave immediately. If their demands are not met at once, they walk out and boycott the offending news source until some kind of acceptable apology is made.

This often forces public relations agencies and other news sources to hold two or three press conferences instead of one. If the conference is of general news interest, they hold one session for Japanese reporters from the various large daily newspapers and a second one for foreign correspondents. If the subject also happens to be of interest to the iron industry, for example, they have to hold a third conference for the benefit of Japanese reporters from the iron media. Magazine reporters representing the lesser-known weekly or monthly trade journals are not recognized by reporters from the leading newspapers.

The press clubs, particularly the ones representing the large national dailies, are run like miniature police states. The members are exceedingly thin-skinned and arrogant toward all nonmembers, making it difficult to stay on good terms with them. Another factor that makes it hard to maintain good relations with the press in Japan, besides the exclusive clubs and the generally antagonistic attitude, is the large number of representatives from each medium and the frequent job-switching among editors, as well as reporters.

Most of the press clubs are closed to foreign correspondents and have rigid rules specifically designed to keep them out. It was not until the mid-1980s, after more than 30 years of effort, that the Foreign Correspondents Club of Japan, along with some diplomatic pressure, succeeded in getting some of its foreign members admitted to the exclusive political press clubs for some special sessions. In most cases, however, they are not allowed to ask questions; if questions are allowed, they must be asked in Japanese.

The press clubs censor the news and also cover up stories that they feel might be damaging to their news source or to Japan. They are therefore one of the major reasons many Japanese have a distorted image of themselves and the world at large.

One advantageous factor in practicing PR in Japan is the fact that Japanese editors appreciate receiving free material on subjects of interest. It has to be in Japanese, though; otherwise, they won't pay any attention to it. Because of the number of reporters representing Japan's news media, even a minor press conference will attract 50 or more reporters. Many small receptions draw over a hundred newsmen and photographers.

Role of the PR Man

An American PR executive in Tokyo noted that there were many errors in stories appearing in Japanese media about foreign firms and foreign products. Thus, they need PR services if only for reference purposes. All of his accounts, he added, are foreign, and his major effort is counseling management. "I am convinced that the average foreign executive sent to Japan is of the highest caliber. He soon finds out, however, that things are not done here like they are back home, and his biggest problem becomes the necessity for getting this across to the head office. In addition to needing a sounding board, my clients need information that is not available from ordinary sources," he said.

"One of the most common pitfalls we help the foreign business-man avoid is the time-wasting preliminary ceremonies that occur when he first approaches a Japanese company. When you don't have an introduction to the 'right' man in the company, it is custo-mary for the Information Department, or whomever you first happen to contact, to call either an official greeter or a man from General Affairs. He will take you in, listen to your story (which may take hours to tell) and then inform you, sometimes on your second or third visit, that some other department is in charge of your field of interest and would you please get in touch with Mr. So-and-so in the appropriate department."

Another type of peril from which some PR agencies attempt to protect their foreign clients in Japan is the naiveté of their staff. Explained a PR man: "The Japanese side of a joint venture will of-ten make note of when you are out of town. They will then send a clerk to your secretary to tell her he has been sent after your confi-dential file on a particular subject. If the girl hasn't been given spe-cific instructions not to hand out your files, she will very likely do so. In one case, Japanese personnel showed up with photostats of all of a foreign representative's files. When asked by the foreigner concerned where they got them, they readily admitted: 'We sent a boy over and asked your secretary for your files.'"

Industrial Espionage and Professional Spies

One of the most important, but clandestine, functions of public relations agencies in Japan is industrial espionage. Employed by both Japanese and foreign companies, most agencies have devel-oped a number of techniques to ferret out desired information. The most popular techniques include penetration into firms by outsid-ers posing as reporters, visits with carefully cultivated friends to play *mah-jongg*, and "getting to" the favorite cabaret girlfriends of key executives. Inside informers, however, provide the greatest bulk of information sold on the market. A certain percentage of the employees of almost any firm in Japan can apparently be bought for a fee.

One indication of the attitude the Japanese have toward industrial espionage is the fact that there are "schools" for such spying. One of the schools, located in Yotsuya, Tokyo, was founded by a woman. More interesting, however, is the fact that the woman was a former intelligence agent with extensive prewar experience with the Japanese army in China and Manchuria.

Courses at the spy schools are offered at two levels—introductory and advanced. American firms that reportedly engaged the services of spy agencies were said to have been astounded by their efficiency and detailed accuracy.

Japanese businessmen are interested in maintaining good relations with the public and other businessmen, but they naturally see this as an exercise in personal relations—not public relations. As a result, very few Japanese firms conduct public relations as we know it. In their press conferences, for example, it is mutually understood that there will be no embarrassing inquiries by reporters and that their stories will automatically reflect the common Japanese image of sincerity, harmony, and righteousness.

From the American newsman's point of view, one of the primary functions of a public relations agency or PR department within a firm is to prepare and make available detailed information on key personnel and company activities. In Japan, this is still rare because the idea of revealing such information to outsiders as a routine responsibility is still alien to the thinking of Japanese businessmen. Second, the superior-inferior, group-above-all code under which they operate negates the idea of singling out anyone except the top executive to speak for the company or receive public attention.

It is true that almost any person or any department in a Japanese company will pass out printed statistical information, and if a foreign investigator personally visits the company with any type of respectable credentials he can often get the information he wants. But the idea of having a public relations man impersonally and regularly release company information is still unusual.

At present, the first thing the average Japanese businessman says to himself when he wants to explain some factors or enhance his firm's public image is: "What connection can I use to get free editorial space in what media?" In making the proper contact, the

Japanese businessman often will spend considerably more money than an advertisement or some public relations effort would cost. Writing in the *Mainichi Daily News* on what Japan needs to compete with the West, economist Dr. Yoshitaka Horiuchi said: "Lack of effective public relations is Japan's biggest bottleneck in both business and diplomacy." Lack of good relations can be just as critical for the foreign businessman in Japan.

Chapter 16

Japan Tomorrow

Guidelines for Foreign Businessmen

The question of what will happen to Japan in the future is of consuming interest to the Japanese. Future forecasting is now a major industry, and "Great Life Forecasts" are published regularly. A recent forecast appearing in *Japan Marketing/Advertising*, a publication of Dentsu, the huge advertising, market, and social research company, was especially provocative.

The forecast was divided into five categories: society, cities and culture, life, the marketplace, and marketing.

There were ten key points under societal changes:

(1) The "nostalgia syndrome." The Japanese will become disillusioned with hard work and affluence and will begin looking back to the 1950s, trying to recapture the romantic dreams of the period when they were rebuilding a nation in a spirit of extraordinary energy, effort, and enthusiasm.

(2) A new consumer class will be formed. People living in the major metropolitan areas who have received most of the benefits of the economic miracle of postwar Japan, including the accumulation of cultural information, will form a new society, almost totally different from any that existed in Japan in the past.

(3) A cadre of "superwomen" will appear. More and more women with unusual talent and drive will break away from the traditional pattern of the passive woman in a male-dominated business world and will achieve great success and popularity in many fields.

(4) Japan will become a nation of Neros. The Japanese will indulge themselves in an orgy of pleasure, in food, in fashions, in the flesh. The mass media will become a "grand colosseum" presenting sadistic performances, and the people will be transformed into a "faceless tyrant."

221

(5) A "serious youth" syndrome will develop. In a backlash to the hedonism of society, idealistic youths will appear on the scene and will seek to develop new goals and a new set of rules for the Japanese, much like the young *samurai* who brought the downfall of the shogunate government in the 1860s.

(6) Welfare activities based on volunteers will become a major force and the ultimate symbol of an affluent society. The Imperial Household will set an example in the rapid growth of service and welfare activities, which will assume great social importance in fashion, as well as in spreading the benefits of affluence.

(7) The incidence of information-related crimes will grow rapidly. With the entire economy of the country based on computer manipulation of information and control, crimes involving the theft, alteration, or destruction of information will become a major social problem.

(8) Female university students will prefer sexual liaisons with older men. University women, seeking greater stability and status in their lives, will increasingly turn to middle-aged men not only for a "mature feeling," but also as part of a yearning to return to the age when women relied more on men for their welfare.

(9) A new class of computer technocrats, who make a sport of playing with information and view the world through cathode ray tubes, will emerge.

(10) Housewives will take up part-time intellectual work. More women with children still in school will join the labor force as part-time workers at home, using word processors and other forms of electronic equipment—some starting their own businesses.

The forecasts for cities and culture were:

(1) More and more areas around transportation terminals and other strategic locations will be designated for high development, while areas not chosen for development will suffer serious problems.

(2) Tokyo will become a major world center of super intelligence and talent that will rival if not surpass New York.

(3) Tokyo's traditionally famous Asakusa and Ueno districts are being renovated and will recapture much of the popularity they had during the long Tokugawa Shogunate period (1603–1868), but more recently enjoyed by the Ginza, Shinjuku, Roppongi, Akasaka, and Shibuya.

(4) Japan's millions of neon signs and outside lighting will take on the quality of art and evolve into a kind of illumination fantasy-land, with a parallel rise in interest in other forms of art as performance.

(5) Super urban centers will continue to develop. As more and more factories are concentrated in industrial areas, present urban centers throughout the islands will be linked together in growing information networks, contributing to the rapid development of an information society.

(6) Avant-garde cultural movements will develop. Leading enterprises and wealthy individuals will sponsor the development of new art and cultural activities that will enrich the lives of the people.

(7) Youth will turn from sports to arts. Growing numbers of the young will opt for art instead of sports in their extracurricular activities and leisure time. Literature, movies, and dramas will become increasingly sophisticated.

(8) Renewed interest in books and plays by Yukio Mishima will result in a boom in his traditional, *samurai*-like dedication to art, "Japanese spirit," and Japanese culture.

(9) A new age of "resort culture" will appear in Japan. The heyday of the great pleasure districts of Shogunate Japan will be rivaled by the appearance of hundreds of elaborate summer resorts around the country that will develop their own culture based on Japanese traditions and the new computer-controlled information society.

(10) Calligraphy will experience a new boom. The ancient art of calligraphy—once the criterion by which the Japanese judged education, refinement, and culture—will experience a revival as the ideal way to develop a refined aesthetic sense and spiritual enlightenment.

As for life-styles, the following developments were predicted:

(1) In their efforts to become gourmets of Western foods, the Japanese will become a major market for high-quality wines. Detailed knowledge of vintage wines and the variety of brands will become an important status symbol in Japan.

(2) Arranged marriages in Japan will come back into vogue as more and more young Japanese realize that "love matches" more often than not end up in divorce as soon as the bloom wears off.

They will be far more "rational" in their choice of mates, utilizing new methods of determining compatibility of experience, education, personality, and goals.

(3) Fashion will become bipolarized. The present trend in Japan among many fashion designers to use apparel as an art medium will continue to grow until there are two entirely different concepts of clothing, distinctly bipolarized and independent of each other.

(4) Money will become a game. Young people with large cash savings will begin playing the money markets as a sort of fashionable game, and older people with excess funds will begin using data bases to help them make their investments.

(5) A boom will occur in northeastern Honshu. The new Bullet Train express line from Ueno, Tokyo, to Honshu's northeastern Tohoku district will result in an industrial and tourism boom in that area.

(6) Country "villas" will come into fashion. As the cost of land increases in Japan's major cities, more and more urban dwellers will use their surplus money to purchase second homes in easily accessible rural areas where land costs are not as high.

(7) Private bathrooms will enjoy a boom. The traditional love of the Japanese for daily hot baths will result in a boom in highly individualized home baths that reflect the new affluence, interest in health, and desire for self-indulgence in luxurious settings comparable to the great, elaborate public baths of *shogun* days.

(8) Seafood will reemerge as popular fare. Growing interest in natural, healthy foods, along with a tendency to develop a gourmet approach to eating, will spur the present rehabilitation of seafood in the Japanese diet.

(9) The traditions and pleasures of Old Japan will be rediscovered. As the population of Japan ages, more and more people will rediscover the aesthetic refinement and joys of living on tatami floor-mats and experiencing the naturalness of Japanese tea and other traditional products, such as confections. This will have a substantial impact on the Japanese market.

(10) The travel industry in Asia will receive a significant boost as more and more Japanese make pilgrimagelike visits to the other countries of Asia in what might be called a search for their roots— an experience that will refresh them and sensitize them to their kinship with Asia.

Changes in the Consumer Market

Dentsu's future-casters saw the following developments in the marketplace:

(1) There will be an overall advance in image technology, parallel to the spread of compact disks and home video.

(2) Market deregulation will go into high gear. The pressure for the Japanese government to privatize public corporations and liberalize its controls on marketing will increase, with the introduction of free marketing principles, resulting in a more vigorous and efficient business climate.

(3) There will be a distribution and software "revolution." The distribution industry will undergo a revolution as computers and marketing software come on line, altering the way people shop.

(4) The "silver market" will become a major economic segment. As Japan's population ages, the need for welfare services and other services for senior citizens will become a major factor in the economy.

(5) Biotechnology will boom. New drugs and other breakthroughs in biotechnology will play an increasingly important role in the lives of the Japanese.

(6) Interest in office renovation will grow rapidly. The transformation of Japan's hundreds of thousands of offices into computerized "information centers" and a growing interest in making the offices more user friendly will develop into a major economic activity.

(7) Cross-generation shopping will develop. The tendency for large numbers of shops to cater to young people only will give way to shops based on a sense of status that transcends generations and will result in both shopping streets and shops having an entirely new look.

(8) Telephones will spawn new businesses. Liberalization of the use of telephone lines will result in the development of many new businesses dealing in information that will impact on the use of offices and also on services provided to older people.

(9) Gasoline stations will be redeveloped. The nation's hundreds of thousands of gasoline stations will be redesigned and redeveloped as diversified retail outlets, resulting in significant changes in the cityscape.

(10) Mental clinics will proliferate. Because of a new attitude toward stress and other mental problems, clinics specializing in psychiatric services will spread throughout the country, and it will

become routine for busy people in high income brackets to patronize them for help in overcoming stress.

These are among the most significant changes in marketing seen by the future-gazers:

(1) Market information will become available on a daily, even hourly, basis, making it possible—and mandatory—for businessmen to tailor their marketing programs accordingly. Management that is not creative will not succeed, and such enterprises will fail.

(2) "Radical" marketing will come into use. As the marketplace becomes more competitive, marketing programs that make use of radical techniques that shock the consumer will become commonplace, bringing a new kind of energy to marketing.

(3) Direct marketing will take off. Department stores will take the lead in developing direct marketing via catalog, telephone, and computer sales, helping people save time and the expense of shopping in stores.

(4) Video will create new activities. The creativity and talent inspired by video software will result in a flow of this new talent into the mass media, causing and speeding up revolutionary changes.

(5) Television will gain more popularity among the young. New types of "midnight" programs and the linking of television with video will attract large audiences of young viewers.

(6) Society will become more stratified on the basis of consumption patterns, and advertising media will develop programs designed to appeal to specific classes. Magazine publishers will continue to make strong efforts to fix their readership by class.

(7) Information will be increasingly used as a weapon. The power of the people who create new information will increase, giving them extraordinary leverage.

(8) Intellectualism will enter the newscaster's studio. People will no longer be satisfied with announcers who simply read the news. News people will be expected to provide background information and in-depth analyses of events. Intellectual newscasters will be the new stars of the media.

(9) Interest in space will grow. As the finiteness of the earth and its resources becomes more clearly recognized, interest in outer space will become a prime motivating factor in many areas, from advertising to electronics.

(10) CM video software will debut. Video software consisting solely of CMs will appear and will make the most of images and music to attract young audiences.

The American Dream

One of the great American dreams is that we can, should, and eventually will Americanize the rest of the world. This dream was a significant part of the American policy toward Japan during the postwar Occupation years, from 1945 to 1952, and we have never fully forgiven the Japanese for changing our dream to suit their own purposes and being more successful at it than we have been.

But all is not lost. Even though our transplanted dream has been Japanized, enough of it still exists to be easily recognizable, and there is ample evidence that it has become part of the psyche of the Japanese born after 1965.

Dr. Jeanne Binstock, a marketing consultant in Tokyo who has specialized in Japan's first mass-market generation (those born after 1965), says that this generation of Japanese is becoming both modernized and Americanized in quantum leaps.

Hired by Marplan Japan to direct a multiclient study of the values and life-styles of Tokyo teenagers, Binstock found that there has been an accelerating shift toward American values and life-styles among teenage Japanese born after 1965, a fact voluminously corroborated by studies sponsored by the Japanese government and by major news media.

Said Binstock: "Television has made them aware of the pursuit of success, fantasy, and hope. Older teenagers want more looseness in their lives, more choice, more rich experiences."

This generation of Japanese, Binstock adds, has been conditioned by American television and American movies, and every program they watch is a lesson in how Americans think, feel, and behave, their goals, their work preferences, and their sense of meaning in life.

"American movies implicitly reveal American values and role models. American movies have taught them that the good guy wins, even if he is younger. Inevitably, he wins over authority, or if he doesn't he will live to fight another day. He wins, too, if he has better ideas or he represents decency—Western decency, of course, which rarely includes loyalty (except to friends) or filial piety," Binstock said.

In Binstock's words, the post-1965 generation of Japanese have learned their lessons well. They are first-rate consumers. They work to get money to buy the things they want. They are much more interested in stimulation and rich experiences than in harmony and doing what is expected. "Tranquility doesn't bear much

227

weight compared to communication. They prefer action," she added. "They no longer believe in 'beat the nail that sticks out.' Television has told them that that is nonsense, that it is okay to stand out, and that creativity and imagination are desirable personal attributes leading to achievement."

Binstock says the second "megatrend" exhibited by post-1965 Japanese is replacement of the salaryman-generalist mentality with a strong desire to specialize and be as independent as possible.

In Binstock's view, the most successful American export to Japan has, in fact, been the American life-style. As this spreads throughout the country—and it is spreading, inexorably—opportunities for American companies to do business in Japan will gradually increase.

Xenophobia and the New Japan

The evolution of Japan into a world economic power and the inroads made by American attitudes and life-styles has not eliminated the traditional xenophobia of the Japanese, however. Besides the small percentage who have become internationalized by living, studying, and working abroad or working for foreign companies in Japan or depending directly on foreign tourists for their livelihood, most Japanese prefer not to get involved with foreigners, and many of them go to rather extreme lengths to avoid any kind of contact.

Even in cosmopolitan Tokyo, there are thousands of landlords who refuse to rent to foreigners. Many real estate agents are notorious for their rudeness to foreigners who contact them for rental properties. Said one American businessman: "Two house hunts in three years have convinced me that the average Tokyo landlord is profoundly racist. We're still the 'hairy barbarians' who forced Japan to open its doors in 1854. In other advanced nations, their actions would be illegal or at least hidden. In Tokyo, proprietors don't hide their prejudices!"

Stories of foreigners being refused entrance into bars, clubs, and massage baths are commonplace, especially in Nagoya, and are growing in other areas, as well, including the popular international hangout of Roppongi in Tokyo.

Most Japanese who refuse to do business with foreigners or refuse to hire them or otherwise get involved with them have a stock excuse. They say foreigners cannot speak Japanese, do not know or follow Japanese customs, and therefore would cause serious problems. They have a point, but only up to a point, because most foreigners in Japan go out of their way to fit in and do things the Japanese way.

Another Losing Proposition

Some American high-tech firms that import Japanese-made components or products place their orders with Japanese sales offices in the United States. This, noted Jon P. Schrag, General Manager for GTE Far East (Services) Ltd., in Tokyo, is a serious mistake.

Schrag said that requiring their American customers to deal only with their U.S. offices is a carefully thought-out strategic policy of the Japanese that helps them accomplish a number of goals. Schrag details these goals as follows:

(1) By having their own sales people in the U.S., the Japanese learn a great deal about the American market. Their U.S. affiliate marks up the product price and uses the resulting revenue to hire experienced American engineers to help them further penetrate the market. "By purchasing Japanese products in the U.S. instead of in Japan, American firms are literally financing their own demise," Schrag adds.

(2) By preventing American companies from consolidating their worldwide purchases, the Japanese deprive American companies of concentrated buying power.

(3) By controlling and monitoring the shipment of needed components to American companies, the Japanese can deduce the American company's production plans and marketing strategy, thus gaining a competitive edge.

(4) By selling their own products in the U.S., the Japanese tend to keep American companies out of Japan, thereby preventing them from developing any firsthand knowledge about or expertise in the Japanese market.

Schrag said that only a few American companies were smart enough to recognize the importance of their purchasing policy as an easy first-step solution to market problems. He lists three obvious advantages gained by the American companies that do their own purchasing in Japan:

(1) They are able to buy in volume by consolidating their purchases in Japan for their factories worldwide, thus getting huge

discounts and top priority on delivery.

(2) Since the American buying office does the shipping, the Japanese vendor has no idea where the products are going. Thereby, sensitive marketing information is kept secret.

(3) When technical support is needed from the Japanese manufacturer, the American company would control the technicians, not the seller.

Schrag added that if the top 100 American electronics firms were in control of their own buying in Japan, it would significantly slow down high-tech development in Japan. "Not only would competitor margins go down, but control and market information would become more expensive (to the Japanese)."

Trade Discrimination Continues

The Japanese are masters at stonewalling and continue to make use of this technique because there is still no mediator or arbitrator that can act as an unbiased referee or judge in matters of trade disputes. Clyde McAvoy, vice president, Far East, for Continental Airlines, and one of the most outspoken critics of the Japanese trading system, said that what is needed is a small claims court.

McAvoy recited a litany of practices, as well as legislated abuses, by the Japanese government that make doing business in or with Japan either more difficult or impossible. He cited one problem Continental Airlines faced when it tried to get permission to operate charter flights out of Japan. It would be the same, he said, if a Japanese TV maker that wanted to export a larger-than-usual number of sets into the U.S. for the Christmas sales season were told that it had to fill out a form giving the name of each individual it wanted to sell a TV set to and that it would be informed one or two days before Christmas if the extra sales were approved.

McAvoy added that one of the primary problems in attempts by the American government to work out a better relationship with Japan is that each administration seems to have only a four-year attention span, while American businessmen involved with Japan have to contend with a Japanese system designed to keep them just short of equal market access and also keep our government just barely tolerant.

McAvoy said that the business of Japan is business, while the business of America, for better or worse, is world security. "The

U.S. would be undercutting its own national goals if it permitted the political destabilization of a friendly and strategically placed nation such as Japan because we want to sell them more oranges. Now all that remains is to convince the Japanese that they are undercutting their own national goals by exploiting America's open markets without reciprocating," he added.

Intellectual Invasion by the Japanese

American attorney Warren G. Shimeall, who has practiced law in Japan since the 1950s, observed that one of the greatest challenges the U.S. faces from Japan is in rights to intellectual property. Noting that it was ideas and new products that made American great, Shimeall made the point that close to half of all the patents now granted in the U.S. go to foreigners—not to Americans—and that the biggest majority of the patents are now going to Japanese.

His obvious implication is that if this situation continues, the United States will be in even more trouble in competing with Japan.

Summary

Smart marketers are now going to impressive lengths to tailor their products to the specific demands of Japanese consumers. Johnson & Johnson (Japan), for example, changed one of its toothbrushes seven times before releasing it. "There is no magic in marketing. It's how well you meet the needs of the consumer that makes the difference between a successful product launch and a failure," said Masami Atarashi, president of Johnson & Johnson (Japan).

Nippon Lever, marketers of Lux brand soap, has six different brands on the Japanese market. Explained marketing services manager Roger Brooking: "Sixty percent of the soap sold in Japan is bought as gifts, and customers want a variety of designs and packaging to choose from on different occasions."

The number of foreign companies who have recognized the advantages of establishing factories in Japan—and becoming a part of the local scene—continues to grow. A spokesman for Fairchild Semiconductor Corporation, which opened a $100 million plant in Nagasaki in 1986, noted that Japanese society is very closed and that to succeed in Japan you have to come in and become a part of the culture.

The message is simple. The Japanese prefer to buy things made in Japan even if they have a foreign name on them. Japanese customers want to be sure of a guaranteed source of supply, and they prefer to buy from companies that are nearby so they can develop and maintain a close personal relationship with them.

In the case of Fairchild, it was deliberately designed to be more Japanese than American. It has quality-control circles and suggestion programs, operators do their own maintenance, morning exercises are obligatory, and there are company sports meets, mandatory baseball, tournaments, and temple festivals.

Wisdom Gathering

Learning how to do business with the Japanese requires a specific commitment to new ways of thinking and behaving—a process that begins with wisdom gathering and goes on to include a variety of personal experiences that range from becoming adept at exchanging business cards to sitting on *tatami* (reed-mat) floors.

The first commitment, however, is to the seriousness of your goals. Doing business in Japan is not something that can be undertaken lightly. Your success will be determined to a considerable extent by the firmness of your decision and the extent to which you are willing to go to achieve success. A major part of this commitment is that you take the learning itself seriously. It is typical of many Western businessmen to ignore or laugh at the cultural customs of others, particularly when these customs seems so inconsequential—so unrelated to the business of business. That is a serious mistake.

The second commitment is to time and personal involvement. You must be willing and able to spend time at preparing to do business with the Japanese and at developing a personal involvement that goes well beyond what is ordinarily necessary in Western countries. The Japanese are extremely sensitive to personal behavior in private, as well as business, relationships. The rules and expectations are minutely defined. Proper behavior requires the kind of skill and stage presence associated with professional acting.

The Japanese do not automatically expect foreigners to know or follow their rigid rules of behavior, but they are ill at ease with foreigners who do not, and they are unable to develop close relationships with them. This, of course, results in a constant strain on both sides.

The first and most practical step in beginning the process of wisdom gathering is to read carefully and synthesize several of the better books on Japan. I recommend the following titles (there are many others):

Japanese Etiquette and Ethics in Business, by Boye De Mente (Passport Books, Lincolnwood, Illinois)

Passport's Japan Almanac, by Boye De Mente (Passport Books, Lincolnwood, Illinois)

Shadows of the Rising Sun, by Jared Taylor (Charles E. Tuttle Company, Rutland, Vt./William Morrow)

Miracle by Design, by Frank Gibney (New York Times Books)

The Japanese Mind: The Goliath Explained, by Robert C. Christopher (Linden Press)

From Bonsai to Levis, by George Fields (Macmillan)

There are also several very worthwhile English-language magazines on Japan that you should subscribe to and read:

Japan Journal (a monthly general interest magazine on Japan that emphasizes business topics), Suite 305, JACC Bldg., 244 S. San Pedro St., Los Angeles, CA 90012. $28 for one year.

Journal of Japanese Trade & Industry, published bimonthly by the Japan Economic Foundation, 11th Floor, Fukoku Seimei Bldg., 2-2-2 Uchisaiwai-cho, Chiyoda-ku, Tokyo 100, Japan. Available in the U.S. and Canada from Elsevier Science Publishers, 52 Vanderbilt Avenue, New York, NY 10017, and other areas from Elsevier Science Publishers, P.O. Box 211, 1000 AE Amsterdam, The Netherlands.

Tokyo Business Today, published by Toyo Keizai Shinpo Sha, 1-4 Nihonbashi, Hongokucho, Chuo-ku, Tokyo 103, Japan.

Journal of the American Chamber of Commerce in Japan (see Other Sources in the back of this book).

Name Card Reminder

It is absolutely essential that you have name cards if you want to do business in Japan. Having the cards printed in both English and Japanese gives you a significant advantage—and you need every advantage you can get. To find out if you can get Japanese-language typesetting in your area, contact the local chapter of the Japan-American Society (if there is one), the nearest office of Japan Air Lines, the Japanese Consulate, Japanese Yellow Pages, the local branch office of a Japanese company, etc.

If you are in Tokyo and need name cards in a hurry, you can get same-day service at Nagashima Associates on the ground-floor rear of the Imperial Hotel and at Sun Ace in Nihonbashi (tel. 667-4936). Sun Ace delivers.

Have your cards printed on good-quality paper and carry them in a cardholder. They are valuable business tools and should be treated as such.

When you receive the name card of one or more persons prior to or during sit-down meetings, it is customary to place the name cards on the table in front of you, to study them intently for a few seconds and then leave them on the table for additional reference until you have learned the names and titles of the individuals involved. Laying them out on the table according to the seating arrangement of the various individuals is a good way to keep track of who is who.

Introductions

The importance of going into Japan with introductions cannot be overemphasized. The introduction gives you instant recognization, both as an individual and as a representative of your company. There are, of course, two kinds of introductions—from one person to another on an individual basis and from an individual in a company to a contact or colleague in another company.

Before you approach any individual or any company for an introduction to someone or any company in Japan, it is very important for you to have already done a lot of homework and to have identified the Japanese company or companies with which you would like to do business. The reason for this, obviously, is that you want an introduction that is as specific and as targeted as possible and that will be recognized by the recipient.

Effectively identifying a Japanese company includes pinpointing its group relationships—its bank, its association, its suppliers, its customers, its ownership. Each of these group relationships offers a point of contact that is acceptable to the Japanese. While direct contact is certainly not out of the question, particularly if you represent a larger, better-known company, the smaller you are and the less well-known you are, the better your chances will be if you approach the Japanese company of your choice through a traditional contact point.

The easiest of these points of contact to identify is usually the bank, since virtually all Japanese companies and company directories list their banks. The next step is to find out if your own local bank happens to have a correspondent relationship with the Japanese bank concerned. If so, an introduction from the international department of your bank to the Japanese bank is a good place to start. If not, your bank should be able to tell you which local bank does business with the Japanese bank.

When you approach any Japanese company with the intention of establishing a business relationship, you must be prepared to answer a number of specific questions before you can expect to engage in any meaningful dialogue. The questions include: Where did you get their name, how long has your company been in business, how many employees are in your company, what are your annual sales, how do you promote/market your goods, what is the level of your technology, do you regularly introduce new products, have you done business in Japan before, what is your business plan for the Japanese market, why are you approaching them?

You should make sure that any written introduction you receive from your bank or elsewhere answers as many of these questions as possible. It will encourage the Japanese bank or anyone else to react more favorably on your behalf, impress the Japanese company concerned, and greatly enhance your prospects.

Japanese banks traditionally play the role of go-between for their clients and often initiate new ventures on their behalf. If you cannot for any reason decide on which Japanese trader, manufacturer, importer, or distributor you should approach, Japanese banks are often in the best position to advise you.

With the number of Japanese banks, agencies, trading firms, and subsidiaries now operating abroad, it is often possible to begin the process of entering the Japanese market by approaching local offices. A majority of the Japanese firms overseas are in fact on the lookout for new products, new ventures, or new relationships that they can introduce to their home office or to an affiliated company in Japan.

Establishing Your Network

The more time, effort, and care you take in establishing a network of pertinent contacts in Japan, the better are your chances of success in any endeavor. This network should include key government officials, executives of appropriate industry or trade associations, any research labs or industries involved in your area, news media covering your industry, bankers, any service club you may be a member of, a private club (for recreational/social activities), the American Chamber of Commerce in Japan, etc., plus, if possible, a well-known professor, researcher, or doctor, depending on your product area.

One of the best investments any foreign company that wants to enter the Japanese market can make is to retain the services of a respected consultant who has a long successful background of activity in Japan, someone whose contacts go back 20, 30, or more years. The more prominent this individual is in the Japanese community, the easier it will be for you to achieve your goals.

Identifying Your Market

Failure to pinpoint your market precisely can be an especially costly and often fatal mistake in Japan. Once your market has been identified, the next step is to make sure your product is constituted and packaged to fit the market. Next comes creating and implementing a launch program—steps in which your consultant and network should play key roles.

The Human Element

Keep in mind that to succeed in Japan you must emphasize the personal and human side of business. Pushing product merit and profits will generally get you nowhere fast. To sell to the Japanese, you must understand their likes, dislikes, and idiosyncrasies and cater to them. Working effectively with the Japanese requires even more sensitivity and skill in coping with human relations in their cultural context.

Follow-up and Nurturing

One of the biggest weaknesses of foreign companies approaching the Japanese market is their failure to appropriately follow up on the various contacts they make in the earlier stages of any relationship. It is essential to keep in mind that regular personal contact is vital in developing and maintaining a market in Japan. This nurturing process never ends and must be built into the philosophy and practice of the business.

It is, in fact, this personal nature of business in Japan that helps make working for a living more tolerable here than it is in many countries. The *aisatsu* courtesy visits, the year-end office parties, the New Year's office parties, the company trips, the nighttime entertainment system—all these add to the special ambience of the world of Japanese business and help make the effort worthwhile for people who have an affinity for Japanese culture.

Chapter 17

Living in Japan

Myths and Realities

Living in Japan for the foreign businessman may not be what the home office or envious friends and relatives generally consider it to be. It does not give the businessman a financial advantage. It does not allow him to have more free time. It does not allow him to keep up with what is going on in the industry back in his home country. It does not always enhance his chances of moving up in the company hierarchy once he finishes his tour of foreign duty. It does not mean an easygoing, comfortable life of leisure beyond the boss's sight.

What it does—almost invariably—mean is a drop in the businessman's standard of living in terms of both convenience and comfort. What it may do to his mental state is even more serious. His chances of developing an ulcer or having a nervous breakdown are increased tenfold. He is far more apt to become an excessive drinker, to have family troubles, and to fail at his job. Records show that the average stay for American executives in Japan falls some 40 percent short of the expected tour because of the above factors.

There is an important difference in whether the man comes out here voluntarily or is sent by his company. Those who want to come are self-programmed to like the place, get along, and be a success. The other category is more likely to dislike Japan and to have a lower tolerance and frustration level.

A. C. Pinder, long-time resident of Japan and writer of the popular *Trials of Our Man in Tokyo* column in *Shipping Trade News*, found that "wife trouble" was one of the major reasons why American businessmen in Japan fail so often. The wife often finds it difficult, if not impossible, to adjust to local conditions. She cannot communicate with her Japanese neighbors and must do her shopping and run her house in an altogether different manner than she is accustomed to in the United States or elsewhere.

Another factor that is a frequent source of friction between foreign businessmen and their wives in Japan is the presence and general availability of so many very pretty Japanese girls.

Answering a survey on attitudes of American businessmen in Japan, the president of a leading United States firm in Tokyo said: "Wives who are enthusiastic about Japan on arrival frequently become dissatisfied with a schedule that often keeps husbands out of town or involved in entertainment that does not include them. A wife who is constantly complaining and urging her husband to go back home is little help to the man who is trying to cope with all the unusual problems involved in running an office in Japan.

"Vacation areas are also generally packed with people, unless one is prepared to pay astronomical prices for those rare elements in Japan—seclusion and quiet." The same man then added: "Yet, most of us will remain in Japan. The opportunities are tremendous, and in spite of the disadvantages the balance sheet indicates that Japan is still a pleasant, as well as a challenging, place to live." In this added comment, he was, of course, expressing the viewpoint of a businessman/male.

The Cost of Living in Japan

The mid-1980s saw an influx of foreign families into Tokyo, as American and European businessmen flocked here to take advantage of the new trade and financial liberalization measures. This resulted in a high demand for Western-style housing and a subsequent leap in the cost of suitable rental accommodations. At present, rental properties in the Yoyogi, Uehara, Komaba,and Harajuku areas go for ¥20,000 to ¥25,000 per square meter per month, while in the closer-in districts of Azabu and Akasaka the rate is even higher.

This means a 60-tsubo (200 square meter) Western-style home that would be suitable for a foreign manager with a family goes for one million yen or more per month.

The demand for foreign housing is expected to grow in Tokyo as Japan becomes more international, and this has led to the construction of a number of housing projects designed for foreign occupancy. One such compound, called Lares (from the ancient Roman god who watched over homes), includes appliances imported from GE, Westinghouse, and Magic Chef, with sports club memberships, an English-speaking doctor, and grocery delivery for residents. The homes in the compound were designed by a French architect, are two stories, and have four bedrooms, two and a half baths, fireplaces, and built-in cable TV hookups.

A recent report prepared for the American Chamber of Commerce in Japan showed that 90–100 square meter, two-bedroom homes in Tokyo were going for $3,000 to $3,500 per month. For a 120–160 square meter apartment, the average was $4,000 to $4,500. Three and four bedroom homes and apartments ranged from $5,000 to $8,000 per month—not including a deposit equivalent to anywhere from three to six months' rent. Part of this deposit is normally regarded as "key" money (*kenri ken*) and is not returnable.

Houses and apartments that do not include the major appliances may be available at lower rents than the above. This means, of course, that the renter must either buy or lease the necessary appliances.

Finding a Home

The most important problem facing the newly arrived businessman in Japan is finding a home. Since this means more to the wife than to the husband, I enlisted the aid of several wives in studying this subject. Their comments reflected almost identical experiences and views. Said one:

"Blessed are the foreigners who come to Japan with a company that provides housing—either company-owned or leased on a long-term basis for rotating employees. The hotels are full of families not so benignly treated, and just the mouth-frothing frustration of house hunting is enough to drive the less persistent ones back to a waiting plane—even before the hotel manager decides the children are more of a nuisance to the hotel than to the parents and tells them they have to leave. Obviously, the best place to go if one wants a house is to a house agent. This is a fine idea, provided there are acceptable houses available, but often there aren't, even if the prospective tenant is willing to pay up to $5,000 a month and still not have adequate housing."

The For Rent ads in the daily English-language newspapers make it sound easy (if expensive), but a house they describe as "gorgeous" is usually anything but, by American standards, and its location may be something else. Real residential areas, as Americans think of them, hardly exist in Japanese cities. There are many areas of Tokyo where most of the buildings are residential, but, with a few rather distant exceptions, they are minuscule in size, irregular in shape, and exceedingly cluttered in appearance.

There are many large Western-style apartment buildings in Tokyo that provide all the modern conveniences—central heating, air-conditioning, built-ins, and so on. They are usually more expensive than houses if more than one bedroom is needed. Again, depending on location, degree of plushness, etc., these range from around $2,000 to $8,000 per month.

There are cheaper houses and cheaper apartments, if you are willing to live more or less Japanese style (no central heating or cooling, little furniture, small rooms usually with straw-mat floors, often a nonflush toilet, and frequently no bath); or if you are willing to live an hour and a half or so from the downtown area.

It is common for Japanese landlords to require several months' rent in advance. The minimum is usually three months, and the maximum is one year. (Smaller, relatively inexpensive Japanese-type bachelor apartments are usually rented for just one month's advance rent.)

If the foreign businessman is transferred to Japan without housing already arranged for him and his family, it is often advisable for him to come alone and send for his family only after he has found a home. This, of course, means that his wife has to trust him to find one that she and their children will be willing to live in.

Transferees arriving in Tokyo without a house or apartment waiting for them now have a number of viable options. There are short-term and long-term "apartment hotels," as well as "weekly mansions," that are fully equipped with furniture, kitchen utensils, TV, telephone, electrical appliances, and other essentials for temporary or permanent living.

Among the apartment-hotel chains, Asahi Homes Ltd. is one of the largest, with facilities in several major Tokyo residential areas, including such close-in and popular districts as Roppongi, Moto-Azabu, Sendagaya, Akasaka, Nihonbashi, and Takanawa. For current vacancies and details, contact Asahi Homes, 3-2-19 Roppongi, Minato-ku, Tokyo 106, Japan—tel 583-7551.

The best known of the "weekly mansion" groups, which are limited to furnished rooms (single or double), is Tsukasa Weekly Mansion, 1-24-17 Higashi Gotanda, Shinagawa-ku, Tokyo 141,

Japan—tel 440-0111, fax 440-3801. Tsukasa has some two dozen multistoried mansions spread around the Yamanote Loop commuter train line that encircles central Tokyo.

Other Tokyo companies that offer furnished apartments include Fuji Flats, Homat Regina, Kioicho Court, Kitano Arms, Kojimachi Sanbancho Mansion, Sanbancho Hilltop Mansion, Aobadai Homes, Akasaka Dia, Azabu Court, Azabu Heights, Castle Azabu, Harajuku Park Mansion, and Palace Aoyama. There are at least two dozen similar apartment complexes in the central Tokyo area.

Rental Information Center

One valuable source of apartment and housing information in Tokyo is Nippon Jutaku Joho Co. Ltd. (NJJ), or the Japan Housing Information Company, which provides free information on apartment rentals, offices, office buildings, store facilities for lease, and so on. Those wishing to use the services of NJJ have only to call in (or fax) and specify their needs, including their budget—tel (03) 476-1191, fax (3) 476-2261. You may also register with NJJ by writing to the company at 1-12-18 Jinnan, Shibuya-ku, Tokyo, Japan.

If you are moving into an unfurnished home, you may want to bring most of your kitchen things with you. Whether or not you bring other main household items (beds, couches) is a matter of choice. All these things can be obtained in Japan, although desirable items are much more expensive there than when they are bought elsewhere.

Home electricity in the Tokyo area is 50 cycles, 100 volts, which means that some American appliances, made for 60-cycle current, will not operate properly or at all without adapters. American-made washing machines, TV sets, and phonographs all have to be adapted. Cooking appliances usually work, but you have to set the heat indicator higher.

Furniture Rental and Leasing

Virtually any household or office item needed on a temporary basis may be rented or leased. Among the rental companies in Tokyo are Heart International (Fujiyoshi Co., Ltd.), 302 Town House Moto Azabu, 1-5-24 Moto Azabu, Minato-ku, Tokyo, Japan—tel 444-

4051, fax 444-4053 (which specializes in office furnishings); AID Leasing Service, 707 Takanawa Grand Heights, 2-14-14 Takanawa, Minato-ku, Tokyo, Japan—tel 445-4650 (furniture,refrigerators, and TV sets); and Rents (Taiyo Rental System), 1-17-16 Higashi Yama, Meguro-ku, Tokyo, Japan—tel 719-3721. Rents' slogan is that it rents anything. It also has an outlet in Osaka—tel 306-3147.

Another major rental service, which also caters receptions, ceremonies, and sporting events, is Tokyo Soshoku Ltd., 2-8-3 Yazaike, Adachi-ku, Tokyo—tel 856-2333.

Sky-High Prices

It has been conservatively estimated that it costs up to three or four times as much for an American executive to live in Tokyo if he attempts to live on the same level as he did in the United States. This comes as something of a surprise to firms making their first contact with Japan. Most have heard that Japan has become a relatively expensive place to live for foreign businessmen, but it is difficult for them to believe just how expensive it has become. (A cup of coffee in a hotel coffee shop costs from $3 to $5 per cup; a small glass of orange juice, from $4 to $6.)

Many head office firemen visiting Japan underestimate the cost of living there because about all they pay for, in addition to hotel expenses and some gifts, are a few restaurant and nightclub bills. These are high, but the visiting executive observes that "such tourist expenses are not routine for the resident who lives in a private home and 'knows the ropes.'" As it happens, however, any American living in Japan who wants to maintain some semblance of the living standard he left at home is forced to patronize the same places that cater to tourists. These are the only places offering Western services.

Junior-grade foreign executives in Japan often have a particularly tough time of it. They generally make quite a bit less salary than the top managers make, and their fringe benefits are also proportionately less. Yet, it costs them just as much to eat, to send their kids to school, and to join in the limited social life of the foreign community. Unless their company is able and willing to give them a liberal living allowance and foot bills for such things as club fees (golf club memberships range from $5,000 to $500,000), the junior executive is relegated to a kind of third society—several rungs below the ranking foreign executive and off to one side of middle-class Japanese.

"In many ways," a young executive said, "we are forced to compete directly with both Japanese and foreigners who are on large expense accounts. Since practically all of the facilities that Americans find adequate or acceptable are designed and priced for those who are wealthy or have unlimited expense accounts, our out-of-the-office activities are limited, and this puts us in an awkward position when it comes to accepting and returning social obligations."

Orientation Programs

More and more foreign families moving to Japan are taking advantage of the extensive orientation and counseling services offered by such companies as Oak Associates of Tokyo, which seeks to provide businessmen and their wives and children with a suitable understanding and appreciation of their new environment. It is especially important that entire families participate in these programs because if any member of the family is unhappy about living in Japan it can spoil the experience for the whole lot.

Oak Associates notes that it can often take several months to find the right home for a family and that selecting schools can be equally time-consuming. Other points in the orientation program: Parents are warned that children in Japan have easy access to alcohol; wives become less concerned about the late-night hours their husbands spend in bars and cabarets with Japanese businessmen after they have visited such places themselves.

Companies whose employees have participated in the Oak Associates program say the fee is far less costly than having to relocate a family because one or more of its members could not adjust to the Japanese environment.

Japanese Taxes

There are several kinds of taxes—direct and indirect—imposed on individuals and companies in Japan. To foreign businessmen and foreign residents, the most important of these taxes are (1) taxes on incomes and profits; (2) taxes on consumption (restaurant and club taxes, automobile taxes, legal stamp taxes, electrical and gas taxes, etc.); (3) inheritance and gift taxes; and (4) taxes imposed on manufacturers and retailers. Although the laws are revised in the spring of each year, the basic structure usually remains the same.

Individuals in Japan are subject to national income taxes and to a prefectural or municipal "inhabitant's" tax, which is usually referred to by foreigners who live in urban areas as "ward taxes."

There are three categories of foreigners who must pay taxes in Japan. These are (1) nonresidents—that is, individuals who do not live in Japan but have income in Japan; (2) nonpermanent residents, or those who have lived in Japan for one year but do not intend to live there permanently (most foreign businessmen); and (3) permanent residents.

The nonresident with income in Japan (from royalties, business interests, etc.) must pay a flat 10 percent to 20 percent in national income taxes. The nonpermanent resident must pay taxes at graduated rates (unless otherwise specified) on all income earned in Japan or remitted to and paid in Japan. The permanent resident must pay taxes on all income, regardless of its source.

The national and local (prefectural and municipal) taxes are lower in Japan than they are in the United States for those with lower incomes. The minimum taxable is 2,015,000 yen (family of four). The rate of taxation, after deductions, begins at approximately 23 percent and escalates rather rapidly to 75 percent. In recent years, the average amount of taxes paid on a per capita basis has been around 436,000 yen (of which 287,000 was national tax). The overall ratio of national income to tax has been 24.2 percent.

Local or ward taxes are figured on a percentage of the national taxes and are graduated downward. That is, the higher your national income taxes, the lower percentage you pay as local taxes. Those whose national taxes are very low must pay as high as 65 percent of the amount as their local taxes. Those with high national taxes pay as low as 24 percent of their national taxes as local taxes.

Several categories of income are nontaxable. These include transportation allowances, special cost of living allowances, business travel expenses, interest on postal and other savings, and casualty insurance payments. Resident taxpayers are also entitled to a series of deductions from their gross income, beginning with a basic personal exemption and including employment income deductions, life insurance premiums, residential property damage insurance premiums, dependent allowances, old age allowances, medical expenses, and social insurance premiums.

246

Corporation income in Japan is taxed in three different ways and is quite complicated. These three ways are corporation taxes, corporation inhabitant taxes, and enterprise taxes. The final rate of taxation is determined by whether income is distributed as dividends. When income is distributed as dividends the corporation tax is 23.21 percent, the corporate inhabitant tax is 3.41 percent, and the enterprise tax is 10.71 percent, for a total percentage of 37.3 percent. When income is not distributed as dividends, the rates are 32.82, 4.82, and 10.71 for a total of 48.35 percent.

Because of the complexity of the business tax structure in Japan, the importance of an expert tax accountant can hardly be overestimated. A number of well-known American accounting firms have branches in Tokyo, and some Japanese accountants specialize in handling the tax obligations of foreign firms. An English-language *Guide to Japanese Taxes* is published each year by Zaikei Shoho Sha, 1-2-14 Higashi, Shimbashi, Minato-ku, Tokyo, Japan.

Personal Transportation

Perhaps the next most important problem facing the foreign businessman setting up housekeeping in Japan is what to do about personal transportation if he has young school-age children. Neither owning your own car nor utilizing the public transportation system is a completely satisfactory solution. While plentiful and fantastically punctual, Japan's commuter trains and subways are unbelievably crowded for two hours in the morning and two hours in the evening. To the foreign commuter unused to such conditions, especially where women and children are concerned, this can be intimidating.

Another important factor in considering the use of public transportation is whether your home is close to a station or stop. Chances are that the foreigner's home will be located anywhere from a 5- to a 25-minute walk from the nearest transportation. This can be an annoying problem not only because of time, but also because it rains from 30 to 90 days a year in Japan. The majority of the streets outside downtown areas have no sidewalks. In many outlying districts, the small lanes leading to private homes may not be paved at all.

Raincoats, umbrellas, and boots provide only a minimum amount of protection, so businessmen who have to dress well have little choice but to use private transportation or taxis on such occasions.

Private ownership of a car in Japan is almost a full-time job for the Japanese. For the foreigner, it is even more of a problem. You may bring one car with you duty-free when you enter Japan to establish residence, as part of your household goods. There are dozens of very specific requirements and qualifications that you must satisfy before you can actually bring a car in, however. Seven book-sized pages are necessary to list and explain these requirements and provisions. After you succeed in getting your car in, there is an annual road tax—based on the size of your car—which runs between $200 and $500 a year, plus compulsory auto inspections that can cost double or triple this amount.

This compulsory inspection (sha ken) is required when you receive your license plates, when renewing your registration, and at regular intervals, depending on the age of the car. The car inspection itself is not too bad, but the mandatory procedure that must be followed before the inspection is something else. You must take your car to a designated car service center where, no matter how good its condition, it will be thoroughly reexamined and tested by the center mechanics, who mark each part they check with a daub of yellow paint (to show that it has been inspected) and then prepare a detailed report of the inspection. For a fee, the service center will also take your car through the official inspection. These authorized garages invariably find something on your car that needs to be fixed or replaced, and you seldom get by without a sizable bill.

Automobile insurance is compulsory in Japan, and you must have it before your license will be issued. Since the driver of a car involved in an accident is held responsible for the injured person, it is a good idea to carry more coverage than the law requires. It is also recommended that the car owner, as well as his firm, be named as the insured party.

If you have a valid United States driver's license or an international driver's license, you are not required to take a driving test, but you must pass an eye test, a color-blind check, and a written test on driving regulations and traffic signs. If you do not have one of the above licenses, you must take a "mechanic's test" to demonstrate your knowledge of the engine and other parts and how to repair them. This applies to everyone! This test is fairly difficult, and many people, particularly girls and women, have to take it over and over again before they manage to pass it.

If you should end up having to obtain a driver's license in Japan the same way the Japanese do, you are in for an extraordinary experience. Before you can apply for a license, you must attend a government-regulated driving course at one of 1,500 licensed driver's schools around the country. Before being allowed to drive, you must attend 25 hours of classroom lectures, including five hours on the construction and operation of a motor vehicle. Next comes dry runs on a simulator. Finally, there are 17 sessions at the wheel of a car on a driving range, accompanied by an instructor who monitors your every move.

Successful completion of this part of the program gets you a learner's permit, which allows you to drive on selected roads and streets. You must log ten hours of off-range driving in these designated areas.

A typical driving course takes six weeks and costs $1,500 or more. Schools located in resort areas, where various recreational activities are combined with the study, are substantially more expensive.

Approximately half of all Japanese who take the driving test, after having completed the driver's course, fail and have to take additional instruction. But despite all this care and preparation, automobile accidents are common.

When you go to get your license, be sure to take your passport, your alien registration booklet, two photographs that are no bigger than 33mm size, and your current license. If you move after getting your license be sure to report your address change to the local police station within ten days so it can be shown on your license. It's the law!

Japan uses international traffic and highway signs, and they are easy to understand even when you see them for the first time. The main difference between driving in the United States and driving in Japan is that in the latter you drive on the left side of the street or highway (British style). Another equally important difference is that many Japanese drivers do not obey traffic regulations. They speed, veer back and forth, switch lanes, cut into traffic from side streets without waiting for a gap in traffic, and pass on hills and curves and in tunnels. About the only rule you can go by is that any vehicle in front of you by as much as one inch—no matter how it got there—has the right of way.

It is possible for a foreign businessman in Japan to import a new car from his home country, but the requirements are so strict and discriminating that few people do it. If you do not bring your own car with you as household goods, you may buy a used car from someone who is leaving or from a car lot. Remember that if you buy a car from some one who works for the United States government and the car has not been in Japan long enough to be duty-free (two-years), the person buying the car is responsible for paying any import duties concerned.

Rather than go through the problems and expense of trying to import a car into Japan or buying a used one, many residents buy Japanese-made cars, which are much less of a hassle and more suited for the narrow streets and lanes.

Another thing to remember is that before you can register a car in Japan you must have a certificate from the police station in your local district attesting to the fact that you have either a garage or some other non-public area in which to park your car off the street.

Once you finally get a car and your license and begin driving, there are so many places in the major cities where you can't turn left or right or park that much of the initial irritation continues. Fees for the limited public parking facilities in major cities are high—several dollars an hour. Businessmen who can afford drivers simply get out at their destinations and let the drivers worry about what to do until they return.

Shopping for Food

There is a wide variety of stores available that carry basic food items, including the neighborhood shops that cater to Japanese families and, of course, sell mostly domestic products (rice, fish, vegetables, canned goods, fruit, eggs, oils, meats), along with self-service convenience markets, such as 7-Eleven and Circle K, supermakets, chain stores, and the huge food sections of department stores.

With the exception of domestically produced vegetables, fish, rice, and fruits as tangerines, food items in Japan are likely to be more expensive than the average price abroad. By very careful shopping—and acquiring a taste for basic foods—one can get by fairly reasonably by shopping in the small neighborhood stores.

It also pays to know when to shop for daily perishables, as the price tends to drop as the evening draws to a close—with some real bargains available just before closing time.

The food sections of department stores (more expensive than local shops) carry a wide range of gourmet-type foods and many prepared and partly prepared foods, along with the regular everyday grocery items. Department store food sections also usually carry selections of imported food items.

The supermarkets, where most foreign families do their shopping, carry both imported and domestic merchandise in a fairly wide variety. They are expensive, even by high standards. Imported items are at least double the overseas price.

Most foreigners who become residents in Japan eventually develop a taste for a number of Japanese dishes that are both inexpensive and delicious, and this can do much to prevent the food budget from growing to astronomical proportions. These include some of the noodle dishes (*O'soba, ramen*) that can be ordered from neighborhood shops and are delivered to your home steaming hot, along with rice dishes, and seafood dishes, such as fish, shrimp, and oysters.

Any imported item is expensive, and if you prefer to stick to foreign-made tobacco, cigarettes, cosmetics, drugs, liquors, and wines you must be prepared to pay from two to three times what you would pay for the same items outside Japan.

Shopping for Clothing

Shopping for children's wear in Japan is an adventurous experience. There are many styles and price ranges to choose from, and just about anything that a child might need or want can be obtained at fairly reasonable prices—unless you choose to do your shopping in prestigious stores.

Shopping for adult Westerners in Japan is a different matter. While there is a fantastic array of men's and women's wearing apparel beautifully displayed in department stores and specialty shops, it is not made to fit the Western frame. Women who are size eight and under can make out fairly well, as can men who are no more than five feet, nine inches in height and weigh no more than 160 pounds. This, of course, eliminates many Western men and women.

On the other hand, most department stores feature small "Corners" of imported apparel and accessories, primarily high fashions for women. But prices on these items generally run from two to five times as high as prices outside Japan. Good quality men's outerwear and various types of women's dresses can also be readily tailor-made in Japan at bearable prices. Some tailors cater almost exclusively to a foreign clientele.

Shoes are a special problem for adult Westerners in Japan. In the first place, one can seldom find a pair of domestic-made shoes any larger than a man's size nine. Furthermore, at this time shoes made in Japan for domestic sales come in only three widths, the widest of which is usually not wide enough for the Westerner. Imported shoes are available in numerous specialty shops, but, as usual, the price is about double or triple the price elsewhere.

There are a number of shoe shops in Tokyo that cater to patrons with large feet. These include Big Shoes Akasaka, 3-21-18 Akasaka, Minato-ku, Tokyo—tel 586-6234; and Ten (Big Shoes Collection), 7-8-13 Nishi Shinjuku, Shinjuku-ku, Tokyo—tel 369-7511.

Because of the difficulty of obtaining suitable Western-size clothing in Japan at reasonable prices, many foreign residents make shopping trips to Hong Kong as often as possible and usually stock up on their trips home.

Schools

There are schools offering American-type curricula in English, from kindergarten through high school, in Tokyo, Yokohama, Osaka, and Kobe. American families may enter their children at one of the few United States military dependent schools still being operated in Japan when space is available. Tuition at the commercial (non-United States military) schools is very high—from $600 to over $1,000 a year for a kindergarten student and $2,000 or more for high school students.

Schools in the Tokyo area include the American School in Japan, which includes grades from kindergarten through senior high school; St. Mary's International School for Boys, which also has grades 1 through 12; Sacred Heart International School for Girls, and the privately run nondenominational Nishimachi International School. All are expensive.

There is usually a waiting list for these schools, and it is necessary to register early (registration fees are extra and run up to $300 or more). The tuition generally includes books and insurance. An entrance examination or placement test is usually required.

Along with the scarcity and expense of Western-oriented schools in Japan, foreign parents of school-age children are faced with the problem of getting them to and from whatever schools they attend. Children who are too young to make use of local transportation on their own have to be escorted both ways every day. Some parents assign this duty to their chauffeur; in other cases, the mother drives the children to school. Families without personal cars have to use taxis or utilize local transportation, with a maid or the mother acting as escort.

One example, not as unusual as it may sound, emphasizes this problem. The wife of one of my friends has her maid stay at home to do housework and look after her three-year-old daughter, while she takes her six-year-old son to and from school each day. The trip there includes a five-minute walk to a bus stop, a 30-minute bus ride, a transfer followed by a 15-minute train ride, and then a 10-minute walk from the train station to the school. After seeing her son safely to school, the mother returns home, having spent two hours traveling. In the afternoon she repeats this roundtrip. Not surprisingly, she will be very happy to return to the United States.

Babysitting Services

Professional babysitting services are available from a number of organizations in Tokyo. These include I Baby Sitter in northwest Tokyo—tel 930-0504, Nihon Baby Sitter in Urawa-shi—tel 822-8058, Sugamo Babies Home in Toshima-ku—tel 947-7481, and Tokyo Baby Sitter in Komazawa, Setagaya-ku—tel 410-3496. The services are licensed by the Labor Ministry and under the control of the Tokyo Metropolitan Government.

Getting Around in Cities

Just getting from one place to another in a Japanese city—especially going to a place one has never been to before—is a major accomplishment for the newly arrived foreigner who usually does not speak or read Japanese (which helps, but not that much!). The reason is that streets and lanes in Japanese cities are normally not named. There is no systematic pattern to the layout of most streets outside downtown areas. The addresses of places have absolutely nothing to do with the street they are on. Buildings and houses that adjoin each other may have absolutely no relationship between their addresses.

253

Japanese cities are therefore labyrinths, more baffling than any ever deliberately devised. Japanese cities and towns are divided up into areas of irregular shape and size, some big and some small and most of them odd-shaped. Buildings and homes in these areas were originally addressed according to the chronological order in which they were built. In other words, the first house put up was designated No. 1, and the second was designated No. 2, but the second house or building might be some distance away, and it can be behind, in front of, or somewhere off to one side of the first. Furthermore, as the cities became more and more crowded, houses and buildings went up in between those that were consecutively numbered, completely scrambling the order.

In the 1960s, considerable effort was made to eliminate some of the chaos in the Japanese addressing system, with some success, but it is still the most complicated, cumbersome, and confusing system in the world. Time and time again, it is a problem of elimination to find the desired address—and this holds even if you can read the Japanese address signs and ask questions in the vernacular. Newcomers to Tokyo or Osaka (which is not as bad as Tokyo) therefore may actually need a guide for the first few days and sometimes weeks, until they become familiar with just a few routes that they have to take regularly. This situation is another reason why many foreigners, especially the wives and children, feel so isolated and frustrated in Japan.

The Cook, Maid, and Chauffeur

Foreign families who can afford the expense have a maid, a cook, and a chaffeur. Some can afford only a maid and a cook or just a maid who does a little bit of everything. Many American wives feel they could not get along in Japan at all without a maid to take care of all the tradespeople who come to the door; to answer the phone when the caller is Japanese; to do a lot of the shopping, to pay the bills, which are usually in Japanese; to help with the children, etc. For their part, the executives of American companies in Japan are finding a chaffeur more and more of an asset, primarily because of the time and wear and tear a driver saves them.

Some maids cook, as well as do housework, and help with other chores. Such "cook-maids" receive from $800 to $1,500 a month (along with room and meals). A general maid who doesn't cook receives from around $500 to $1,000 per month. Monthly wages for nursemaids range from around $500 to $1,000 per month, depending on their experience and the number and ages of the children in their care. Wages for chauffeurs run from $1,200 to $2,500 a month (or more), plus food and lodging if they are required to stay away from home. Both maids and drivers generally receive seasonal bonuses amounting to one to three months' pay. The employer is also usually responsible for uniforms, medical expenses, and severance pay—all of which must be discussed and agreed on at the time of employment.

The best way to obtain maids and chauffeurs is to advertise in the Help Wanted sections of the English-language *Japan Times* and the *Mainichi Daily News*. In Tokyo, it is also a good idea to check the bulletin board at the American Club. Families leaving Japan generally put up notices in an effort to place their domestic help with newcomers.

There are numerous temporary-help companies offering the services of maids and other domestic servants on an hourly, daily, weekly, and monthly basis.

Leisure Time and Entertainment

Most foreign businessmen in Japan have less leisure time than they had at home. Because of the traditional Japanese system of mixing business and entertainment, the businessman is forced to spend many of his evenings at receptions and parties or in restaurants and nightclubs. Most foreign representatives here are also called on to entertain visiting "firemen"—in extreme cases, several times a month. For a while, many newcomers like this emphasis on entertainment, but it soon palls for most of those who have to keep it up month after month, and it eventually becomes a form of excruciating torture. For the few men who have no saturation point, however, Japan can be a modern day Bacchanalian paradise.

In addition to keeping business commitments that require an inordinate amount of outside entertainment, many Western businessmen in Tokyo also attempt to keep up with a self-perpetuating whirl of social activity that, for the most part, is masterminded by their wives and much of which centers around the American Club. The importance of the American Club to many foreign families cannot be overemphasized. Said one man: "The families here would be lost without it. It is their haven of sanity, their anchor to normal life."

One businessman observed: "My home life is constantly inter-rupted by visitors. And the entertainment climate is naturally up-setting to most wives because they are not included when it is business-related. I'm not home enough, and when I am I'm usually so tired that I don't even want to talk, much less play with the kids or take my wife out."

Vacations in Japan are far more expensive than might be imag-ined. Not being conditioned to Japanese food and Japanese-style accommodations, the Westerner has little choice but to pay first-class, tourist prices wherever he goes. (First-class Japanese ac-commodations in resort areas and in cities like Tokyo and Osaka are more expensive than Western-style accommodations, for that matter.) Friends of the author who vacation in Japan say they bud-get $100 a day for each member of the family requiring a separate seat and bed. On this basis, four people might spend $2,000 on a five-day trip. Of course, if the same family wanted to "rough it" and go second- or third-class Japanese style, which usually includes communal sleeping, they could get by for about half this amount.

As for home radio and television entertainment, the only day-long English-language radio broadcasting in Japan at this time is done by the American military station, Far East Network (FEN). This isn't much, but it's something. There is very little commercial English-language TV broadcasting in Japan. Such programming means only an hour or so of English-language viewing. Many movie houses, however, regularly feature American films in En-glish. Some hotels and luxury apartments have English-language cable-TV.

There is, of course, a great deal of Japanese entertainment avail-able to foreign residents. In fact, Japan is one of the entertainment capitals of the world. The choice ranges from the famous night-clubs and cabarets to go-go bars, hot-bath/massage parlors (now called Soaplands), traditional Japanese theater (*kabuki* and *noh*), stage musicals, symphony orchestras, puppet shows, burlesque shows, and all kinds of sporting events. *Sumo*, traditional Japanese wrestling by huge men in G-string-like costumes, is the most spectacular and colorful. There are also such participation sports as swimming, skiing, and mountain climbing.

As it happens, however, a great deal of the more readily acces-sible entertainment in Japan is either limited to men or to those who speak some Japanese and are turned on by strictly Japanese food, customs, and pleasures. This again eliminates many West-erners, particularly the wives and children.

The Japanese do not entertain in their homes the way Western- ers do because their homes are usually much too small (and often too fragile), and they usually are not equipped to take care of the needs of more than the members of the household. The Japanese system, developed over the centuries, is to entertain friends and others in public places, like inns, restaurants, and theaters.

Psychological Problems Facing Foreigners

In addition to experiencing daily misunderstandings and friction resulting from such vital cultural differences as language and val- ues, foreigners in Japan are also faced with a wide range of minor irritations that prick away at their most sensitive spots. One of the smaller, but often acutely annoying, problems is the time it takes to obtain and update visas and identification booklets.

Other things that may grate on the nerves and sensibilities of foreigners include the tremendous concentration of people in Japan's large cities, with the resulting crowds of humanity in the streets, stores, and theaters and on all forms of transportation. There are also the narrow, twisting, sidewalkless "streets" that ac- count for some 80 percent of the thoroughfares in the country; the fact that these so-called streets are choked with traffic much of the time; the scarcity and high cost of housing; the time it takes to commute to offices, stores, and schools; the potential danger from fires, earthquakes, and typhoons; the red tape connected with everything involving the government; and the difficulty of getting what you want when you want it from carpenters, repair shops, and handymen.

Many wives, never having had maids before and not knowing how to treat servants, are also constantly embroiled in some kind of hired-help problem.

All these irritations are made more galling because, not knowing the Japanese language and having little, if any, affinity for more than a taste of the Japanese way of life, most short-time foreign residents in Japan are isolated to an extreme degree. Some feel the Japanese rub salt into the foreigner's wounded pride and feelings by always carefully discriminating between foreigners and Japa- nese and by keeping foreigners on a sort of pedestal that has some advantages but at the same time exposes them relentlessly to public scrutiny.

How to Do Business with the Japanese

Foreign residents in Japan never lose the feeling of being outsiders and being discriminated against in some way. This hurts deeply, particularly among the businessmen who have labored for years and contributed more to the development of the country than they could ever be paid for. These people feel they have a rightful interest in Japan and are disappointed and frustrated when they meet indifference, discrimination, and opposition.

It is obviously true that the relationship between Japanese and foriegn businessmen living and working in Japan has changed considerably since the early 1950s. And there is no doubt that it will change further. The foreign businessman in Japan today is more likely to be looked at both as an outsider and as a dangerous competitor. Except in technological areas, the Japanese are convinced that there is very little, if anything, they can learn from the West. The pendulum has, in fact, swung the other way. The Japanese firmly believe that it is their turn to teach the West the joys and advantages of Japanese harmony in business, as well as in all other human affairs.

The newcomer arriving in Japan would be well advised to leave his superiority complex or his "Occupation" complex at home and to regard the Japanese as his equals who are not going to change their attitudes or values to suit his; who, indeed, may be more capable in their own milieu than he is in his; and finally, that he is in their territory and that in most cases the game is played according to their rules. If his success depends on bringing about changes in these rules, then he can expect it to require extraordinary receptivity, flexibility, patience, sincerity, intelligence, and perseverance—on his part, not theirs.

Glossary of Interesting and Useful Terms

BIKANYUSO (Bee-khan-yuu-so)   This is a word, or catchphrase, coined in 1984 by Shinji Fukukawa, then director general of Japan's Industrial Policy Bureau, in reference to the cultural values he said Japan's new industrial society should seek. *Bi* means beauty or fashionable; *kan* means feeling or taste; *yu* means pleasure or play, and *so* refers to creativity and innovation. The word caught on quickly not only among the young, but among future-oriented businessmen, as well.

HITO-KETA (Shh-toe kay-tah)   In marketing parlance, *hito-keta*, or "single-digiters," refers to people born during the first nine years of the Showa era (the reign of Emperor Hirohito, which began in 1926), who suffered during the war years and whose work ethic was primarily responsible for the rebirth of Japan as a major economic power. Those who were born from 1936 on, grew up after the war, and now make up the bulk of Japan's new, affluent consumer class, are known as *Futa-keto*, or "double-digiters."

IJIME (Ee-jee-may)   This word originally meant to tease or annoy in a relatively harmless way, but now it is used in reference to growing violence in Japan's schools—physical, as well as psychological, violence perpetrated by students on each other and sometimes by teachers, as well. The incidence of such violence in schools is indicative of the pressure children are under to achieve and the breakdown of the old concepts of group behavior and cooperation.

JITSU RYOKU (Jeet-sue rio-kuu)   This refers to an ideal type of manager in Japan—one who is quiet, unassuming, and reserved, but is competent, dependable, and loyal.

259

JIZEN KYOGI (Jee-zane k'yoe-ghee)   This phrase means prior consultation, something that is very important for employers to engage in when contemplating changing the work rules.

KANBAN (Kahn-bahn)   This is the famous "just-in-time" production control system developed by Toyota Motor Corporation in the early 1950s. The term actually means "signboard," but here it refers to a job instruction chart—covered with plastic—that shows what parts are needed where and in what quantity. Some companies have two types of *kanban*—one for internal use and the other for its outside suppliers. The very first *kanban* was in fact a large signboard erected in the predecessor of the Toyota Motor Corporation (Toyoda Loom Works) in the 1930s to tell delivery personnel what parts to take to the various assembly-line workers on a daily basis.

KANRI SHOKU (Kahn-ree show-kuu)   This phrase means "management status," any manager from the rank of *ka cho* (section head) on up.

KAIZEN (Kie-zen)   Translated directly, *kaizen* means "change/ improve" or "innovation/goodness." As typically used, it refers to both an attitude and an actual, desirable change in some process or solution. Some Japanese say that the Japanese themselves are imbued with a strong sense of *kaizen*, that it is responsible for their penchant for rapid change—in technology, fashion, etc.—and that this characteristic is one of the main factors responsible for Japan's economic success.

KIBO TAISHOKU (Kee-bow tie-show-kuu)   This means voluntary retirement. It generally refers to the situation in which employees are persuaded to retire voluntarily to avoid being dismissed.

KOROMOGAE (Koe-roe-moe-guy)   In Japan's Edo Period (1603—1868), the Tokugawa Government designated the specific date on which the population changed from winter to summer clothing in the early spring, and from summer to winter clothing in the late fall—regardless of what the weather happened to be like on that particular day. Although the edicts governing *koromogae*, or "apparel-changing," have long since been scrapped, both the term and the custom are coming back into use in the world of fashion—as a fashionable thing to do, as well as a marketing ploy.

KOSHIN JO (Koe-sheen joe)   This is an investigative agency that specializes in checking out the backgrounds of prospective employees—a very important step before hiring and one that foreign companies in Japan often failed to take.

MADO-GUCHI (Mah-Kuu sot-chee)   Literally, "window entrance," this term refers to a contact (company or person) through which one reaches someone else or accomplishes some action. If you want to get into a particular company, organization, or system, you must have a *mado-guchi*.

MAKU SATSU (Mah-kuu sot-sue)   This term literally means "to kill with silence." The Japanese have a long tradition of using silence as a means of communicating and as a tactical ploy. Its use is generally intended to achieve a desired purpose, and it may or may not be negative or malicious. The Japanese regularly use silence as a normal and natural part of their method of negotiating, without any devious intentions. It is therefore important that the foreign businessman be familiar with this custom and know how to interpret and react to it.

NOMI-NICATION (No-me-nication)   Made up of the first part of the Japanese word *nomimasu* which means "to drink," and the last half of "communication," this Japlish word refers to business conversations and socializing that takes place in bars, cabarets, and other drinking establishments, and it is one of the institutionalized ways of "wisdom gathering" in Japan.

NYUSHA SHIKI (Nyu-shah She-kee)   The *Nyusha Shiki*, or "new employee ceremony," held by larger companies in April each year when new employees join, is a very important occasion. Company executives tell about the history of the company, its products and services, its philosophy, and so on, including how the new employees are expected to talk to customers.

SABISU (Saah-be-sue)   From the English word "service," *sabisu* generally refers to things that one does for good customers or potential customers that are extra and free and may include price discounting. The Japanese are usually generous in their extension of *sabisu*, and they expect as much in return.

SHA KEN (Shah-ken)   On the surface, *sha ken*, or "vehicle inspection," suggests nothing more than auto inspections that are mandatory in other countries, but in Japan *sha ken* has a distinctly Japanese flavor. Under Japanese law, all vehicles must undergo an inspection when they are three years old. Those that are between three and ten years old must be inspected every other year, and those that are ten years old and older must be inspected annually.

On each inspection, more than 1,000 parts have to be checked, including such major components as the electrical systems, brakes, underbody, shock absorbers, engine mounts, and tires. Only licensed garages are permitted to make these inspections and any repairs needed. There are some 35,000 such inspection/repair garages in the country. The minimum cost that any car owner gets by with is about ¥60,000 and the average runs to ¥120,000, or more than $700. One garage owner in Tokyo says he averages 55 inspections per month and that the minimum cost to drivers is ¥110,000.

One of the effects of the *sha ken* system is that it encourages owners to buy new cars every three years to avoid the cost and trouble of the inspections. The system also requires that car owners have automobile insurance, and car coverage is the most profitable area of the insurance business. It is estimated that 30 percent of all insurance payments in Japan are for auto insurance.

The *sha ken* system is very unpopular in Japan with car owners, but the powerful licensed garage lobby keeps the law on the books.

SHIMAGUNI KONJO (She-mah-gooney kone-joe)   Literally, "island-country complex," this refers to the feelings of isolation and exclusivity that have traditionally been characteristic of the Japanese and accounts for much of their attitude toward the outside world.

SHIN JIN RUI (Sheen jeen ruey)   Affluent young men and women in Japan who were born after 1955 and make up a new leisure class whose life-styles differ radically from those of their par-

ents, are often referred to as *shin jin rui,* or "new human beings."
The term connotes that this generation of Japanese is so unusual,
so different from anything that has been known in Japan in the
past, that they are totally different people.

SHOKUTAKU (Show-kuu-tah-kuu)   Temporary employees.

TENKIN (Tane-keen)   This is a word more and more Japanese
dread to hear. It means "job-transfer" and often also means having
to move to less desirable offices or cities in outlying areas.

ZENMEN HENKO (Zen-mane hane-koe)   A complete change of
the work rules of a company. If there is only a partial change, it is
known as *bubu henko* (buu-buu hane-koe).

Other Sources of Business Information in English

American Chamber of Commerce in Japan

The American Chamber of Commerce in Japan, which dates from 1948, can be of extraordinary help to American businessmen going into Japan for the first time (as well as to those already established there). Its regular seminars and briefing breakfasts for newly arrived and visiting businessmen are especially worthwhile.

In addition to conducting seminars on doing business in Japan, the Chamber also publishes a number of books that are updated frequently, along with its monthly *Journal*. Two of the Chamber publications that foreign businessmen will find unusually helpful are *Manual of Employment Practices in Japan* and *Living in Japan*. The Chamber also maintains up-to-date listings of attorneys, CPAs, and consultants—a particularly useful service for newcomers.

The Chamber address is: Fukide Building No. 2 (7th Floor), 4-1-23 Toranomon, Minato-ku, Tokyo 105, Japan—tel 433-5381.

Commercial Branch, American Embassy (Tokyo)

The primary function of the Commercial Office of the United States Embassy here is to help American businessmen who want to do business in Japan. This service includes current information on Japanese economic trends and commercial developments—often on a product-by-product basis—and information and advice on United States Eximbank and other financing, FCIA and other insurance, Japanese customs procedures and rates, United States and Japanese patent requirements and regulations, trade dispute procedures, and similar matters of commercial interest.

The Commercial Branch of the Embassy also helps American businessmen establish contacts and negotiate with appropriate Japanese Government officials on matters of commercial importance; provides descriptive and background information on individual Japanese companies; and assists in locating suppliers, buyers, licensees, and joint venture partners. For a very nominal fee, the Embassy will canvas the local business community to locate prospective distributors or licensees for an American company. This service can be requested through the United States Department of Commerce in Washington, D.C. A similar service is provided at no cost to new-to-market exhibitors in the United States Trade Center in Tokyo or participants in United States Trade Fair Promotions in Japan.

American businessmen may also get commercial news of available products included in the monthly *Commercial Newsletter* the Embassy sends to over 2,000 Japanese businessmen and officials.

For additional information about these or a wide range of other services the Embassy offers American businessmen, contact the United States Department of Commerce in Washington, D.C., or the Commercial Branch, American Embassy, 1-1 Akasaka, Minato-ku, Tokyo, Japan—tel 583-7141, extension 681.

Socio-Economic Institute, Sophia University (Tokyo)

Sophia's Socio-Economic Institute publishes a variety of books and bulletins on business in Japan, researched and written by both scholars and businessmen. For a catalog of titles and prices, contact: Sophia University Socio-Economic Institute, 7 Kioicho, Chiyoda-ku, Tokyo, Japan.

The Japanese Government

Several ministries and bureaus of the government, including the Economic Planning Agency and the Bureau of Statistics of the Prime Minister's Office, produce a number of publications on a periodic (usually annual) basis. These include: *Statistical Handbook of Japan, Social Welfare Services in Japan,* and the *Annual Report on the Family Income and Expenditure Survey.* These publications are available from Government Publications Service Center, 1, 2-chome, Kasumigaseki, Chiyoda-ku, Tokyo, Japan.

Japan Chamber of Commerce and Industry

The JCCI publishes *Standard Trade Index of Japan,* one of the most detailed of the business directories available on Japan. The directory includes basic information about manufacturers, trading companies, wholesalers, and retailers, plus commodities and services, as well as brand names classified by commodity and listed alphabetically.

The *Trade Index* is available at shops specializing in books on Japan, and from the JCCI, Suite 505 World Trade Center, 2-4-1 Hamamatsucho, Minato-ku, Tokyo 105, Japan—tel (3) 435-4785.

Associations and Banks

Most of the banks and dozens of trade associations in Japan publish reports, magazines, and/or books. Many are of interest and help to the foreign businessman. Among them are the *Japan Supermarket Directory, Basic Statistics of Large Stores in Japan, Management Japan, Economic Picture of Japan,* and the *JFEA News* (published by the Japan Federation of Employers' Association).

Also available are a number of handbooks of special interest, including *How to Prepare Rules of Employment,* published by the Labor Department of the Tokyo Metropolitan Government; and *Health Insurance Law, Japanese Labor Law, Welfare Pension Law,* and *Workmen's Accident Insurance Law*—all published by the Trade Bulletin Corporation.

Yano Research Institute

Founded in 1958, Yano is a major research operation that provides customized research, regular industry reports, and company profiles for foreign and Japanese clients. The company also sponsors marketing seminars and does management and marketing consulting. Yano is also a major publisher, producing several dozen studies and reports each year on a 10-day, monthly, and annual basis (on Japan's electronics, computer, and communications industries, etc.) For a catalogue of the firm's English-language publications, contact 4-59-3 Yoyogi, Shibuya-ku, Tokyo 151, Japan—tel 370-4474; fax 370-0656.

Guide to All English-Language Publications

Because of the large number of publications involved and the fact that prices change, new titles come out regularly, and old titles become unavailable, the best bet for the foreign businessman is to obtain a subscription to the *Japan Publications Guide*, published monthly by Intercontinental Marketing Corporation, IPO Box 5056, Tokyo 100-31, Japan.

The JPG attempts to list all books and periodicals published in English in Japan that are on sale to the general public. The listings include the title, the publisher, a short description of the publication, whether it can be bought directly from Intercontinental Marketing Corporation, the price, the frequency of publication, and whether it is new or revised. A current catalog, plus 12 monthly issues, costs $8 if sent by sea mail, $15 if sent by airmail.

There is no extra charge for most of the publications available directly from Intercontinental Marketing Corporation, but a small fee is added to most orders to cover postage and handling. If Intercontinental cannot supply a particular publication, it will provide the publisher's address without charge to JPG subscribers and for a small fee to others.

Other Publications of Special Interest

Key Players in the Japanese Electronics Industry, by Dodwell Marketing Consultants, CPO Box 297, Tokyo, Japan. An in-depth analysis of the top nine Japanese electronics companies; the market shares of the major 40 electronics products; and a comparative analysis of the top nine Japanese companies and key multinationals. ¥80,000.

Labor Pains and the Gaijin Boss—Hiring, Managing and Firing the Japanese, by Thomas J. Nevins. The Japan Times Ltd., Publications Dept., 4-5-4 Shibaura, Minato-ku, Tokyo 108, Japan. This is a very important book for any foreign businessman contemplating operating or already working in Japan. Written by a well-known labor consultant based in Tokyo, the book covers such topics as how to attract and recruit staff; how to design payment packages for Japanese employees; how to gain and maintain control of your Japanese staff; how to keep out and control unions; how to create rules of employment; how to control retirement liabilities; how to discipline employees; how to communicate and work with a Japanese staff; how to bring uncooperative managers into line; and more. ¥3,100 (including domestic postage).

Retail Distribution in Japan, by Dodwell Marketing Consultants, CPO Box 297, Tokyo, Japan. A 450-page directory of the leading wholesalers, retailers, and importers in Japan, by category, with an analysis of current retail trends. ¥80,000.

Tetraplan Corporations' Guide

Nihon Tetra Ltd., in cooperation with 250 of Japan's leading companies, operates a 24-hour Corporations Guide system, whereby anyone may dial a telephone number that accesses a computer-controlled data bank of information on the member companies. The system also allows the caller to request additional information, as well as leave messages for return calls from the companies concerned.

For details on how to access the data bank, contact Nihon Tetra, 11th Floor, Shiba Diya Bldg., 2-4-5 Shiba Daimon, Minato-ku, Tokyo, Japan—tel (3) 432-1988; fax (3) 432-5390.

Detective Services

Several detective agencies in Tokyo specialize in industrial information and advertise their services to company clients. These include Kokusai Keizai Chosa Company, or International Economic Research Company, Shinbashi Rainbow Bldg., 2-15-17 Nishi Shimbashi, Minato-ku, Tokyo, Japan, tel 503-4621; Teikoku Detective Agency, Machiyama Bldg., 3-15-22 Roppongi, Minato-ku, Tokyo, Japan, tel 479-5503; and Teikoku Private Detective Agency, 4-20-1 Sendagaya, Shibuya-ku, Tokyo, Japan, tel 403-5151.

About the Author

Boye De Mente first went to Japan in 1949 as a member of the Army Security Agency, assigned to an intelligence processing unit in Tokyo. Since then, his involvement with Japan has been intimate and ongoing, having worked for the Japan Travel Bureau and been editor of several major publications in Japan, including *Preview* magazine, the *Far East Reporter, Today's Japan,* and *The Importer.* De Mente has written more than a dozen books on Japan, its culture, and language. Today, in addition to writing and consulting on Japan, De Mente is senior editor of *Far East Traveler* magazine in Tokyo. De Mente makes his home in Paradise Valley, Arizona. He is married with two daughters.